A
Private View
of a
Public Life

Also by the author

The Creative Woman

A
Private View
of a
Public Life

Dorothy Goldberg

CHARTERHOUSE
New York

Library of Congress Cataloging in Publication Data

Goldberg, Dorothy Kurgans.
    A private view of a public life.

    Includes index.
    1. Goldberg, Dorothy Kurgans. 2. Goldberg,
Arthur J. I. Title.
E840.8.G58A34   973.92'092'4 [B]   75-22221
ISBN 0-88327-047-1

MANUFACTURED IN THE UNITED STATES OF AMERICA

Foreword

This book, a view of public life reflected within the personal life of one family, offers a piece of the action of government. It comes from a life shared with a Cabinet officer in the Kennedy administration, an Associate Justice of the U. S. Supreme Court, and the U. S. Ambassador to the United Nations.

Yes, it is biased. But then I think every autobiographical work is written with the late John L. Lewis's words in mind, consciously or subconsciously: *Them that tooteth not their own horn, their own horn shall not be tooted.*

I suppose it is too much to hope that Arthur will be accorded neither the blame nor the credit for what I have written here—though I am grateful for his cooperation once he realized how serious I was. But it was hard to get even verification of a fact from him until I was fairly deep into the Court period. He claimed: "It's your book, not mine." He has an allergy to writing memoirs. I acknowledge indebtedness to him for his patience and for some valuable insights and for my own widening horizons about public life.

So here is my account, a view from backstage, neither worshipful in the beginning nor denunciatory at the end. The details of these times, as well as the period itself, may be as casually forgotten as most other periods in history, but I hope this account may contribute toward restoring public confidence in government. I can only chronicle the events that touched our lives during the years when we lived through several careers, through a private life permeated with public concern, and a public life permeated with change—sometimes good, sometimes ill-advised.

Here is some of our talking together and talking with others, and more of what made us laugh, and some of what made me cry and certainly worry and sometimes agonize about. I wrote this book from my journals, mostly, and from memories. Obviously I had no access to the Court's records; nor to behind-the-scenes papers and classified documents of the State Department. Since I abhor wire-tapping I never listened in on Arthur's phone calls except once when he spoke to President Johnson, after he had left the government. Arthur was outraged by the President's totally inaccurate version of why he had left the Court, and he asked me to listen in, telling the President that I was on the line.

The various phone calls that I report in the book, then, are only what I heard on Arthur's end. Thus, "even-handedness" (a word Arthur was prone to use too often) is not a characteristic of this book. "Even-handedness" is impossible either for a writer or a man's wife, so I ask the reader to accept my book for what it is: a sketchbook of where the Sixties touched our lives. Although I did not have the benefit of a professional research staff, I have made every effort to be accurate.

Jonathan Grossman, librarian of the Labor Department, and Catherine East, executive secretary, Citizens Advisory Council on the Status of Women, furnished me with helpful documents. Others gave dedicated secretarial assistance. My thanks go to Sarah Alami, Sophia Fleischer, Nancy Passemante, and to Catherine Waelder, a student at Georgetown Law School, for transcribing the manuscript. The latter's help in verifying some data is also appreciated.

I am thankful too that Carol Rinzler, then editor-publisher, Charterhouse Books, discerned the potential for this book in my voluminous journal notes. Her perceptive editorial assistance and that of Grace Shaw is greatly appreciated. However, I take responsibility for the contents and writing of this book.

Contents

A
Private View
of a
Public Life

1

From the
Princeton Station

The unusually heavy snowfall that locked us in the Princeton Inn that December 13, 1960, was a surprise. The few steps from the inn to the walk became snow-covered as soon as they were shoveled; the walk became only a narrow single-file path leading between waist-high snow to the street. The streets were impassable; the airport was closed. Everything was stopped.

If I had phoned Weather before leaving Washington, I would have gracefully declined accompanying Arthur to the Carnegie Endowment for International Peace. And if not for my mother, I probably would not have accompanied Art so frequently on his travels. She always urged me to accept. "When he invites you, go. Go. You should be glad he invites you." The children were grown. Robert was in his first year at Amherst. Barbara was enrolled at the Graduate School of Social Service at the University of Chicago. My own gallery responsibilities were fairly well discharged.

But since I had not phoned Weather we were both trapped, completely blocked by blizzard when President-elect Kennedy phoned Arthur to ask him to be his Secretary of Labor. Arthur called him Mr. President, though he had always said "Jack" before. "Thank you for the confidence you have in me. First I must talk this over with my family and then talk further with you."

On the train back to Washington we talked about what might come, and Art wondered if he could afford to make such a change. Money had never stopped us before—not that we had so much that we could afford to be cavalier about material things; we had none of the really substantial security that would long since have been ours if he had been a corporate lawyer, and for the first time he was earning enough to provide for future contingencies. Eight years out of his life would reduce his later earning capacity. Arthur was certain the administration would be in office two terms, and that he would never return to his labor constituency because of the conflict of interest. But he was weary of the petty bickering within the labor movement, and he wanted to work for the larger public interest. We could manage very well on a reduced salary.

Another consideration was his being a Jew. There were Jewish senators and representatives, but no Jews in the Cabinet. Perhaps there was an obligation when a door opened to keep one's foot in it, so that it might open even a little wider for others. (Later a friend told us that when her son had heard the first rumor of Arthur's appointment he had said, "It just *isn't* likely. Can you imagine the name *Goldberg* in the Cabinet?" I asked Art if the names Abe Ribicoff, Wilbur Cohen, Arthur Goldberg were possibly considered for political appearance. "Put that out of your mind. Kennedy thinks of nothing but the office and the right person for the office.") It all might be worth the lessened income, but still Arthur was not sure.

For my part, I was stunned. Certainly I felt pride that he should be recognized and chosen for the President's Cabinet, but beyond that I could not see how our lives might be affected. I probably would no longer be able to count on him for helping with my Monday evening class at the gallery in contemporary art—but anyone could operate the slide projector.

We were plunging over the dam of fairly comfortable routine. I had not really expected that he would be so involved in the new administration—though I suppose I should have. I had scarcely attended any meetings or spent time at the convention headquarters, frequenting art galleries instead. At the convention sessions in the evening, I sketched everything from the chandeliers to the large steel structures on which the press photographers and television cameras were perched to strawhatted people marching with placards. Perhaps not much would change for us because we lived in Washington already.

From the beginning of our marriage, shortly after Arthur had passed the bar examination, his idea of his work had been the law in its wider, justice-seeking scope rather than in a law practice in one specialized field. Even as a bride, I had been glad of our joint decision to give up the certainty of a financially successful future. I was proud that he disliked having his law work revolve around the foreclosing of mortgages and was glad when he became a lawyer's lawyer—hard work that it was—before his own practice grew. Gradually an increasing amount of his work was in the labor field. At that time, there was a sense of mission in the trade union movement. (We saw it again during the Sixties when young idealists turned to the civil rights movement.) And young lawyers who were idealists turned to labor law. Perhaps that same idealism made Arthur suggest that I give up my night school classes in advertising and marketing techniques at Northwestern University and return to my art studies and for a degree in art education at the University of Chicago.

When the depression closed public school art departments, I worked instead as a social caseworker in the steel mill area of south Chicago, continuing with graduate studies in the School of Social Service Administration. A year after his appointment in 1948 as chief counsel to the Congress of Industrial Organizations and the United Steelworkers of America we moved to Washington where we lived a quasi-public life. Arthur's name was often splashed on front pages of the news, especially during the Supreme Court case of 1952 after President Truman ordered government seizure of the steel mills. In 1955 he was the architect of the combined AFL-CIO. During all those years I pursued my art work full time. Our children, Barbara and Bob, were enrolled in public school, and they and I were home by 3:30.

By the time of the Kennedy administration, I had exhibited widely in local area and regional shows and had had several solo exhibitions, including one in New York. I was also involved with the newly organized Associated Artists Gallery, of which I was program director, and with the classes that I was teaching there. It did not occur to me to expect radical change in my own life.

In Philadelphia, where we had to change for the Washington train, the slushy, narrow platform was crowded with delayed passengers, and the two suitcases Art was carrying kept bumping into people. He did not carry them close to his body, but let them swing out widely. Naturally, people glared, and one muttered, "Get the hell out, will you! Watch where you're going!" I was worried that there might be a fracas or that one or both of us might be thrown off balance and trip onto the tracks. There was no porter, nor any sign of one. Apparently, we were supposed to descend—maybe cross over to the other side. It was baffling.

Then a warm, cheerful voice boomed, "Mr. Goldberg! What're you doing here? I hear you're being mentioned for Secretary of Labor." Strangers paused to look curiously at Arthur. After exchanging courtesies, this kind person, whom Art recognized as somebody from the Shipbuilders Union, thrust his own brief case under his arm, grabbed both of our bags, and said, "You two don't move, stay right here. I'll find out for you and get you first-class reservations. It's an honor," he kept saying. "Imagine, the Secretary of Labor."

Then he returned, guided us down the steps and up again to the proper track, pleasantly telling whoever happened to be blocking the way, "Look, this is the new Secretary of Labor, can you make room, please?"

At the train doors, the conductor was watching our luggage and expecting us. He extended his hand. Then Arthur grabbed the bags, carrying them in that same wide-out way, walking ahead of me sideways through the aisle, bumping each passenger he passed on either side, but they were smiling at him now instead of glaring.

Back in Washington it appeared that Arthur was not quite Secretary of Labor. Arthur learned that George Meany had submitted to the President-elect a list of candidates for the Labor post that did not include him. Arthur told Kennedy that a Labor Secretary needed the approval of the head people in the labor movement, that he had to work with them. "Apparently I don't have that, but remember, I am not an applicant. *You* called me. So you had better ask someone else."

And they *were* thinking of someone else. Robert Kennedy called Arthur to ask him what he thought of Martin Donohue, another important labor lawyer. Arthur asked the President's brother, "Why are you calling me? I'm not a candidate and you surely don't need my approval. Choose anyone you want."

Then the President-elect himself called and asked to see Arthur at his N Street house again. "You don't need me," Arthur repeated. "Apparently you're going elsewhere, but I do have something to say to you because I care about this new administration, and it has no relation to me and this Labor post. You are the elected President. You'd better start acting like one, and not as a supplicant to every special interest group. The fact of the matter is, once you've made up your own mind and say so, they'll all go along." Arthur continued, "And I am resentful, yes, that my name has been tossed around this way." (I thought he ought to regard it as a tribute to have his name mentioned.)

"So, pick yourself a Secretary of Labor," he told Kennedy, "and Meany will approve it, and I am not telling you to pick me or anybody else. But *you* pick him. Don't go around asking. You tell, you don't ask." Later, an aide, Ralph Dungan, was sent to find out if Arthur would consider being Deputy Attorney General. Arthur replied that he couldn't consider being a deputy to anybody and reminded Dungan that he was not an applicant for any job.

The next month, on December 16, the President-elect called to ask him to the N Street house. Arthur was not expecting to be designated or, I am sure, he would have worn something more fitting than a slouchy old brown suit and his light coat to address the press and be photographed on the steps. I was conscience-stricken later about not having remembered to have had them pressed. When Kennedy informed Arthur that he had decided to appoint him, Arthur said, "Look, I am still of the same frame of mind." The President-elect said, "Okay, you can act like Adlai Stevenson if that's what you want, and you can say you haven't decided whether or not you will accept. Do whatever you want to do, but you told me to act like a President and right now I am acting like one, and I am going to tell George Meany I'm appointing you."

Arthur left, and later in the day the President-elect called to say he had told George Meany that he was appointing Arthur, and

George had said, "Okay," and had intimated that he would like to be present at the designation. Arthur said yes.

The period before the inauguration was full of anticipation and preparations, learning to meet interviewers and to cope with lessened anonymity—our pictures were frequently in the news.

It was eerie being recognized by strangers. I could no longer dash into Franklin Simon, just a few blocks away, as casually dressed as before. Once, when taking a bit too long deciding on the relative merits of a $2.95 wallet compared with one at $5.95, the patient clerk queried, a bit archly, I thought, "Is it really such a problem, Mrs. Goldberg?"

Arthur was always photogenic. But my own image, when it appeared, dismayed me. The daily studio sandwiches munched before an easel had added weight, and that made me grimace. Something would have to change.

(Later I learned that the age of the camera people and possibly even their politics sometimes made a difference, too, in how one was photographed. Also, no matter how friendly the photographer, no matter how many pains he may have taken, if the editor happened to have a distaste for wives, or Democrats, the picture would not be one to clip and send to relatives. One kindly photographer sent me strips of seventy-two frames he had snapped—almost all better than the one the editor had chosen for publication.)

I still had no firm idea of what might be expected of the wife of a high official, but Charlotte Drummond, the wife of Roscoe Drummond, the columnist, told me how to help my husband remember names and faces. "Just clip the news photos and tape them to the medicine cabinet mirror when he's shaving, then take them off and check him for accuracy." But there were too many new faces and too many new names for that. Soon the newspapers were filled with names that were no longer always of strangers. My picture, it occurred to me, was now a stranger in the news to others.

The New Year's Eve dance we had planned for our children and their friends was a joyous, noisy party, but too crowded. Though it frequently made me fume, I had grown quite used to Arthur's habit of inviting an additional five or ten or twelve people, but this time the fifty invited guests became almost a hundred and fifty. But Arthur was not to blame this time. Friends had cheerfully, and not even apologetically, brought houseguests and relatives. All of them were so anxious, they said, to meet Arthur and congratulate him that they were sure I would not mind. And that time I really did not mind too much.

The period was filled with public hope, but I had private misgivings about time for my own work.

I would have to enter a canvas in the Baltimore Museum's area exhibition before January 20. Other work needed framing. The gallery's holiday show required a portfolio of freshly matted new drawings. There still were necessary arrangements to be made for forthcoming shows for which I was responsible. And then there were all those extra-painting obligations—the various classes at the gallery required preparation time and visual aids. The experimental pilot program for the aging at Sargent House, funded by Agnes Meyer, for which I had been asked to provide a group of art teachers, meant added work too—though voluntary.

At a dinner we gave for our friends, the outgoing Secretary of Labor, James P. Mitchell, his wife, Isabelle, told me that almost every day would begin with a coffee-committee meeting about 10:30, then go on to a luncheon, a tea, one or more cocktail receptions, and a dinner.

"I don't know about Democrats," she said, "but the Republicans expect us to do all that." She was enviably composed and unhurried; to me, such a program sounded impossible. Throughout the entire campaign I had not even bothered to read more than headlines, because of my own work.

In the early bewildering weeks after Arthur's designation, announcements were received almost daily from the Inaugural Committee, together with requests for numerous appearances. One came from the National Business and Professional Women's Clubs, inviting me to a luncheon in honor of distinguished women in Congress. When I asked a friend whether it really was necessary for me to accept, she said that if I felt strongly about it, certainly it could be skipped. "But you might want to accept." Why? Because so many votes were involved.

"Votes? What votes? Arthur's not running for office!"

"No, but the administration is."

I was abashed to think that I had needed to be told.

Then, recognizing as I did that although Arthur hadn't said anything about my suddenly having to become political, it was expected of me now, I reflected that I had better agree to stand in the receiving line.

I had assumed they would never miss me—not from any undue sense of humility but because there was an overabundance of "distinguished women" already available. I would have preferred not to attend, knowing that it was because of Arthur, not myself, that I would be standing there.

Then, I thought that Arthur was an artist too, of another kind, and I was glad that he had been recognized by the Kennedy administration for his cool, logical, dispassionate attitude toward his work and his reverence for it. He was also fervently and determinedly protective of the interests of working people. I wanted him to succeed in transferring all that enthusiasm to the wider public good, even if it required my standing in a receiving line like a mannequin to shake all those public hands.

Who were the "distinguished women" that so many other women were willing to stand so long in serpentine queues to see? They were the incoming Cabinet wives, the women of the Kennedy family, the wife of the Vice-President, the new sub-Cabinet wives, Bess Truman and Margaret, senators' wives, representatives' wives, two sisters of the Speaker of the House, the wife of the House Majority Whip, the wife of the chairman of the Economic Advisors. Lines of people waited patiently to greet the wife of the Air Force Secretary, the wife of the new Undersecretary of Defense, the wife of the Navy Secretary-designate, the wife of the Army Secretary-designate, and the wife of the director of the National Gallery of Art. Then there were the outright political wives—the wife of the chairman of the Democratic National Committee, the wife of the chairman of the Inaugural Committee.

A few women were "distinguished" because of their own offices, not their husbands': Esther Peterson, Assistant Secretary of Labor; Elizabeth Smith, the Treasurer of the United States; Representatives Julia Hansen, Martha Griffiths, Kathryn Granahan, and Leonor Sullivan; Margaret Price, vice-chairman of the Democratic National Committee.

Who were the people standing in line, slowly moving forward? According to Daisy Cleland and Amelia Young of the *Washington*

Star: "Around the rotunda could be glimpsed the galaxy of faces you'd see at a county carnival, a Georgia State Fair or a tourist attraction in the Nation's Capital." If the guests came from county carnival hinterlands, they dressed as fashionably as some of those in the receiving line, if not more so.

On my way to the receiving line, walking under the Mellon Gallery through the basement corridors, I caught a glimpse of white azaleas in a room filled with drawings I could not stop to see. Then, before being ushered to our places, we marched through a room with Renaissance bronzes. Soon the originals disappeared and only reproductions were on display. I clutched at them with my eyes too, and I regretted the indignity to the works of art. Nobody really looked at them. Having this reception at the National Gallery was like using the Philadelphia Symphony Orchestra to play background music in a cafeteria.

My turn was from four thirty to five, relieving Ethel Kennedy; I was to be relieved at five by a congressman's wife whose name I did not know. It must have been so disappointing, I thought, for that long, winding line of waiting women, standing so patiently for blocks of inching up to where the "distinguished women" were, to find what they were finding. I felt I had to seem really glad to see them. A teen-age girl curtsied; I felt so sorry for the aged ladies, though all politely said it was worth it.

I had always enjoyed meeting people, but now the meeting was so bewilderingly passing. How did I know that I had not met these people before—on the street, or halted at a stop light, or standing in line waiting to have a package gift-wrapped? They all had names, which I often mispronounced. They all had family, friends, experiences that would have been interesting to hear about. Being civil begins with just giving someone who comes to shake your hand your whole attention even for one brief moment, recognizing that he is not a digit on a clicking measuring device but a human being sharing a precious moment of a day, when one of us may not have the next moment. But for all the apparent unimportance of occasions like these, they really were not sham, but ceremony. There are only a few occasions when it is possible for the public to participate, to come nearer, to feel themselves included in the same time continuum that sweeps certain persons into power—and that occasion was one of them.

*   *   *

Dressing for inaugural events would not be too much of a problem except for a long ball gown. I already had everything I needed. Usually, I brought my dressmaker an early issue of *L'Officiel*, the Paris publication of current designers' work, and she would reproduce any couturier number I selected. Now, there would be no time for such pattern-making. Instead, I selected a good American fabric and a pattern from one of the better books.

Added to all the new experiences was the possibility of having to return to an abandoned one—entertaining crowds of strangers again. When a couple enters a new field of work or moves to a new city, a certain amount of entertaining is required of them. But all that was long behind us. In the early Chicago years I had not balked at receiving twenty-five young lawyers and their companions. Even on a mere day's notice I would take it in stride, young enough to offer them nothing but potato chips and a slightly spiked punch. But what may be acceptable to young guests when a hostess is their own age is not the same a few decades later.

Not that I minded entertaining. Once I stumbled on an attractive combination, I kept repeating it. That worked satisfactorily with occasional guests, though the children, Bob and Barbara, voiced objections: "That's your 1957 dessert again." I enjoyed going to parties and liked giving them, though I preferred small dinners or informal buffets. Fortunately, there generally was enough help. Until Barbara and Bob went away to school, they were, of course, expected to pitch in, and we had a dependable cook-housekeeper too. My mother, who lived with us, used her own culinary talents for an occasional apple strudel or cheese blintzes. Our interfaith Seders had become so popular that we had waiting-list requests from one year to the next.

I was under no delusion, however, about the new group of strangers. Their friendships, as our own, had already been established. Charming as they were, I did not anticipate that our relationships would be more than purely business.

Our daughter, Barbara, was amused by the sudden interest in her by some former high school classmates who had shown little interest before, but she refused to reject the few who persisted in calling in the midst of hectic days—such as the morning of our dinner on Christmas Day. The press photographers from *Life* magazine were to come. The rugs needed vacuuming; clutter was everywhere. I was vexed.

Barbara said, "But you yourself said not to upstage anyone, particularly those who weren't nice before." She was in love, engaged to be married, and had a detached tolerance about everything else. It reminded me, though, of when she as a kindergartner had come home from a friend's house to ask me, "Why aren't Jews good citizens?" Her playmate had quoted her mother. I fumed. "Go back and tell Mrs. Beale that good citizens don't talk that way."

"I won't. Her mother's not my friend—she's my friend and she knows me better."

Bob went about muttering that our whole family was a bunch of frauds because Art said he would have to wear a jacket. Why were we getting all dressed up if it was just a typical dinner? Art said, "No New Frontier informality for us. The others are young enough for that casual stuff. At the table you'll look presentable. Period."

During dinner, as the photographers snapped Art carving the turkey, mother, who was never in awe of the new situation, said, "Hmm. The turkey looks underprivileged to me."

The Sunday before the inauguration, we gave a brunch for the Cabinet families and new White House people who had moved to Washington from out of town. We had a splendid log fire. The room needed a bit more light, so I did not feel self-conscious about illuminating my paintings *The Wall* and *The Year Beginning with Younger Hope Than Ever,* which I had made for Barbie's going to Oberlin (but she had said, "Do you mind, mother, if I take something else?"). Over the fireplace on bristol board I had painted the quote from Ben Franklin that Joe Fowler had sent Arthur when he was designated:

> We must not in the Course of Publick Life expect *immediate* Approbation and *immediate* grateful Acknowledgment of our Services. But let us persevere thro' Abuse and even Injury. The internal Satisfaction of a good Conscience is always present, and Time will do us Justice in the Minds of the People even of those at present the most prejudic'd against us.

My mother took having the Cabinet to brunch for granted. "Very nice people," she said.

Arthur insisted I read the poem Mary Zon of the AFL-CIO had sent us.

In the year one-nine-six-one,
Comes a new, most favorite son.
Chimes erupt in every steeple,
Jack gives Arthur to the people.

Up the tempo, mark the date.
Encomiums accelerate.
The enchantress at his side
Is his captivating bride.

Panegyrics from Walker and Al Adams,
The Messrs. Reuther and their Madams.
Gushers from Knight, sparks from Carey,
Praise from David and Rosemary.

Potofsky sends a courtly bow,
A courteous nod from Roger Blough,
Tributes from Truman and Talloo.
Zsa Zsa whispers, "Arthur-who?"

A sunny, Caribbean grin
From Governor Muñoz Marin,
Erasing the Antillian growl
Emitted by Fidele and Raoul.

Small, brave smiles from Dick & Pat,
Hurrahs from Tom and Peggy Harris.
From the By,Y.'s—Lois and Nat—
A hot and pungent Kosher haggis.

All join hands and celebrate
With Henry, Leila, Bob and Kate.
Approbation in a shower
From Mary's—Loftus, Zon & Maurer

Long-stemmed roses—minus thorns—
From the Zacks and Roscoe Boern's.
A ten-foot pole, complete with flag,
From Chester, Dean, Adlai & Dag.

Cheers from Nossiter and Sokolov,
Caviar from the House of Romanoff.
Votes from Lawrence, Wagner, Daly,
Ballot boxes from John Bailey.

Unsolved problems from Jim Mitchell,
From Adenauer, a wiener schnitzel.

Ten free lessons in the rhumba
From Kasavubu and Lumumba.

Godspeed from Shelton, Ross and Kroll.
A happy song from Nat King Cole.
Girlish squeals & handshakes manly
From Saul, Betty, Gertrude & Stanley.

Gather round the festive board—
Cakes from Bierne & ale from Abel.
Shashlik on a flaming sword,
Lindy's lox & Snitzler's bagel.

A yellow polka-dot bikini
From Shirley Temple and George Meany.
A lacey, paper valentine
From baby Jack and Caroline.

A singing telegram and cable
From Golda Meir and Betty Grable.
A warm and friendly press to bask in
From Walter Lippmann & Abe Raskin.

Blaring trumpets, crashing cymbals,
Macy's glad and so is Gimbel's.
(But nothing in the mail today
From Hoffa, Beck, or Joey Fay.)

Blessings from Monsignor Higgins,
A two-inch head from Russell Wiggins.
Something green from DeValera,
A rainbow from I. Rice Pereira.

Shouts of joy, paeans of praise,
Syncopated rondelays,
Ring the welkin, deck the hall,
Love and kisses from us all!

(Mary Zon has talent.)

In almost no time, Ted Sorensen had composed a verse he titled
Men of New Frontiers.

All hail the men of new frontiers,
The hardy Kennedy pioneers:
The Georgia cracker known as Rusk,

The courtly Hodges, never brusque,
Orville Freeman, farmer's friend,
To Stu' Udall, a sleeping bag lend,
Send racey books to Edward Day,
Send lazy crooks to Bobby K,
Take health needs to Abe Ribicoff,
It's Dillon's fault if your checkbook's off,
McNamara's Ford is in his past,
Art Goldberg's not least tho mentioned last.

That night, in the dark, before falling asleep, Art chortled: "Well, Perle Mesta would give her eye teeth to have snared a Secretary of State, a Secretary of the Interior, a Secretary of Agriculture, the Postmaster General, the President's counsel, the Budget Director, and three top Presidential assistants."

"That doesn't happen to be an objective of mine—besides, the Secretary of the Treasury wasn't here, nor the Secretaries of Commerce, nor Defense."

"That's because we should have made the brunch on Wednesday; then they all would have been in town."

I found it amusing the way verse was breaking out all over in the most unlikely places because of jubilation over Art's appointment. I thought perhaps this might be the traditional way people welcomed others to public office. Some were really proficient, such as James C. Hill, an arbitrator friend who wired Arthur:

When Stevenson and Bowles hob-nob
With Freeman, Rusk and Brother Bob,
And Goldberg takes on Mitchell's job,
C'est magnifique, c'est formidable.

To which Arthur replied:

When arbiters wish well to me,
Along with unions, industry,
I know I will not friendless be
In my job as "Secretree."

It all bespoke a certain light-heartedness. The mood was festive. I thought, perhaps this is the jubilance that accompanies all new administrations upon their achieving power. Our friends surely rejoiced with us and kept us busy being honored guests at parties.

Friends rejoiced—yes, but some anxious to hear the "inside" of the political changes were continuing to drop in as usual on Sunday mornings. Coffee had been ever ready previously, and we ourselves liked the informality of it. For those with children in a nearby Sunday School it was also convenient. But after Arthur's schedule became so tight that even our few evenings at home were interrupted by work, callers, and continuous telephone messages, I realized that to share our Sunday mornings as frequently as before meant that I was the loser—having markedly less time with him, while friends enjoyed the same routine as ever.

That seemed an unfair arrangement. Thus, although I found it most distasteful to finally have to tell one or two point-blank to please be understanding about calling before dropping in, being forthright saved the Sunday morning situation.

During the inaugural parade, as the red, open cars traveled down Pennsylvania Avenue with the Cabinet members and their wives, the people along the streets called out, "Hey, Goldberg!" I waved happily to them. For a few minutes, Arthur returned their greetings, but then he slumped down in his seat and just looked grimly at the avenue.

"Did you ever see such a dump? What a street!"

"Sit up," I muttered between my teeth. "They're recognizing you, listen." And the freezing onlookers were shouting, "Hey, Goldberg."

He sat up, looked around brightly for a few minutes, returned their waves, then continued in an undertone:

"Look at that floozy building, those dirty second-story windows. Some street for a ceremonial parade."

I paid him no attention and waved cheerfully to the onlookers. This was as satisfying as being Queen of England, dispensing smiles to the populace. Here a wave, there a wave; here a smile, there a smile. I changed the smiles to nods, varied that with hand waves, and in my growing exuberance even would have extended both hands, prize-fighter fashion, but Art said, "What's got into you?"

"Listen how they're calling your name. Sit up and wave, for goodness' sake." But he gave them only a feeble, absent-minded gesture and kept commenting about the buildings.

(*Architectural Forum,* January 1963, in an issue devoted to

Washington architecture, noted that Arthur's Ad Hoc Committee on Federal Office Space was responsible for two Presidential policy directives to federal agencies. "He [the President] has, as one observer noted, taken more interest in the face of the capital than any President since Jefferson." ". . . the first [directive] was the aforementioned statement of architectural policy on government buildings . . . drafted under then Secretary of Labor Arthur Goldberg. This directive also set in motion the current study of redevelopment along Pennsylvania Avenue between the White House and Capitol Hill, the messy stretch sometimes called the nation's Main Street. The second key Presidential order came six weeks ago, directing federal agencies to observe the guidelines set forth in the Year 2000 plan."

Later, Arthur's Metropolitan Opera Award paved the way for subsequent developments in the art field. He recommended several federal and state aid programs that were precursors of current government programs.)

I subsided too when the motorcade slowed down as we approached the reviewing stand and I could hear better what the crowd was calling to him.

"Hey, Goldberg, don't forget that raise!"

"Goldberg, remember our raise!"

The inauguration of a new President is like a commencement, and his inaugural speech, like that of the commencement speaker, is usually quickly forgotten. The sophisticated politicians and newspaper columnists think the oath-taking avowals more of the same blather heard every four years; the incoming team of Cabinet members and government officials seems to be pawing the ground like horses before a race, impatient to be off and running and showing how they can outdistance the previous administration.

But something was very different in this inauguration—the youth of the President, the youngest in our country's history. A new word also entered with him—"vigor." Midway through his address, the cynics seemed to become a little restive. After all, it was cold on the Capitol steps, and besides, there had been so many preliminary theological blessings that even the true believers squirmed.

"All this will not be finished in the first one hundred days. Nor will it be finished in the first one thousand, nor in the life of this administration, nor even perhaps in our lifetime on this planet. But let us begin. . . ."

We began the decade by loving the way he dispelled our own suspicions about people in high places. He had a capacity to feel, because, though wealthy, he had known suffering. Politics in the Kennedy administration would once again be a tenable consideration for idealists and for young people. All politicians, apparently, were not corrupt and self-seeking. Some could be trusted to try to make government more responsive to the needs of the people. Kennedy was not promising total success in four years or eight years but urging the country to care enough to begin trying to effect change. The will to change precedes the act, and for that, people must be inspired.

His speech was not filled with glowing promises never to be fulfilled, as critics later were to charge. All we were asked to do was to begin. The President was ready to lead—and so was Arthur in the Labor Department—but first we had to plow through the ritual and rites of the Inauguration Day, through that snow incessantly falling.

Almost every writer has paid due respect to that initial snowfall in commenting about the incoming administration. For Arthur and myself, it meant, among other mishaps, missing the gala symphony concert and the gala something-or-other at the Armory. The young military aide assigned by the Inaugural Committee to drive and escort us to the restaurant where Joseph Kennedy was hosting a gathering could scarcely maneuver the car. Waiting for the Presidential party, the guests chatted with an unsuppressed excitement. Perhaps this air of expectancy was, for the politicians, no more than the satisfaction of coming in from the cold of the Eisenhower years, but for me everything was new.

In 1948 Art and I and the children had attended President Truman's inaugural festivities, but we were not invited to as many events; and in 1944 we were present at the Roosevelt inauguration.

At that time, I was invited to a women's tea at the White House and well recall the crowd and Mrs. Roosevelt's smilingly allowing herself to be engulfed in their reaching out to her. I remember, too, my own reluctance to come forward to talk to her, and when it was inevitable, as she moved directly in my path, I murmured a few words about a mutual friend whom she may not have remembered at all, but she smiled and at least seemed to recognize the name, saying, "Oh, yes, and how is she?"

She had seemed so much older and so removed from my sphere of interests. I had admired her unhurriedness then and her own lack of excitement about the flurries of excitement she herself was obviously arousing. I thought she had a natural, unaffected sense of self-possession.

Now, President Kennedy entered to "Hail to the Chief" music. Everybody rose. Jackie was immediately whisked onto the dance floor. Arthur had met her several times before, when the President had asked Arthur to his home for advice. Our son, Bob, had been included in one meeting, but when I asked him about Jackie, he had said, "Very nice, but you ought to see Pamela!" That was Mrs. Kennedy's young secretary.

It was the first time I had met Jackie. Her height surprised me; it gave her a womanly bearing that contrasted with a childlike look of continual semibewilderment. It was a musing, questioning look, with very wide-open eyes and slightly parted lips permanently fixed in a third-of-the-way smile. I think she used that look as an instrument for guarding her privacy, that she reserved her full dazzle for more intimate friends.

Mrs. Kennedy seemed altogether at ease with men old enough to be her father; but even later, on the other occasions when we would meet, and when I would be near enough to observe, she seemed less comfortable with their wives.

I commented once about the way Arthur so cavalierly gave up his rightfully earned Steelworkers pension ($25,000 a year after he reached sixty); he had served the Steelworkers Union from 1938 to 1961. Other Cabinet officers found acceptable ways to hold their pensions for later; Arthur glared when I remarked about that. Arthur gave up his pension, in the form of a long-standing deferred compensation agreement, because he thought that the public would not understand a Secretary of Labor intervening in a labor dispute involving the Steelworkers Union, which he foresaw was bound to happen, and at the same time remain the beneficiary of an agreement by which the union was obligated to pay him money on his retirement. "You can't have your cake and eat it too," he shrugged it off. What cake? I didn't think it made sense either for President Kennedy to magnanimously waive his salary because his father was a rich man. People should be paid their rightful earnings.

But Arthur was determined to protect the President with all his skill and expertise and without having to disqualify himself for any reason. He had already detected storm clouds arising in the steel industry-labor area and wanted to be in an unequivocal position to dispel them. If he were to maintain his rights to a pension, the public might regard his tenure as they did Martin Durkin's in Eisenhower's Cabinet; he regarded himself as on leave from his real work as president of the Plumbers Union; Arthur did not care to have his tenure so beclouded. He also sold the small share he held in San Juan's Condado Beach Hotel, since he might have to apply the Minimum Wage Act in Puerto Rico and that would involve employees of the hotel.

This was a disadvantage of public office, but the ethical principle took priority. I hoped that the Steelworkers Union would be similarly ethically motivated and reinstate Arthur's pension after he had returned to private life. Even his own labor-law associates accused him of acting holier-than-thou. But Arthur did not go about his business as a holier-than-thou person, and certainly he showed no symptoms of that at home. In fact, he admitted, too cheerfully I thought, to a strong sympathy for sinners, because saints rarely walked on earth.

On Friday, January 13, in the meeting of the Committee on Labor of the United States Senate held in the New Senate Office Building, the President's nominee for Secretary of Labor said, "I have completely parted with all of my connections with the labor movement. I do not intend to return, although there is nothing dishonorable in returning after a period of government service."

Then, when he told about giving up his pension, he continued, "I do not recommend this as a procedure to anyone else, and I do not want to sound more pure than anyone else, but the labor scene is a sensitive one and I have felt, because of the nature of the labor scene, the public was entitled to assurance from me that I would act in the best interests of the public."

At the Senate Labor Committee hearing on his nomination,

Arthur replied to a question from Senator Everett M. Dirksen of Illinois about a possible conflict of interest because of his long association with the labor movement. Arthur answered that he could not say that "at this moment I have brainwashed myself and have departed from all the views and convictions which I had throughout the years. It would not be honest if I said that to you."

Both Senator Paul Douglas and Senator Dirksen endorsed Art's nomination. Senator Dirksen, a Republican, summing up, said, "In my opinion Arthur Goldberg can certainly be counted upon to advance the legitimate rights of industry—upon which the welfare of labor is, in the last analysis, very dependent."

Later, an editorial appeared in the AFL-CIO *News* that gave us some pleasure after all of Mr. Meany's early hedging on the nomination:

> It is this honesty and forthrightness that have contributed to Goldberg's successful role in the American labor movement, that have gained him the respect and admiration of management representatives and of leading public figures, the press and the courts. He brings to his new post the tradition of American labor—that union members are citizens first and trade unionists second, that the public interest always comes first. In this tradition there can be no conflict of interest.
>
> Congratulations, Mr. Secretary

I arrived at the reception at the Labor Department a little late because I wanted to hear with my own ears the speech Senator Dirksen was making and then the solemn "advise and consent" of the Senate. Everybody we knew in the labor movement was at the reception, as well as our family and various officials from the new administration and the department heads of the Labor Department. The party was in the large conference room adjoining Arthur's office that other Secretaries of Labor had used as their private quarters. Art, however, preferred a more intimately proportioned, but nonetheless dignified, room. That reception in the conference room marked the first of many meetings there at which I would be either in the receiving line with Arthur or greeting guests on my own.

The reception provided an intimation of pressures to come, both private and public. So many of the new officials were already there, chatting busily with the labor people. I had insisted to Arthur that we include as many members of both sides of our family as possible, because nothing like a Presidential inauguration had ever happened for any of them before.

I found it difficult, however, to introduce them all to the various dignitaries and was conscious that the feelings of my three younger nieces, aged nine, eleven, and thirteen and a half, were becoming bruised. Their dark glances and pointed comments about my paying more attention to strangers than to family made me aware of the far greater pressures carried by the Cabinet families with children living at home.

My mother, generally a retiring person, was intent only on meeting Adlai Stevenson. "I don't care about anyone else, I must meet him." When I introduced them she said, "Governor Stevenson, this is truly a great moment in my lifetime. I thought *you* should have been the President, and I still think so, but I was the only one in our family, I am sorry to have to say, who voted for you." Whereupon Adlai Stevenson cupped her face in his hands and bestowed two warm kisses upon her cheeks.

As for Arthur's eldest sister, Mary, who always carried herself with dignity and always held her head so high that the family called her "Queen Mary," she walked with her head even higher. In Elgin, Illinois, when Arthur's designation was announced, the headline was "Mary Greenberg's Brother Made Secretary of Labor," because she was active in so many community projects. Obliquely, as I moved through the crowd, I could see Arthur already at a telephone in his office, engaged in trying to settle the New York tugboat strike.

I had begun keeping detailed, though one-sided, records of his telephone conversations with the leaders involved. The next morning Arthur, still in his pajamas, began telephoning before breakfast.

I sat at the edge of our bed scribbling in a notebook. Bob entered in *his* pajamas and admiringly and lovingly tried to hug his dad's head as Arthur sat at my dressing table, telephoning. Art had to put one hand over the mouthpiece to say, "Cut it out. Can't you see I'm operating?" It did not occur to me for even one moment to worry that Bob might be feeling rejected. He was chuckling and had seated himself on my dressing table, swinging his legs in Art's direction, so that to prevent his shins getting hit, Art had to move my dressing-table chair out of the way while trying to talk into the phone. Then Barbie willingly rushed to comply after she was given orders to phone for reservations. Then Bob was designated to get the tickets. All of us helped to throw some things into a bag for Art, and off he went to New York. A settlement was reached after fourteen hours of bargaining.

Business Week announced to its readers that that was an indication of things to come: "Speedy intervention, pulling out all the stops, a drive for fast settlement." They failed to mention that on the plane to New York Arthur scribbled the terms of the settlement on the back of an envelope.

2

We Plunge into the Maelstrom of Public Life

I did not give up my painting from any sacrificial sentimentality about wifehood taking priority over a woman's professional work. I gave it up—temporarily, I thought—for several reasons, but perhaps largely from an innate egocentricity. For one thing, I thought my work was too good to ride to public recognition on Arthur's celebrity coattails; and for another, I had carried the fusion of word and graphic image (which was all I wanted to work on in paint) as far as I cared to go at that particular time.

While my work was not "famous," as some columnists stated to my subsequent embarrassment, it was serious and departed from what my contemporaries were doing. I was not "giving it all up," rather I was taking time to refuel in another medium that promised to be also interesting—that is, everyday life as lived in the public official world.

Arthur asked me for some of my own paintings to hang in his new Labor offices, but that created a conflict of interest. It made me professionally uneasy. Although previously all the walls of his offices had been covered with my paintings, to hang them now in the Labor Department was not the same. It was too public, savoring too much of patronage. "Besides," I told Arthur, "some of them might sweep the administration out of office." I reminded him of all the adverse talk when President Truman pushed his daughter Margaret's singing talents forward.

"That's different," he said. "You're already recognized as a professional, and, besides, no one else I know paints labor subjects. I want them, and that's all."

I allowed only a few of them to be hung. Then I arranged with the Museum of Modern Art and the Baltimore Museum for loans. Mary Lasker had suggested that the Museum of Modern Art might agree to make some art loans. When I met René d'Harnoncourt he was enthusiastic about the idea.

(I also asked Mark Rothko, whose work I so admired. He replied that only if all the walls could be appropriated for his work would he consider such a loan. This was a great temptation, but had to be discarded lest it be my choice that determined the single artist to be so represented in a federal department. Later I regretted my timidity: if an artist does happen to be even peripherally near the seat of power, he or she should strike out more boldly on behalf of the artist who makes a singular statement, despite a general popular lack of understanding.)

Entries in my appointment calendar were more non-gallery matters. A typical schedule for several consecutive days looked like this:

Mon., Feb. 6

Morning—Remind Art his coat needs fixing if he goes to Cincinnati

Afternoon—Lunch at the Army Navy Club 12:30

[This with an admiral's wife who was on the Symphony Board. She had called to ask if we would entertain the Howard University Chorus after a symphony performance at our home. I gladly said yes, but privately wished they had delayed for a few weeks to give me time to get organized because of my gallery responsibilities.]

Evening—Eric Johnson dinner at 7:30

Tues., Feb. 7

Morning—Barbara arrives

Afternoon—Mrs. Romulo, Tea for Cabinet wives at the Philippine Embassy

Evening—6 to 8 Reception in honor of the Speaker by the Clark W. Thompsons

Wed., Feb. 8

Morning—Hairdresser

Afternoon—Assemble at 4:30; 5 to 7 White House reception

Evening—Preview of Marilee Shapiro's show at our gallery

Thurs., Feb. 9

Morning—10:45 A.M. Dr. Stites Gallery Tour for Cabinet wives at National Gallery [An excellent tour, but after that I did not go again because of my own art series taught at the Gallery.]

Afternoon—12:30 Lunch at Phyllis Dillon's for Cabinet wives

Evening—Bill Walton's house 6:45 to 7:15 Cocktails with the Caccias [British Ambassador] Opera at 8:00

Fri., Feb. 10

Morning—Choose upholstery material for large chair

Afternoon—Lunch for Esther Peterson by Mrs. Frank Moss [wife of Utah Senator]

Sat., Feb. 11

Free

The days were filled with new experiences, going to strange places or finding myself in action-filled rooms as a bystander.

We attended a Red Mass for the President and the leaders of the government at St. Matthew's Cathedral on Rhode Island Avenue. I had frequently seen the outside of the church. Now inside, I stared at the grayed plum marble of the altar section that looked like a Mark Rothko painting with a purpled, mottled opacity.

At first, I thought that all the people rushing up for communion were trying to stare at the President. He was in the first pew on the left. He remained on his knees throughout, and I watched over him as if I were the guard watching everyone who passed him— but no, the people passing him did not stare. They really were intent on their own devotions. Having reassured myself that the crowd was not being pious to pry, I relaxed, realizing it really was not my concern and regretting my uncharitable thoughts. After all, they, not I, belonged there.

But Robert Kennedy's absence was noted. Perhaps he, as a Catholic, was absent for the very reason we, as Jews, were present. Attendance was optional, but if we had stayed away it might have been misconstrued. Perhaps Robert Kennedy thought that his presence could be misconstrued and seen as justifying the preelection misgivings of some about the long arm of the papacy. He could decline, while the President could not, lest it appear that he was leaning over backward to prove something that didn't need proving. Later I wondered if perhaps the brothers had not planned it that way. Speculation like that had a savor when it was aroused by incidents of one's own day—when it was not merely something earnestly harangued in the correspondence section of *Commentary.*

The next day there was a joint session of Congress to which the wives were invited. Considerable gymnastics were required of the audience. As the dignitaries entered the House, the crowd would rise to applaud. This was difficult to do while carrying a heavy coat, but no one had told me where to leave it. Mrs. Kennedy and her entourage were crisply trim and unencumbered.

To kneel or not to kneel was the question in the church, here it was to applaud or not to applaud. (In the beginning sessions I applauded everything and everybody.)

Typical of the new experiences was a Red Cross luncheon at their headquarters. The outside was familiar enough as part of the Constitution Avenue landscape. I had often passed the building on my way to the Corcoran Gallery, but it had never occurred to me that I would be invited to sit with the "pillars of the community" at the launching of their annual campaign. Columnist Sylvia Porter chaired that particular meeting, and whenever I read her column later I would remember my wonder that she would send me a telegramed invitation to attend an urgent meeting.

The Red Cross office probably learned from Art's secretary that he could not be present that day and, having asked both of us originally, my name was probably left standing on the list like the occupied chair in a going-to-Jerusalem game. Or, the value of his name even with the Mrs. preceding it could have been the consideration.

None of these events or places would have involved me before, and I rather enjoyed the sense of floating along on an ocean of situations, none of which I had chosen for myself, waiting to see where the tide was going.

*　　*　　*

My orientation toward politics had opened up some years before when Arthur was teaching a labor course at the University of Chicago Evening School. When I visited his class once, I recognized a judge and his wife, friends of ours who had recently become separated, attending the lectures in opposite corners of the hall. I was thinking how amusing was the paradox of their possibly being reunited in a course in management-labor conflict, and so I was not listening to Arthur. Then, from far away, I heard his voice remarking, "And this evening, we have with us a guest specialist in labor law from the University of Wisconsin: Mrs. Goldberg, when would you say we have had government by injunction?"

There was a pause and it stretched. It became a silence, and I became conscious of sixty-seven strangers staring at my inattentiveness. Worse, I could not think of the slightest piece of glibness to turn the moment with a light touch. Though I knew, of course, about John Lewis' Mine Workers Union having been enjoined from striking during the Korean War, I suddenly found myself completely tongue-tied.

After class the program director consoled me. "Don't worry, Dorothy," he said. "If you ever want a divorce, you have sixty-seven witnesses."

I do not doubt that Art intended to show me off proudly to his class, not to show me up, and that he had fully expected me to know so simple an answer. In fact, Margy McNamara grumbled to me about virtually the same thing later at a farewell party for Ted Sorensen. I think it was when Art called on her with no warning, after everyone who preceded her had delivered clever, prepared little quips. "That man of yours expects every woman to come up with a speech one-two-three."

His high expectations of me prompted my reading more diligently the same journals of opinions his friends read—the ones who always had pertinent comments to make about current happenings; I discovered that much of what passed for original thought at cocktail parties was merely a warmed-over T.R.B. column from the *New Republic*—or *Wall Street Journal* editorials, if the group were somewhat more conservative.

What knowledge I had was largely based on my labor-management understandings, achieved at the large labor conferences and political conferences, and the nonacademic but interest-arousing classes at the University of Wisconsin's Summer School for Workers. My own interests were largely in art, and I found myself often vexed and impatient with political liberals who could not extend themselves similarly to modern art. At least Arthur had learned a little something about that.

In February, Margaret McNamara, wife of the Secretary of Defense, invited the Cabinet wives and Lady Bird Johnson to luncheon at her home. We were to discuss allocating our time in a way that would avoid duplication of effort and, if possible, to make one joint contribution that might be more productive than merely accepting honorary chairmanships.

Some of the women had had considerable experience, notably Lady Bird Johnson and Martha Hodges, whose husband had been a governor of North Carolina before he became Secretary of Commerce. Jane Freeman, wife of the Secretary of Agriculture, also knew about public-life demands from personal experience, having been a governor's wife, as did Ruth Ribicoff, wife of the Secretary of Health, Education and Welfare, whose husband had been governor of Connecticut. Lee Udall's husband, the new Secretary of the Interior, had formerly been a congressman, and Phyllis Dillon's husband, now Secretary of the Treasury, had been an Undersecretary of State in Eisenhower's administration. Mary Louise Day's husband, the Postmaster General, had served as Illinois' Commissioner of Insurance when Adlai Stevenson was governor.

Each Cabinet wife, of course, already had commitments to various projects of her own that she still hoped to honor. So there were some diffident silences as each contemplated her particular commitments; the calendar pressures were already beginning.

There was some talk about the futility of merely lending one's name to a work, but the clamor for Cabinet-wife representation was insistent and steadily accelerating. Women with young children and minimal household help, such as Lee Udall—her six children ranged from one and a half to eleven years old—carried an added load because the children took priority. (Lee later organized a gallery for the exhibition of Indian arts and crafts. The profits provided scholarships at professional schools for thirty Indian youngsters, almost all of whom are now working professionally in the arts.)

Although Ethel Kennedy may have had sufficient help, she was hardly alone in feeling that no paid help can substitute for a mother when a child is ill—particularly when their father is always busy elsewhere—and her active, high-spirited children seemed to encounter every conceivable childhood ailment or disability. Moreover, she was still in the process of completing her family. Early in the administration, her enthusiasm and exuberance, despite her taxing schedule, did much to mitigate her lack of interest in any project that was not the concern of her immediate family.

Jane Freeman was a superb homemaker with as professional a sense of home economics techniques as of party politics, and although she had two young children, she was already working with the very active "pros" of the women's Democratic organization. If she had to add another project, she preferred that it be in connection with the Department of Agriculture.

Ruth Ribicoff suggested that each of us continue with her respective involvements and perhaps, in that way, we could render as effective a service as if all of us worked on one project.

I liked the way the women regarded themselves as also being responsible to the wider public trust their husbands had been sworn to serve. Perhaps they wanted to help because of the affection and regard everyone felt for the young President. After all, he had admonished everyone to ask not what your country can do for you, but what you can do for your country.

The ceremonial obligation expected of high officials and their wives is a convenience for the men, who frequently cannot attend because of work pressures. That a wife shares protocol rank allows her participation to signify her husband's recognition of the importance of a given project, activity, or organization; it signifies due respect for diplomatic protocol if a wife attends an embassy function. Of course, it takes a bit of finesse, on occasion, to provide the hostess with a graceful out if she would rather invite another couple—Washington was at that time, and remains, a couple-oriented society.

This ceremonial aspect may be boring and inconvenient; it may also be interesting, pleasurable, and not without a certain glamour. This crumb from the cake, which might be called consort status, can, to a degree, be quite satisfying. From my observations,

I think it provides almost a fair half of the cake for a woman who has a close and communicative relationship with her husband; her observations and appraisals of people can be interesting and valuable. And, of course, it provides added opportunity for a shared relationship.

Some career women who accompany their husbands to Washington—even though they may have such a relationship—take an appraising glance at the whole system and get themselves employed at once. Professional women are provided with an immediate solution to the conflicts of the public versus private life; they can respond graciously with regret to the many luncheons and fund-raising events while still being able to attend White House dinners, State Department receptions and embassy events.

I had never given much thought to the wives of public officials before; judging from the newspaper photographs, they seemed to be merely tea-pouring smilers with perfect coiffures, so I was a bit surprised at the earnestness of this group. I wondered how much of their motivation was political expediency.

Virginia Rusk seemed wholly nonpolitical. She really should have been paid by the Department of State for representing her husband and the Department so well at the many diplomatic functions that the Secretary himself could not attend. She had only occasional cleaning help, and her daughter Peggy was only twelve then. Apparently Peggy was a self-sufficient youngster who could be trusted to be cooperative and understanding, as was her thirteen-year-old brother, Richard. Later, when I knew Virginia better, I learned that the Rusks almost never ate dinner at home. If an embassy dinner was not on the day's schedule, they went at the hors d'oeuvres, a situation they regarded with some amusement. That expedient may well explain the appearance Virginia gave of never being in a hurry, being able to take all the time needed to assure whomever she was talking to at those unending functions of her engrossed attention. Perhaps the fact that she never wore a wristwatch may have been an added advantage. Virginia had a daily, open-house coffee hour in the mornings for the women of the various foreign missions, and she made herself particularly available to receive the newly arrived diplomatic wives at her home. At that time, there were ninety-five embassies and six legations in Washington.

All the embassies recognized that the Secretary of State would be represented by Mrs. Rusk at the almost daily receptions to which they were invited. The Secretary himself would more likely appear at dinner parties, although even then he would enter very late, or not at all during especially demanding periods. Virginia's presence in his absence was almost obligatory, lest some of the smaller nations regard themselves as slighted by the State Department. She also assumed the duty of attending the national holiday celebration of every embassy—ninety-five celebrations a year.

She was very much liked and that was an asset to her husband and the administration, for the Secretary had a certain remoteness. (When Robert Kennedy died, I discerned a sensitive and somewhat bruised person beneath that arm's-length reserve. He called to ask if he might accompany us to the funeral services, diffident about his reception by the Kennedy family because of his loyal support of President Johnson.)

Virginia Rusk, with the aid of Eleanor Israel, a person of unusual organizational ability and a full-time unpaid volunteer consultant to the Chief of Protocol, initiated THIS—The Hospitality and Information Service—for diplomatic families. Virginia Rusk also helped Mrs. Angier Biddle Duke in the 1964 restoration project of Blair House, although, for Robin Duke, the Blair House project was a labor of love that she directed with enthusiasm and zeal.

Everyone agreed that Virginia Rusk carried the heaviest burden among the Cabinet wives. She had a formidable daily correspondence, invitations to accept, regret, or to extend to others; she oversaw protocol visits of foreign notables' wives, saw the foreign service wives on home leave, and contributed to orientation sessions for foreign service wives going overseas. While much of the detail was handled by the Department of Protocol, the thank-you notes Virginia sent were personally written. They were never mechanical but sparkled with personal comments and spontaneity; they flowed more smoothly, perhaps, than her conversation, because the precise word was important to her and warranted her taking the time to seek it. She spoke slowly, even with a halting deliberateness, so people would stop to really listen until a sentence was finally completed.

She had an open smile and conveyed a human interest that was undoubtedly effective with foreign visitors. Gwen Gibson wrote of her in the New York *Daily News* of February 17, 1962: "For sheer devotion to duty, Washington's dollar-a-year men are being obscured by a clique of ten enthusiastic women—the Kennedy Cabinet wives. Without a suggestion of salary, these women behind the men who run the capital are working full time—and then some —for the taxpayer."

Virginia's sense of form kept her from indulging in any unseemly merriment at some of our early conversational gropings for a common meeting ground with a particularly taciturn visitor, but sometimes it was an effort for me to be similarly controlled. Particularly when, after one or the other of us had made a rather banal remark at a State dinner, the interpreter seriously translated it. Then, not receiving any glimmer of understanding from the guest, he would retranslate, and both Virginia and I would wait in a state of poised attention for the visitor's delayed bewildered response. I would hastily swallow a chunk of dinner roll and pretend to be suppressing a cough.

Virginia thoughtfully helped by sending to our home a copy of the briefings that she herself received, so that in the afternoon before a given dinner I might be prepared for any conversational exigency. I found it was helpful also to make a point of studying the morning's newspaper more carefully on the day of the visitor's arrival—at least to know what subjects to avoid. Arthur, however, could not always prevent himself from plunging into controversial depths with his dinner partner. Once, Arthur asked the ranking woman guest an innocent question about her country's borders that caused her to look so startled at her own interpreter—a charming woman seated on the other side of Arthur—that the latter laughed and said in English, "It's all right, the Secretary is only asking a geographical question, not a political one," whereupon Arthur concentrated his attention upon the interpreter.

Virginia told Gwen Gibson that she enjoyed the extensive traveling with her husband because, "It gives me a rare opportunity to visit with him. At least, when we're alone in the cabin of the plane, he can't very well go out any place."

She enjoyed her role, having always maintained a lively interest in what she called "current events." (I could understand. It is so much more interesting to be seated near someone at dinner who can provide instant background on his country and its problems than to pore over ponderous books and articles. And dinner at the State Department, or the White House, or Blair House occasionally provided enough momentum to send me searching through the stuffily written articles the following day looking for an opposing or more explanatory version of my dinner partner's comments. At first, it seemed incredible to find oneself seated at dinner near someone who was a shaker of trees of power. How did he get to be what he was? And what plums was he reaching for and why now? Afterward, it became altogether natural not to skip foreign news reports from that person's part of the world—however remote it might be.)

Lady Bird Johnson, of course, had been an experienced business woman and had always shared in the obligations of her husband's public offices. Her constructive contributions are already too well known for any comments here. She held "doers" in high regard and later, as First Lady, would invite women "doers" to be honored at White House luncheons. It was thought that, next to Eleanor Roosevelt, Mrs. Johnson was the most activist of all the First Ladies.

Phyllis Dillon's experience included having been a diplomat's wife; her husband had been ambassador to France. Her interests were largely in art—her home with its Impressionist paintings was made available for various benefit tours. The few dinner parties we attended there were exquisite in all the many perfect details. No matter how many people may be employed to provide so excellent and smooth-running a performance, one person is generally responsible, and in her Washington home that person was Phyllis Dillon.

Career women may dismiss the creative talent that enters into such social events as unimportant compared to being, let us say, a lawyer, and they tend to avoid being labeled a "hostess-wife" by making only minimal gestures. New feminists may say that similar talent went into Marie Antoinette's plannings at Versailles. But our time has seen the development and execution of a new form of art called "conceptual," in which the artist gives orders to subsidiaries in the same manner as the head of an advertising agency gives orders to the copywriter, the layout artist, the graphics director, the illustrator—all the others. A conceptual artist may drape tens of thousands of square yards of plastic curtaining materials over cliffs in Australia, or suspend a mile-long banner between two peaks in the Rocky Mountains. In a free society one has a right to choose which conceptual art one prefers to practice. Whatever Phyllis Dillon may have regarded as her personal art would have been executed with craftsmanship and skill.

She was helpful in organizing weekly National Gallery tours for Cabinet wives, led by Dr. Raymond Stites of the National Gallery. This was a leftover activity from the Eisenhower administration. I remember Phyllis willingly accepting a YWCA request to serve as an art judge for an amateur exhibit that I also was asked to judge. Later, in New York, she would be an active board member of the International Council of The Museums of Modern Art.

Margaret McNamara, an intense person of great drive and sensitivity, suffered keenly from the public criticism of Vietnam, believing her husband's role misunderstood and misinterpreted by various columnists. To mention their names would arouse a cold wrath in her and elicit a caustic comment. So strong were her feelings, torn as she was between her children's rejection of the war and their father's reported role, that she developed an alarming ulcer requiring hospitalization and long bed rest for many months during the Johnson administration.

Her recurring comment to mutual acquaintances was "Watch out for Dorothy Goldberg; she'll get you to whitewash her fences like Huckleberry Finn—with her 'everything's the greatest, the best, most fun'—then she dances off somewhere else." I forgave her because she herself was the most committed of Cabinet wives to the school project. She volunteered when I was recruiting in the Labor Auditorium; when all were asked to stand up to identify themselves, her voice emerged from a far recess of the room, "Margaret McNamara, former teacher." I had not even known she was there.

She was jesting, of course, about my "dancing off" once a project was moving smoothly, but I never regarded any specific project with a proprietary interest the way many people do who are among the initiators of voluntary projects—clinging to them when others should be taking the helm.

Margaret McNamara, former teacher, took instruction in the teaching of remedial reading for slow readers and volunteered in the schools. Subsequently, she was head of the Widening Horizons program for two years and active in Urban Service work. With Ford Foundation help and that of executive director, Eleanor Smollar Straus, she developed the organization called RIF, Reading Is FUNdamental. It still exists—now international in scope— a project providing nonschool books of its own to children in impoverished areas to stimulate their reading interest. She is a full-time volunteer, and she has also given conscientious service to Chatham College as a trustee.

My own interests were already being channeled toward the public schools of the District of Columbia. I knew from Marjorie Bootin, an assistant supervising director of art in the high schools, and from Jack Perlmutter, a well-known Washington artist who directed the D.C. Teachers College Dickey Gallery of Art, how desperately help was needed.

Yet, the schools were reluctant to accept volunteer help. Years before, Marge Bootin said to me, "There's too much needing to be done. It will just tear your heart out, so don't try. You can't even begin to make a tiny dent in the need." When I persisted then, in 1957, that there must be something I could do to help, she said, "Okay, so you want to feel noble? Then get me the magazines I need for the art teachers' staff meeting next week. There's no money for interior decoration magazines or architectural ones, things like that." Now I resolved to concentrate my attention on the schools of the District, primarily those of the inner-city, to see where and how citizens might be able to help.

Recognizing that the Cabinet wives were already beginning to feel pressured, I merely noted my own interest at Mrs. McNamara's luncheon and refrained from recruiting them. Some of them told me, however, who among the wives of sub-Cabinet and Assistant Secretaries in their husbands' departments might want to help lessen the appalling rate of tenth-grade dropouts.

Jane Wirtz, a sub-Cabinet wife then, was as conscientious in her volunteer commitments as she later was upon her husband's becoming the Secretary of Labor. From the very beginning, she accepted an administrative responsibility for the Widening Horizons program, and in the second year directed it; Texeira Nash, an early volunteer, became co-chairwoman. Jane would willingly accept any chore, saying, "I'll do anything, everything; just don't ask me to talk to more than two people at a time." When she organized and developed Project Earning Power, in connection with the President's Committee for Employment of the Handicapped, she was required to talk before many audiences and became a poised public speaker.

Mary Weaver, whose husband was an Assistant Secretary of Labor, had been an outstanding, gifted professional social worker for many years—a highly paid consultant to state governments on the organization of social welfare programs. She gave up her own work to enjoy, as she put it, volunteer status. But she undoubtedly worked harder and longer hours entertaining. Mary was a full-time volunteer for many years in the Washington International Center, a part of the Meridian House Foundation. She was very much involved on behalf of trainees who came to this country under the auspices of the Cultural Affairs Department of the State Department, either to attend schools here or to visit projects related to their countries' interests. A person of great energies, she also was active on the board of the Washington Youth Gardens, working with Jane Freeman. She developed a luncheon program for senior citizens and was on the board of the Iona Whipper Home (a home for unmarried mothers). She attended the West African Conference of Social Work as a consultant and also was on the Women's Committee for the Employment of the Handicapped.

Mary believed that there is a place in the volunteer sector for the professional who retires or who deliberately chooses to make a contribution as a volunteer, and that such participation provides no threat to one's professional status. She deliberately chose being a volunteer upon her husband's accession to high office in the Department of Labor.

I was grateful to be able to draw upon her professional suggestions in connection with the launching of some of the new volunteer projects.

Thus, Ruth Ribicoff's suggestion was a sage one. Each of us did what we wanted to do as individuals—not as a group.

The Widening Horizons project that called attention to the needs of the children of inner-city schools developed among New Frontier women long before the antipoverty programs that would later include many of their school projects. It began with a series of summer tours arranged for junior and senior high school students through a group of official and private institutions to widen understanding of the city in which they lived, to which tourists came from all over the world. It was the first time that federal officials or their wives, by proxy, had evinced a concern and acted upon that concern for local school programs.

The whole milieu of the new administration's start on getting the country moving again—the theme ad nauseum of the primaries, according to the critics—I found completely spellbinding. At home, from the moment he awoke, I could hear Arthur on the telephone, talking to key government figures; at breakfast, he would explain some of the complexities.

The pace of our lives was assuredly accelerating. I had taken to keeping a journal, but everything was happening too fast. At least four evenings a week, sometimes every evening, we would be dining at the residences of various official hosts. I would bring Arthur his dinner clothes, and he would change in the little room adjoining his office. Then, en route to wherever we were invited, there would be time to tell me the news of that day as it affected him. If my days were taken up with volunteer projects and appearances at various functions, my evenings had broadened as well.

We found ourselves on the Walter Lippmanns' list for parties that I enjoyed, where people in power and people in the writing business mingled. The embassy invitations had begun arriving.

Before we were so closely involved with government ourselves, I used to wonder why Congress would drop the most important business in hand to take so many holidays. It was like an exasperating commercial interrupting a serious program. Now my mother wondered similarly about us. We had so many receptions and dinners to attend. She shrugged a comment our way about the Kennedy administration one evening as we were leaving the house: "Parties, parties, they have. All the time parties, and so many people without work."

But certainly the most exciting invitations of all were to the White House. It meant more than simply meeting the people pictured in the morning's news, seeming very much like anyone else at a dinner party. It meant the corridors and walls of history

—the East Room, the Green Room, the Red Room, the Blue Room—encasing the present moment through which we wandered.

I would strain to see where the greatness was, lest it pass me unrecognized, and I listened carefully, knowing very well that it would not show itself by fashionable dress nor clipped witticisms, nor calculated social grace. And then I would feel an inner pang at my own arrogance for so readily dismissing what I was hearing, to concentrate on what I was seeing.

I relaxed and enjoyed the White House visits, beginning with the guards at the west entrance gates peering inside our automobile. Then the driver would call out: "The Secretary of Labor and Mrs. Goldberg," and I would smile.

Soon the car would pull up before the entrance to the Diplomats' Reception Room on the ground floor, a room that was also used by the President's family for their comings and goings. Mrs. Kennedy had hung an antique wallpaper in that large oval room. It was called "Scenic America," and it showed such places as West Point, Boston, and Niagara Falls; the people in the scene were dressed in early nineteenth-century clothing. If the arrival crowd was as yet not too large, one could look at that, but we generally arrived at the next to the last moment. Only twice did I have enough time to really enjoy the china display in the room adjoining the Diplomats' Reception Room.

Usually, we would be precipitated almost immediately into the hubbub of greetings as we waited to have our coats checked by people who always greeted Arthur with smiles and with some comment about having noticed what he had done. There are, of course, degrees of friendliness, but during the Cabinet days, I thought the warmth was sincere on the part of working people.

There was also a warmth and enthusiasm shared by those who came as guests and who saw one another frequently, but only briefly. The men, especially, knew what their fellow guests had gone through during the day, or could at least surmise. Thus, to meet under the White House roof at night, undisturbed by the pressures and tumult of the day, presumably became a minor triumph for them.

For the most part, nothing more demanding was required of a Cabinet wife than a smile, a handshake, or a peck of a kiss on the cheek, lightly received or lightly offered. Then came the hearty, "How *are* you? Gee, you look great!" And in turn one replied with the usual banalities, "And how are *you?*" "Great." "Great" was the word if a man was doing the exclaiming. The women that year were using "divine." Everything was "divine" at the White House. "Gee, you look divine."

If the line of guests was slow ascending the stairs to the first floor Entrance Hall of the White House, and it generally was because of the long-skirt hazard, then there might be time for one more query and response about where one had spent a recent holiday, perhaps—but not much beyond that, because for even the most urbane among the women, maneuvering the steps in a floor-length embroidered brocade or sequined chiffon demanded some concentration.

If, however, one was able to maneuver the steps, the long skirt, and the polite patter, there was always the possibility of another face intervening, expecting to be recognized. Here one lightly repeated the same pattern with no necessity for extending it, because there obviously was no time. Yet, Arthur was able to accomplish much between the bottom and the top step, turning his head to continue a conversation with whoever was asking questions on the step below, and only rarely stepping on my hem.

The landing at the top led into the large Entrance Hall where the Marine Band, wearing red jackets, was playing. But before that, we were greeted near the landing by a Presidential aide who offered me his arm, while Arthur trailed behind, as we were marched to the little table for the seating-place assignments on little cards. We scarcely arrived there before Arthur was greeting and talking to the poised attendants, the butlers, standing along the north wall. I was impressed with them—their grace and dignity. Their quiet slow-moving bearing and unhurried but warm smiles imparted a true welcoming, as if we were really visiting a home, not a house—and theirs. It was as if they were part of the permanence within that house where Presidents merely come and go.

After talking for a short time to the aide, we were ready to enter the East Room, with Arthur presumably still trailing. But no, he hadn't even entered the Cross Hall yet; he was greeting the musicians, even as they were playing. Then he was shaking hands with the conductor (after the Metropolitan Opera strike every musician had much to tell him). I'm not sure if they were even members of the musicians' union, though one of the men told us he had once met the president of the union, Mr. Petrillo, who had a horror of shaking strangers' hands lest they communicate some germs; he would extend only his pinkie to even the most renowned dignitary. Apparently, there were other risks in all that handshaking, besides the aching ring finger crushed by the overenthusiastic.

Once in the East Room we joined other guests at cocktails, which were served from trays by the White House butlers, and would chat briefly until we were advised by the various aides to form a receiving line for the President and his entourage. The line was formed according to protocol, which meant that the only ones we would talk to for the next ten minutes were Abe and Ruth Ribicoff, at the bottom of the protocol totem pole, and Luther and Martha Hodges of Commerce, one rank above us.

To me it never was a bore. No matter how many times we visited the White House, I never regarded it with other than respect for the tradition it symbolized and the hope it made possible. I felt an indebtedness, and I enjoyed the ceremonial toot-toots that announced the arrival of the Kennedys, as "Hail to the Chief" was played. In the receiving line, Jackie would say "Arthur" with a sweetness and a sort of catch in her voice, and he would melt.

Then we would pass the Cross Hall to the State Room, which gave Arthur another opportunity to tell the conductor of the band to wait and see, that some day the federal government would realize it was as responsible for music and the arts as it was for housing—until I would lose patience and say, "For goodness' sake, we're holding up the line."

Between the second course and dessert, faraway music of the Air Force Strings would grow stronger as they started playing in the Cross Hall before entering in a group. For a few minutes everyone listened, then went on eating. Almost always the strings included "Yesterday." Arthur would generally be the first to start the applause, and if that failed to register, I, sitting at another table, would pick it up, until everyone clapped. (A few years later, at the United States Ambassador's residence in the Waldorf Towers, I would arrange for all entertainers to be seated among the guests. Now the musicians were playing for our dinner and the least we could do was to thank them with our applause.)

The White House never grew tedious—for me, at least. There invariably was something to see, if not to hear, if occasionally during the toasts a visiting dignitary might regard the moment as an opportunity for sounding off on his mission. So I kept looking with marveling eyes at, among other things, the convex mirror in the Red Room, which revealed, in an all-encompassing reflection, the room's potential for more intimately scaled conversation groups.

After dinner, guests emerged from the dining room to spill into the Red Room and the Blue Room. (In the Blue Room there was a pier table, with a large rectangular mirror underneath, ordered by President Monroe from Paris; I assumed it was a "peer" table where hoop-skirted ladies might discreetly peer, on arising from the table, to see if their pantaloons were showing.) The women's press corps was waiting ready to descend upon that day's most newsworthy names. Since Arthur's activities were always making news, they often headed his way. At receptions, they were herded behind a thick, red plush rope and I thought that an indignity to them. I enjoyed watching them and indeed realized that one could learn much from them. It took skill to edge circumspectly near a group and be privy to a conversation that might make the front page. The press never violated the off-the-record courtesy of social occasions, at least not to my knowledge.

I watched the press with interest and tried to compare their observations the next day in the papers with the same sources I had heard. How they could harvest anything pertinent from some of those stodgy, well-fed diners was a wonder, so I tried to include the women reporters if I happened to be with Arthur, or to introduce them to sources having more news potential if he were slow emerging from his table. Later, I dropped all of my own sensitiveness about being in their columns, and exploited them too, for the various school projects that needed publicity; they soon became aware of that tactic.

Some of them—Isabelle Shelton of the *Evening Star*, Wauhillau LaHay of the *Washington Daily News*, Frances Lewine of the United Press, Helen Thomas of the Associated Press, among others—were well-enough briefed to pursue a subject with Arthur beyond the one or two questions of women's page interest. They arrived in attractive evening dress, and it must have been hard on their salaries, attending as frequently as they did. I was more interested in a real Cluny lace collar Maxine Cheshire wore on a plum-colored velvet dress than in her columns, but that was before she suddenly developed the acid pen that had the city standing to attention.

Dorothy McCardle was very much a gentlewoman, and had more than the cursory pleasantries for the wives of important men, having herself been a high official's wife in the State Department. Wauhillau LaHay was kind about listening patiently to news of which volunteer projects needed recruits and therefore publicity (though I would gulp my coffee at breakfast in disappointment when I saw that my story was disregarded and another, not necessarily earthshaking, from Art was elasticized into something important).

I understood what was necessarily the real intent of their presence there, the possibility of a story "straight from the horse's mouth." Moreover, they knew that I always had what seemed to them probably too many projects under way. Certainly, they were most skillful in withdrawing from a nonproductive situation. One could learn from them how to extricate oneself with grace and finesse from a garrulous guest, how not to be held captive during the short period available for guests to talk with one another en route to the East Room, where chairs would have been set up for the program.

I remember one incident during a corridor passage that might have been a scene in a musical. Arthur was surrounded by press and I was pushed onward by people behind me until I found myself at a pillar near the Blue Room where I could lean for a moment. I turned to see the conversational groups that had established themselves in small circles along the corridor walls. For those few moments the circles were open like doughnuts with semicircular "bites" in them that might allow another passerby to be included. I saw a middle-aged woman at the far end of the corridor—the Cross Hall—leave the dining room and stand in place looking baffled. She was unescorted, and there was a tentativeness about her that I assumed was caused by the blockings of the crowd. I noticed her because she had raised her arm but wasn't about to wave her hand, and instead pressed her fingers across her forehead with the palm turned out. It was the sort of gesture that one uses if one is a bit warm; sometimes it accompanies a sense of helplessness. Maybe she was feeling faint? I watched her intermittently as she progressed slowly through the crowded corridor groups.

All the little doughnut-like conversation groups coiled themselves closed as she approached, so that she was entering a tunnel of turned backs. She was being unwittingly excluded along the entire way. I was surprised that no one from either the social secretary's staff or Protocol had been alerted to the solitary guest, to extend a bit more hospitality.

As she approached me, she hesitated and turned around to look about her; then, seeing me, she asked if I knew the way out, the way to the coatroom.

"You're not leaving? Are you feeling all right, may I ask?"

"Yes." But she still wanted to leave.

"There will be a program," and I gestured toward the East Room. She shook her head and again wondered where the steps were to the coatroom.

"Have you been here before?" She shook her head and smiled, I suppose, at my inability to believe that anyone would want to walk out on a White House party.

I introduced myself and told her that directly across the corridor was the Blue Room, where there were two Cézannes, and that everything was being restored.

"My husband would have appreciated that more—and the White House too." He was dead, and she was Mrs. Frank Lloyd Wright. "I feel bad that he was never invited when he was alive, and now I miss him, so I really want to leave."

She brightened, but only a little, when I exclaimed enthusiastically about the great architect. Then I introduced her to one of the women reporters and to Lydia Katzenbach, who happened to be standing near. Mrs. Katzenbach, a naturally gracious woman, introduced her to several others. Soon the circles were loosening as everyone finished their demitasse and strolled into the East Room.

I am not sure whether Mrs. Wright stayed for the program, but by the time Arthur reached my pillar—accompanied by a flock of admirers—I was so glad to see him, so glad that I was able to be there with him, so glad that he was invited to the President's house while he could enjoy the experience, that I forgot about having wanted to poke him for taking so long to join me. Why did I not enter the East Room alone and sit down to await him there? Because alone I would not have been given such good seats. Entering alone with a bright smile and inquiring look on my face, the usher would have said, "Oh, just sit wherever you like, Mrs. Goldberg," but I would have felt it presumptuous to sit in the first row with the President and Mrs. Kennedy. Entering with Art, it would be, "Oh, Mr. Secretary, the President wants you to sit here."

There was no advantage in any delicate humility. To sit farther back offered no exit possibilities if the program were uninteresting —one could not escape before the President left. And when the program was good, and it usually was very good, I enjoyed the unobstructed view of the stage from the front row. But that was not always an advantage. When Pablo Casals played and photographers captured the rising of the audience and enthusiastic applause of the appreciative front row, I was caught applauding rather feebly and looking off somewhere to the left rear.

But the public life was infringing on the private life. We were unable to attend the Bar Mitzvah services of two of our friends' sons because we had to accept a New York Liberal Party testimonial luncheon in honor of Arthur instead. And there was to be a dinner the same evening at Dorothy Schiff's, the publisher of the *New York Post,* and Art thought I should be present there as well.

Other areas of private life suffered: February had been a busy month for Art, but I had not thought that it was so busy that his Valentine for me had to be pulled from his overcoat pocket in a brown, drugstore-labeled bag. When he remembered to thank me for mine (properly mailed to his office for him to find the first thing that morning), I snorted: "*This* is your Valentine?"

> It makes no difference, Honey,
> Where we are or what we do.
> The only thing that really counts
> Is being there with you.
> And, Honey, in this Valentine
> I want to let you know
> That the longer we're together

The more my love will grow.
HAPPY VALENTINE'S DAY

Pink, scalloped, swarming with hearts and floating baby roses and the caption "For My Wife" on it. I knew at once what must have happened.

"You didn't choose this Valentine." I could tell by the limp "mmnn" that I was right.

"Why don't you just admit that you sent Mr. Jackson or Mr. Johnson [his two drivers] to the corner drugstore on your way home to choose one for me while you read the paper?"

"Well, yours wasn't so hot either."

But when Art showed me a copy of the statement he would be making the next morning before the House Committee on Ways and Means on H.R. 3864, the "Temporary Extended Unemployment Compensation Act of 1961"—fourteen pages of pica type and twenty-five pages of tables filled with statistics—I forgave him.

3

I Learn About
the Uses of Power

A magazine once asked Arthur to write an article on how to settle
a family quarrel, inasmuch as he was such an expert in negotiating. Abe Raskin's article in the *New York Times* included Art's
reply in an attention-calling box: " 'No, thanks,' replied the happily married Goldberg, 'but this is an area in which I have absolutely no experience.' "

Arthur's serene facility for arriving at solutions generally allows
for a certain amount of gray area to exist, a certain ambiguity that
permits the hurdling of obstacles to the agreement, providing, of
course, that first there is a will to find a fair peace. Then he is likely
to use such language as, "in a manner to be later determined," or,
"by appropriate procedures," to resolve impasses. And the problems generally get solved.

And they did at the Labor Department, too, but at what a pace!
Even before he was confirmed, Arthur was planning to build
action programs immediately. He knew that the key word was
cooperation. He depended on that and on being able to work with
the heads of the departments of Health, Education and Welfare,
and Commerce, and with the President's Council of Economic
Advisers to devise better techniques than strikes for handling the
human problems of automation. Arthur well knew, from long

experience and particularly from the 116-day 1959 steel strike, that dialogue was needed between labor and management.

Arthur's entire staff was of his own choosing. He picked Bill Wirtz as Undersecretary and Esther Peterson, a legislative representative for the AFL-CIO's Industrial Union Department, to head the Women's Bureau. He chose George L. P. Weaver, director of political education for the International Union of Electrical, Radio and Machine Workers, to be an Assistant Secretary, and James J. Reynolds, vice-president of Alco Products, for industry. The choice of Jerry R. Holleman, president of the state AFL-CIO in Texas, was a concession to George Meany and the AFL people.

When I asked whether others in the administration were also choosing their own staffs, Arthur was not sure. I also wondered whether his wasn't a form of quota system selection—one for industry, one for the black community, one for the AFL-CIO, and one for women's interest. Arthur explained that his conception of the Labor Department was to demonstrate immediately in the very selection of his assistants that the Labor Department was a department for all of the people in the nation, not just for special interests. Each one named, moreover, had merit. The only one he had not known before was Mr. Holleman.

Arthur persuaded Congress to pass a law designating Esther Peterson, head of the Women's Bureau, an Assistant Secretary. Nor did he ask the President-elect for permission when he approached Congress. He said he was making an administrative request. He was the only one in the Kennedy administration to have a woman and a black as Assistant Secretaries, which, at the time, was an achievement.

Kennedy trusted Art. He had already had sufficient dealings with him to know that he was experienced. The senators trusted him too. Indeed, it was only about six months later when, in a poll of the Senate, Arthur was voted the most popular and effective Cabinet officer.

What do you do with power after you get it? Hardly a week after the inauguration, Art pledged that the Labor Department would fight prejudice: "The Department would provide full opportunity for advancement at all levels for anyone qualified to do the job, regardless of any other consideration" and "new vigor would be infused into the President's Committee on Government Contracts," so that no discrimination by employers doing business with the government would be allowed to pass.

He announced, at a testimonial dinner in New York for Representative Adam Clayton Powell, that he had launched a recruitment campaign in Negro schools and colleges to give their students an equal opportunity to find themselves a place in the student intern program of the Department. "In this way, young people of ability will be given a chance to train for positions leading eventually to top administrative jobs." Then the Department began visiting Negro colleges to recruit for employment after Art saw how few blacks were in administrative positions. It was a beginning.

When Art attacked an outstanding social club in Washington that discriminated because of racial bias, a good many liberals thought he had overreached himself. After all, he knew very well that social clubs had a legal right to admit whomever they pleased. Still, an opportunity presented itself permitting him to blast the practice when it discriminated against black ambassadors.

The Metropolitan Club in Washington, one of the wealthiest and most socially prominent clubs, with a membership distinguished in cultural and political life, "turned an insulting face" toward the representatives of people from other lands ("let alone to people from our own land") when they offered all ambassadors from foreign countries except blacks a free membership. Arthur called it "a miserable source of bigotry and prejudice"—something that fashionable club had never before been called publicly. He did not mention the club by name, but all Washington knew.

Arthur's point was that, although the law can do little about private clubs that discriminate, one thing the clubs surely ought not to be allowed to do was to intrude upon the foreign policy of our country. Since the Metropolitan Club's invitation was to all white ambassadors, it was presenting a picture of our country as one that condoned racist attitudes.

Robert Kennedy resigned his membership; the President withdrew his pending application. When he saw Art shortly afterward, the President said jokingly, "You no good so-and-so, now you vetoed my membership in the Metropolitan Club."

After the incident, in July, Arthur appointed George L. P. Weaver, a black, as Undersecretary of Labor for International Affairs to succeed Mr. George Cabot Lodge. Lodge invited

Weaver, who was awaiting Senate confirmation, to be his guest at luncheon at the Metropolitan Club. According to the *Washington Post,* although Mr. Lodge had been rebuffed in his first attempt to bring Mr. Weaver to the club for lunch in March, in July they lifted their ban. Said the *Post:* "Lodge, son of the Republican Vice-Presidential candidate, Henry Cabot Lodge, protested to the club's board of governors. He was joined by a fellow member, Attorney General Robert F. Kennedy, who asked the governors to end the custom of excluding Negroes."

When the encounter led into the Jewish social clubs, Arthur had to be fair with the President. After the President discovered that Burning Tree Country Club did not admit Jews, he asked Arthur to call the Woodmont Club. The Woodmont officials were delighted; they said they would be honored and would give the President an honorary membership. "And we'll give you one too, and Abe Ribicoff." Art said that he was not calling for himself; he was calling for the President.

"Let me ask you something. The President does not feel like playing golf at Burning Tree because they don't let any Jews in. So what's your policy on admissions?" They said, "Well, primarily we're a Jewish club, but we'd accept Kennedy."

"What about Negroes?" It seemed that their membership was restricted to Jews because as Jews they had been excluded. Thus discrimination breeds discrimination.

Arthur then called the President: "If Burning Tree won't let Jews in, and Woodmont won't let Negroes in, you might as well play where you want to play. You can't play on a public course, for security reasons." We did not know then that Burning Tree's defensive attitude extends to women also—even now. Only when a membership looks inward and resolves to change itself can prejudice really be swept away.

Racial bias was not the only bias Arthur attacked. In May, Art issued an order forbidding his department to discriminate against job applicants and employees seeking promotion, because of their age.

It set a good example to private employers and to other governmental agencies, and newspaper editorials lauded him for that. The *Washington Post,* on May 24, pointed out: "Secretary Goldberg is saying that such discrimination [age] must not be used in the Labor Department to discriminate against older persons capable of doing the work at hand. . . . Government has a special obligation to see that the door of opportunity is kept open to all men and women—period."

And that's what one does with power—thrusts a foot in the door to keep opportunity open for those without it. At least one tries.

From the very first day in office, Art plunged into the job of averting strikes with a single-minded concentration on the public interest. He was:

Chairman, President's Commission on Migratory Labor

Chairman, Missile Sites Labor Commission

Chairman, Committee on Youth Employment

Chairman, Temporary Committee on the Implementation of the Federal Employee-Management Relations Program

Chairman, Workers' Advisory Committee on United States Labor-Management Policies

Chairman, President's Commission on Equal Employment Opportunity.

Chairman, President's Advisory Committee on Labor-Management Policy

Member, International Labor Organization

Member, Employers Advisory Commission on the U.S. and ILO

Member, President's Committee on Juvenile Delinquency and Youth Crime

Member, President's Council on Aging

Member, Trade Policy Committee

Member, President's Council on Youth Fitness

Member, Advisory Council on Employment of the Handicapped

Member, President's Committee on Psychological Warfare

Member, Federal Radiation Council

Member, President's Commission on Status of Women

Member, President's Cabinet Textile Advisory Committee

Member, Advisory Commission on Inter-Governmental Relations

Member, Distinguished Federal Civilian Service Awards Board

Member, Cabinet Committee on Federal Office Space

Member, Advisory Committee to the Secretary of Defense

Ex-officio member and ad hoc participant in the National Security Council

And he never was "just a member." Arthur threw himself into the work of the Labor Department with so great a burst of energy that it communicated itself to everyone near him—indeed to the whole Department. The Labor Department was the smallest in the government, but it was asked to bear a staggering load of New Frontier responsibilities. Arthur was nicknamed the Davy Crockett of the administration. In numerous cartoons, a slash of blurred diagonal strokes showed how fast he was traveling. We started framing some of the cartoons and hanging them in the basement on Albemarle Street, but soon even those walls were not enough.

(Our favorite of all was to be that by Les Finnegan about the Metropolitan Opera strike controversy in 1961. First, Arthur was portrayed in the foreground of a Met performance wielding a baton to lead the orchestra and singers. Then, on the stage, he was Figaro in *The Barber of Seville;* Escamillo, the bullfighter, in *Carmen;* Don Giovanni; the Emperor Jones; a coy Madame Butterfly. He was Mephistopheles; a languishing La Bohème on a canopied bed; Wotan in *Das Rheingold* and Brunnhilde in the *Götterdämmerung.* He was portrayed storming, cajoling, pleading, or being outraged and denunciatory. It was Arthur who peeked from within the open jaws of a stage-prop dragon, and it was Arthur, too, as an extra, waving a mace. His face was on several stagehands moving scenery, and there he was as a working member of the Painters Union wielding a wide brush from behind scenery and wearing a jaunty painter's cap askew. He was the seductive Salomé bearing the head of Jokanaan on a silver platter. If you looked closely, it was Arthur's face on the head of Jokanaan, too.)

ITINERARY OF SECRETARY OF LABOR

ARTHUR J. GOLDBERG

FEBRUARY 10–12, 1961

Friday, February 10

8:30 A.M.—Lv. Washington, D.C. via Capital #1 (Breakfast)

10:15 A.M.—Arr. Chicago Midway Airport

10:30 A.M.—Meeting at Midway House, 55th and Cicero (across from Airport) Governor Otto Kerner of Illinois, and local business, labor and community leaders. (Transportation to Midway House arranged by Dennis Church)

11:30 A.M.—Press Conference, Midway House

11:45 A.M.—Leave for Employment Office located at 87th and Stony Island

12:15 P.M.—Arr. at Employment Office, talk with unemployed

12:45 P.M.—Lv. Employment Office for Gary

1:20 P.M.—Arr. Gary City Hall

1:40 P.M.—Meeting in City Hall with Indiana Governor Matthew Welsh and local business, labor, and community leaders. Mayors from nearby cities will attend

2:30 P.M.—Press Conference

2:40 P.M.—Leave for Employment Office

2:50 P.M.—Arr. at Employment Office, talk with unemployed

3:20 P.M.—Lv. Employment Office for Airport

3:35 P.M.—Lv. Gary for South Bend via State Plane

4:15 P.M.—Arr. South Bend Airport. Drive to Employment Office

4:30 P.M.—Arr. Employment Office, talk with unemployed

5:00 P.M.—Drive to Pick-Oliver Hotel

5:15 P.M.—Meeting with Governor Welsh, local mayors, business, labor and community leaders in Rotary Room of Pick-Oliver Hotel

6:15 P.M.—Dinner

6:45 P.M.—Lv. for South Bend Airport

7:00 P.M.—Arr. South Bend Airport

7:05 P.M.—Lv. South Bend in Michigan State Plane for Lansing

8:00 P.M.—Arr. Lansing, Michigan Airport. Drive to legislative meeting of AFL-CIO. Met at meeting by Governor Swainson

8:15 P.M.—Arr. at meeting. Meet with Governor

8:30 P.M.—Secretary Goldberg address AFL-CIO Legislative Conference

8:45 P.M.—Lv. for Lansing Airport

9:00 P.M.—Arr. Airport, lv. Lansing for Detroit Metropolitan Airport in Michigan State Plane. Will be accompanied by Governor

10:00 P.M.—Arr. Detroit

Saturday, February 11

9:00 A.M.—Meet with local business, labor, and community leaders at Sheraton-Cadillac

10:00 A.M.—Press Conference

10:30 A.M.—Leave for Labor Temple to talk with unemployed workers

10:45 A.M.—Arr. Labor Temple, meet with unemployed

11:30 A.M.—Lv. for Airport

12:00 Noon—Arr. Detroit Airport. Lunch at Airport

1:40 P.M.—Lv. Detroit via Delta #433 for Columbus

2:31 P.M.—Arr. Columbus, Ohio

3:00 P.M.—Meeting in Capitol Building with Governor Di-Salle, and business, labor, and community leaders

4:00 P.M.—Press Conference at Capitol Building

4:15 P.M.—Lv. to visit unemployed at AFL-CIO Union Hall

4:30 P.M.—Arr. AFL-CIO Union Hall, talk with unemployed

5:00 P.M.—Dinner

7:00 P.M.—Lv. for Airport

7:30 P.M.—Arr. Airport

7:45 P.M.—Lv. Columbus for Pittsburgh via TWA 546

8:40 P.M.—Arr. Pittsburgh Airport. Met by Pennsylvania Secretary of Labor and Industry William L. Batt and Pittsburgh Mayor Joseph M. Barr

8:45 P.M.—Press Conference, Ambassador's Club, Pittsburgh Airport

9:15 P.M.—Lv. for Pittsburgh Hilton Hotel

9:45 P.M.—Arr. at Hotel

10:00 P.M.—Briefing on unemployment situation by Secretary Batt and George S. McGill, Regional Director of Penn. Employment Security Agency

Sunday, February 12

7:30 A.M.—Breakfast

9:00 A.M.—Meeting with Secretary Batt, Mayor Barr, Pittsburgh Labor-Management Citizens Committee (about 40) and the Mayor's Economic Advisory Committee, and others

10:00 A.M.—Go to Local 1722, UAW Hall, 2325 East Carson Street, to meet unemployed

10:10 A.M.—Arr. at Union Hall, talk with unemployed

10:45 A.M.—Return to Hotel

11:30 A.M.—Lv. Hotel for KDKA Studios, No. 1, Gateway Center

12:00 Noon—CBS Network Show

12:30 P.M.—Return to Hotel, lunch

1:15 P.M.—Lv. for Airport

2:00 P.M.—Lv. Pittsburgh via Allegheny #812

3:58 P.M.—Arr. Washington, D.C. (Final Press Session in Airport Director's Conference Room, Main Terminal Building at Airport with traveling press and others)

On Sunday, February 12, 1961, at 5:40, Art arrived, still borne by the tornado speed of his "whirlwind" trip. "The President called—said it was a terrific job." We rejoiced around a fire crackling for him in the living room. Mother had made her special chopped liver appetizers for him; I fixed him a Scotch. He made one for me, and for mother her Grand Marnier. I had my yellow writing pad at hand and was prepared to save everything for Barbara and Bob. (Bob had called in deep reproach because I had forgotten to tell him that Arthur was on television, and a classmate had had to tell him.)

"Well, I got to the airport early. It was eight thirty, not eight, that I was supposed to be there, so I went in to the coffee place to get a cup of coffee. I hung my coat in the airport restaurant. They announced the plane. I looked for my overcoat—no coat. So I right away called Barbara in Chicago and said, 'You get me a coat from Uncle Abe, honey, and meet me at the airport.'

"The mayor is there with the chief of police, fifty photographers, television, everything, big excitement, and I get off the plane without my coat. Then every radio program, every television, 'The Secretary of Labor is arriving without his coat.' They had another broadcast. So then I got Abe's coat. I kissed Barbie and they had to take a picture, and then they had a room reserved near the airport with a police escort and sirens and Abe too. At the motel, there were big businessmen and labor people. I said in

each case, we'd have a town hall meeting. I gave a little report; then the businessmen spoke, then the labor people. After that a press conference, and on television I said, 'I'm here to express President Kennedy's concern. Unemployment isn't only a statistic, it's people.'

"At the unemployment office I was mobbed and I talked to the people. The people were terrific, very dignified. They spoke very nicely but it was a mob scene. South Chicago was just jammed. One woman said, 'This is my baby.' So what should I do? I took it."

I said, "Well, it did look a little political there."

Art went on: "In the employment office I got up on a chair, told the people the President was with them, that he told me to speak for him. Then I thanked the staff of the unemployment office, said that you were a social worker, and Barbie was a social worker, and I thanked them for their devoted service. I knew they were carrying heavy loads and the work was important. It helped out a lot of people and was appreciated by the President and me." [I had been a social worker in the South Chicago area the year before Barbara was born, after art teaching had been cut from the public school curriculum.]

"Who sat with you?" I wanted to know.

"The mayor sent plainclothesmen, detectives. They sat with me and John Leslie [Special Assistant for Public Relations at the Labor Department]. We had box lunches from the airfield, very good ones, and milk.

"Then we had a police escort to the Indiana state line; then the mayor of Gary was there with a regular cavalcade. Then I transferred cars and rode in to town with the mayor and the senator. There was a big sign: 'Welcome Arthur Goldberg, Secretary of Labor.' Then to the city hall and there was another meeting there. They must have had three to four thousand people, on the stairs, all over—everywhere. They had loudspeakers rigged up. U.S. Steel was there, and Warren Schaeffer, the head of the Gary works of U.S. Steel, and other businessmen. Nobody's done that before —to submit to questions.

"After that, the governor of Indiana took me to the airport and we flew in his plane to South Bend with the senator and the congressman and the newspapermen. And there they had ar-

ranged a buffet dinner in a hotel and the ballroom was just jammed. We just gave them two days' notice, and each time they introduced me, and it was my meeting. I chaired all of them. They asked lots of questions and I tried to answer them."

I wanted to know who paid for all that.

"The Labor Department pays for my travel. The governor for the hotel and the newspapers took care of their own. Then I stopped at an unemployment office in South Bend and each time I said, 'We'll try our best; the President is concerned; we're offering these programs to help, and if what is proposed is not enough we'll have to do more.'

"After that they took us to Lansing. The governor of Michigan sent his plane to South Bend for us. Then we flew to Lansing. We arrived too late. What a nice young governor [John B. Swainson]. He lost his legs in the war. He climbed up the steps of the plane as if nothing was the matter with his legs. All the headlines there: 'Goldberg comes to Lansing, Goldberg comes to South Bend'— those were the headlines everywhere. It was big news. Photographers, local newspapermen—the governor and I had a press conference right there in the airport—like a campaign.

"Then I adopted a new theme in Lansing: 'Everybody says is this a campaign tour? First of all, the President is through with his campaign and I'm not running for anything myself, but if you want to call it a campaign, it *is* a campaign against unemployment, a campaign against distress, a campaign against insecurity—because we tell the facts, because we're candid, don't equate candor with despair.'

"Then Detroit—same thing. Right in the airport. Again I made a statement. Now it's eleven thirty. Then the governor took us in his car to the hotel. They had a beautiful suite; the hotel manager had ordered a hot soup for me and some milk. It was twelve o'clock, so I didn't call you. I had breakfast with the governor, and at nine we had a town hall meeting. And again I presided and Walter [Walter Reuther, president of the United Auto Workers] talked and some businessmen. I had invited the auto companies but they were coy.

"About eleven A.M. I again had a television show, then I went from there to the employment office. It was shut down—Saturday —so I went to a union hall, where the unemployed met with me

and I let them talk. Some are idle almost a year now, and I didn't even agree with them on a shorter work week. I said, 'You'd better get to work first before you start shortening it.'

"Then after that I had lunch at the airport and we took a plane to Columbus, Ohio, and there I was met by Mike Di-Salle [governor of Ohio] and newspapermen and so on. He took me to the State Capitol, where there was a big meeting—another open forum. The governor said: 'This is the Secretary's meeting.' Mike tried to dissuade me from meeting the unemployed. He's such a cautious character, but I said, 'Look, it's not your meeting, Mike, and you don't have to go, but I want to talk to the people.' Oh, I had a sharp debate with one of the Chamber of Commerce people, and then, after we got through, for the first time, we had a real dinner. The governor invited us to his house and we had steak—John Leslie and Andy Hatcher [the President's press secretary] too. They liked that. Until then we had box lunches.

"Then we flew to Pittsburgh. The mayor met me. Big crowds, Steelworkers, Ben and Edna Fisher [friends of ours, Ben was an economist for the Steelworkers Union] in the welcoming committee. The Jewish community is agog. The Fishers have a friend, I don't know her name, but she was so excited, grabs me like a long-lost cousin and says 'I don't know you from Adam, but I've got to express what it means for us to have you. We're so proud, we're busting at the seams.' "

I said, "Hmn." Mother said, "Make a recess, both of you. Stop it. Stop talking; stop writing. Eat." She had prepared an apple strudel for him after seeing him on television at noon. "He's tired," she said to me. "He'll need to rest. I'll make him something special."

"This morning we had a breakfast meeting—same thing all over again, press conferences, also open forum on Sunday—today, they all came out. Then I went to a Steelworkers hall. They told me their problems. Then a television show. They arranged for me to stop at a house.

"You should have seen the house—beautiful, clean—four little children, and he's out of work. They're trying to keep the family together, and I tell you, it's enough, it's just terrible. The Steelworkers are terrific, though. They're wonderful fellows.

"Then when we got to the airport here, in the operations room or something, they had another press conference."

Our friend, Jimmy Griffin, District Director of the Steelworkers' Youngstown area, showed Art the Youngstown paper, all about how the Secretary of Labor came off the plane without a coat. "He had to wear his brother-in-law's coat, Abe Kurgans', and it was too big for him." Someone said Secretary Goldberg's coat was becoming as famous as Adlai Stevenson's shoe, which showed a hole every time he crossed his legs.

Most of Art's work was strictly government business, but occasionally it did take a more personal turn. At one point during Art's tenure, the President called Arthur with the news that Jackie was going to build a house in Middleburg, Virginia's hunt country. She'd found a property, and a local architect in Middleburg had looked at it. The architect told her that she could build a nice house for $50,000.

Arthur said, "Mr. President, if that is what the architect has told you, then it's going to cost two or three times as much. That is the history of all construction. But if you don't mind my asking, why are you calling me?"

"Jackie and the architect have worked out an arrangement whereby the title will be taken out originally in the architect's name, so we don't have undue publicity about it. The architect will engage local labor."

Whereupon Art said, "So now I understand why you called me." At that time, local labor in Virginia meant nonunion labor. "Mr. President, it wouldn't take a week after the property is acquired for a story to break in the *Washington Post* that it is your property. Jackie isn't going to sit in Washington and not take an interest in the construction. Undoubtedly, she's already talked to friends about it. Furthermore, you simply, as President, can't have a house built by nonunion labor."

The President said, "But they tell me that union labor is not available in the Middleburg area."

"That is probably so," Arthur replied, "but we will just have to make arrangements. The building trades in Washington will have a union contractor to build the house."

"I suppose they will charge me a lug."

"I agree with you. They certainly will, President or no President, but there is no other sensible choice."

"Okay. You're right. You arrange it for me."

Art called Jay Turner, the head of the building trades in Washington at the time, and told him that Mrs. Kennedy wanted to build a house, and asked him to take charge. "Also, for God's sake, see to it that the President isn't gouged."

Later, Arthur received another call about Glen Ora from Pierre Salinger. The government was talking about the obvious necessity for a helicopter pad for Glen Ora.

"What's the problem?" Arthur said.

"If it's done at government expense, as planned," said Pierre, "there's bound to be some publicity, but the expenditure is legitimate. There has to be a helicopter pad."

"Why did the President ask you to call me?"

"The President values your advice. He thought it was good advice on the construction."

"Well, Pierre, I have very simple advice. The helicopter pad ought to be built, but by the Kennedys, even though it would be legitimate for the government to put in a helicopter pad."

When Arthur saw Kennedy a short time afterward, the President said, "Incidentally, Pierre told me what you said to him, and I agree with you; that's the way it's going to be."

A long time after the house was built, Art had luncheon with the President in the White House garden. Kennedy looked at Art, smiled as he was leaving to get ready to join Jackie at Glen Ora by helicopter, and said, "You sure know your construction and labor setup. That house cost a helluva lot more than Jackie said it would."

The night of February 14, minutes before his going on television, the President phoned Art for some figures. Then, after hearing about what was being done for the men, what was being done for the children of the unemployed, what was being done for the older citizens, the President said, "Pierre [Salinger] wants to know what you're doing for the young girls?"

I knew that Arthur felt the hollowness and the gravity of the unemployment crisis deeply, because for years he had been intimately involved with unemployment problems. I found myself identifying with Arthur's work for the first time—however peripherally—as if it were my concern too. There was a moral issue involved and there was no avoiding it now. There was no excuse for failing to see what could be done about unemployment.

The Anti-Recession bill had passed in the House by a phenomenally large vote—392 to 30. Art assumed this assured its being noncontroversial and that its security in the Senate need not be doubted. On March 8, he testified before Senator Byrd's Finance Committee, which was expected to act on the President's top-priority request for an extra $1 billion federal program in extended unemployment payments.

Then Arthur left for Minneapolis. He was being besieged by requests to go many more places after politicians had measured the appeal of his previous tour. It gave them a chance to be seen at mass meetings with him, be present at interviews with the press and on television, and to be the beneficiaries of his popularity.

Senator Byrd reached him there by phone and, after the usual civilities, said with gentle Southern courtesy, "Mr. Secretary, we have your bill, and with a very slight amendment, I can get it reported out unanimously."

Arthur, who also used people's titles and names frequently when conversing with them, replied: "Mr. Chairman, would you mind indicating what your slight amendment is?"

"Oh, the same one as during the Eisenhower administration. We'll provide that those states that want extended unemployment compensation can have it, and those that don't want it, don't need to have it."

"Mr. Chairman, that won't be acceptable to the administration," Art said, though he had not asked the President.

Then the senator called him by his first name. "Arthur, I'm terribly disappointed in you. I thought you were a reasonable fellow."

"Well, Mr. Chairman, I think I am, but I can't see the logic of denying unemployment benefits to the unemployed wherever they are, in Georgia, Alabama, Illinois, or wherever."

Then, the senator, with regret in his voice, said softly—and maybe to soften the blow, again used Art's first name—"I'm afraid, Arthur, and I think I should tell you, that we're going to have to defeat your bill."

"Mr. Chairman, I hope and trust—no!" And Art immediately left Minneapolis. The bill was defeated by two votes.

As soon as he came home, he phoned Senator Hubert Humphrey. The following remarks are Arthur's.

"Hubert? Hello, isn't that a terrible thing to do to us? What happened, Hubert? Here I make a speech in Minnesota telling them he's really fighting our battle in the—

"Oh, well, I think we gotta make the fight. Did we have a message from the White House today? Should we get a message from him or keep him out of it? Should I make a statement? . . . What form should it take? . . . Yeah, a letter to the leadership.

"What happened to Hartke? Where was he? You mean he *voted* for this thing? That I don't understand. What's happening to our fellows? They've lost the sense of urgency, that's what. . . . What time you set to go tomorrow? . . . Twelve o'clock. What I think I'll do is to get a good strong letter to Mike Mansfield.

"What will be the parliamentary situation?

"The House bill is the order of business? I see—in other words, I would come out flatly and urge that the vote be for the House bill. Okay, fine. I'll call the President and tell him to do it."

To the White House operator: "You call Senator Mansfield, please." While waiting he turned to me: "The Democrats folded, they didn't show up—Douglas and Gore were the only two who voted with us on the Finance Committee.

"Mike? How are you this evening? Well, I feel clobbered. What happened to our fellas? Is Anderson lined up with Kerr? Uh-huh . . . well. This is worse than the fifty-eight bill. They loaded it up beyond fifty-eight. Seems to me we gotta make a fight, otherwise if we just accede to it, we risk the whole thing.

"We can't let Wilbur Mills down. I haven't talked to the President yet, but either he or I—he'll probably want me to do it—so we can get a letter to you to read to the Senate. Is that the proper procedure? A letter from *him* to you saying he wants the House bill. What's the parliamentary situation, Mike? What will be voted on? Is this a substitute for the House bill? . . . I'll stay there throughout the day so I'll be available for consultation."

The third call went to Larry O'Brien. While waiting, Art told me: "I must say, I'm a babe in the woods. I sure am learning. An old character like Byrd. You know he called me this morning as nice as honey. He said, 'Arthur, I don't mean this in an unfriendly way.' In fact, he told me he was going to cut my throat. At least I gotta know what happened to me. Gotta hand it to that old codger, he told me too."

Then to Mike Feldman, an assistant counsel to the President, who had to check the drafting of the bill.

"Boy, oh boy, they really clobbered us today. How in the world did that happen?" Then an outburst against Gene McCarthy for not showing up. "I'm getting tired of him. . . . Here I tell them in Minnesota that he's out fighting their battle and look . . . yeah. Goddamnit, now, Mike, what do we do? I think we gotta come out against this. I was talking to Mike Mansfield. We gotta get the President to send them a letter.

"Yeah, I was trying to reach Larry, where is he?

"See, I think we have to move fast, before twelve o'clock. We gotta have something written out. I suppose we oughtta talk to the President. Has he been brought up to date? All right, fine . . . right. I'm going on the Hill to see what we can retrieve. Boy, that was a surprise to me. What the hell. I guess these guys know how to put the knife in. Why we lost Kerr and Anderson and Hartke, I don't understand. This is a little mystifying to me. Isn't it to you? You know where I made a mistake? We gotta have a man with the bill and we didn't have that. Wasn't Gene supposed to ride herd? But he never did and walked out on us. That was obvious. That was obvious at the Gridiron the other night. I suppose with this line-up we're gonna get licked. The only ones in trouble are the people outside with no jobs. I guess we have to create a better sense of urgency."

The next call went to Bob Goodwin, a director in the Department of Labor in the division that was supposed to be looking after the processing of the bill. Arthur told him that the letter telling of the administration's opposition and not supporting any amendments should be phrased in such a way that it could be signed either by Arthur or by the President.

Another call then went to Andrew Biemiller, the lobbyist for the AFL-CIO.

"Andy? Arthur, Andy. I see the boys clobbered us. How do you explain it, Andy? I know. I called 'em last night, and I called Lyndon. By God, that's a lot of bull. He's covering up for him. What happened to Hartke? He accompanied me on the trip to

Indiana and made speeches that enough wasn't being done for the
jobless. . . . I don't think we ought to get panicky. Either the
President or I will send a letter to the leadership saying we're
against it lock, stock and barrel and want the House bill. . . . You
think Wilbur Mills will fold, huh? Have we got the votes to win
it? What's the rush about? Why can't they lay it over for a day?
. . . Can't someone object? What about the. . . . See, you're in a
box in a thing like this 'cause they're all voting for unemployment
compensation, and the issue's not clear to the public. So what're
we going to do?

"They can be theoretical about it, but we broke our teeth on it.
. . . So you think the chances are there? . . . He called me last night?
He ran out on 'em, eh? . . . Give him a little cold shoulder that
might help out. Byrd certainly put the knife in this one! . . . But
we got it through so nicely in the House! . . . But they did a quiet
job here. You should've communicated it to me. I thought we'd
be in. Three days! Well, that worried me too a little. . . . Have you
issued any statement attacking the bill? Well, I'm gonna get a good
strong letter up and we'll get you copies to spread around and I'll
be over at the White House and I'll be in touch with you from the
White House."

To me: "I don't think they can swing votes; we're gonna get
clobbered."

Then to Larry O'Brien: "I was on the phone to Lyndon Johnson, to Mansfield. I was on the phone all night. There wasn't very
much I could do there [at the Finance Committee] very frankly."

Between calls, I managed to question him. "But why did *you*
go to Minneapolis?"

" 'Cause I was booked. I'm not a legislator, you know. I'm not
supposed to be a lobbyist. Still, I did try to get it out. Holleman,
Peterson, Bill Wirtz—they were supposed to do the lobbying.
After this, I do it on my own."

To O'Brien, he was reading the Report on Employment from
his own bureau for March 15: "They better not publish this damn
thing. It says things are picking up a little. Insured unemployment
decreased by sixty-two thousand. The President is a better political man than I am because right when we started the bill, I said,
'You know the needs are very great,' and he said, 'Yes, the needs
are great, but there's not much concern about it.' He was predicting a hard time and we have it. Why? The conservatives and the

businessmen control this Congress, that's why. The liberals do not."

Then, when he had hung up the receiver and took a breath, I asked: "But about Lyndon, what did he do?"

"He didn't do a damn thing. Smathers is his boy, and Kerr. He could have lobbied with them and a few others. The time lag has hurt us. Something was brewing. I should have known from their having me up there three days before the Finance Committee. Boy, what a committee!"

Art's letter to Senator Mansfield was full of statistics, but it was easy to understand. It simply said that if people don't have money, it's hard on everyone—their families, their communities, the nation. The fact was that in January, 5.4 million workers were without jobs and about a half million had used up their compensation money and could not yet find jobs.

Then, he examined the provisions of H.R. 4806 as passed by the House. After that, he listed the changes made by the Senate Finance Committee, to which he, as Secretary of Labor, and the administration objected. He analyzed the thinking of the Senate Finance Committee, summing it all up as, apparently, that, "a state should receive no more from a federal tax than employers in the state contribute to it. I believe this principle is not a proper one to meet national needs, and would establish a precedent that could be used in other programs."

Then, he simply told what the bill was intended to do: to meet the unemployment caused by national economic conditions affecting large numbers of workers.

It was a good letter.

The next day, March 16, Art and the administration had to confront what I think was an "ultimate moment," but that sort of language caused him to shake his head at me in an "I-give-up" gesture. For him, a fight must simply be fought when it must be fought. No ultimate moment business, no moment of truth, just a plain showdown was called for, and he and the administration were prepared to meet it. I watched with excitement, recognizing the contest and the drama.

For the first time, I could witness a process of our country's democratic way of life close at hand; I conscientiously tried to keep the journal entries up to date—jotting away frantically, however bewildering my one-sided note-taking might be to me. Nothing could have diverted him. He didn't see me, even when I sat on the bed taking notes right in front of him as he stood at my dressing table where the normal telephone was. The "hot line" was on my long sketching table at the far end of the room. For the most part, he used the White House operators, who were extraordinarily resourceful and cooperative.

For me to accept making myself scarce was to exercise commendable restraint. What wife likes being taken for part of the furniture? Yet, now I was purposely trying to keep out of even his peripheral view and not to ask too many questions.

I learned the details of March 16 from Arthur on his return from the Capitol at 11:30 that night. The objective for the day was to effect a reversal of the Senate Finance Committee's vote when the Senate voted on the floor on the bill, something that rarely occurs.

Art went to Senator Mansfield's office in the morning. At 10:30, the first meetings began with Senators Mansfield, Humphrey, and Gore. Senators McCarthy and Muskie and Haydn were in the back of the Senate Chamber, available if needed. All of them were geared to making an all-out fight. Larry O'Brien was also there, but then he went to the White House. They said the key action was to switch Senator Clinton Anderson of New Mexico, a very influential Senate leader who was a friend of Arthur's, then Senators Vance Hartke of Indiana and Russell Long of Louisiana, the three committee members who had voted against the bill. After that, they would concentrate on Senator Lister Hill of Alabama.

Arthur, in Senator Mansfield's office, reasoned with the various senators. Senator Anderson had thought the Byrd amendment was all right. Art told him he was dead wrong. The senator had wanted to be sure that the bill didn't "federalize" the employment service. He really had to save face. Thus, Art wrote a letter saying that the bill had nothing to do with "federalizing" the employment service, and told Senator Anderson to put that in the Congressional Record for his constituents to read.

He was outraged by Senator Hartke's action, and had the Steelworkers' Chicago director, Joseph Germano, whose office also included the Gary Steel Mills, alert all the labor groups in Indiana. Then, he began calling Senator Hartke's office. Arthur asked Mr. Germano to call Senator Hartke himself.

"What the hell's going on? We supported you, and the Steel-workers need those benefits. Why're you opposing it? D'you want me to bring down five thousand steelworkers to ask you why you're doing this?"

Senator Hartke told Mr. Germano it was all a mistake, then he came to Art's office to say, "Call off your dogs; I'm going to be okay on the floor."

He told Art he had thought the Byrd amendment was all right, but Art said, "You traveled with me in Indiana and told everyone the government wasn't doing enough for the jobless and then you voted against them in the Finance Committee. You're dead wrong."

To convince Senator McCarthy of the urgency of his vote, Art called Earl Bester of the Steelworkers in Minnesota. Bester immediately wired the senator and began the same series of calls as Mr. Germano had initiated for the Indiana senator.

To convince Senator Hill, Arthur first called the Steelworkers' Director, Reuben Farr, and then Buddy Cooper, a friend of ours who had been Justice Hugo Black's first law clerk and was Alabama's leading labor lawyer. He contacted his partner Bill Mitch, who was the son of William Mitch, Sr., the president of the Mine Workers Union of Alabama.

Between the Steelworkers and the Mineworkers, a formidable labor constituency aroused Senator Hill to their urgent need for the administration's bill. Then, Arthur himself phoned Senator Hill, whom he liked very much, and said, "Chief [because he was chairman of the House Labor Committee], are you going to be with me and the angels on this? Look, I hope you can do this for the President, and, yes, for me too. You've got to do this for me, don't you? After all, it's my first bill!"

Senator Hill promised he would "talk to a few of the fellows. I'll see what I can do, but don't worry. I won't let you down." Art felt hungry after he knew the votes were secure and went to the Senate Dining Room. To his amazement there was Gene McCarthy, calmly eating. Art yelled at him, "What the hell are you doing here when we needed your vote?"

"Oh, did they vote? I didn't hear the bell."

"But, Gene, everybody else heard the bell!"

Art bolted his sandwich with the frustration of it and started for home. Passing the open doors of the Senate, he glimpsed a group of senators holding a post-mortem after the vote. They were making speeches, presumably for the record, to include in the newsletters to be sent to constituents. Wanting to thank Senator Humphrey for all he had done on behalf of the bill, Art asked the guard standing in the hall if he would please ask the senator to come out for a moment to talk with him. The guard said, "Oh, Mr. Secretary, you're entitled to go in. Sit here," and he motioned to a couch in the rear of the hall. Ex-senators have a right to sit there, and for State of the Union messages or special ceremonial occasions, so do invited Cabinet officers, but not at other times. But Arthur innocently, unthinkingly, sat down where he never should have been to wait for Senator Humphrey.

He listened to another senator blast the nefarious conspiracy of the Kennedy crowd (and particularly the Secretary of Labor) that had been browbeating senators all day. Out of the corner of his eye, Senator Humphrey happened to notice Arthur, sitting there on a Senate couch. He frantically waved at him to get out and fast. So the Secretary of Labor decamped, telling the guard to advise the senator he would call him from home. Then he came home to tell mother and me the long account of that day's work until finally: "I can't talk anymore. I'm going to sleep."

And mother turned to me: "See, this is what they mean in the papers when they say a bill went on the shelf. It means no one fought for it; no one cared enough to fight like this."

Arthur persisted in ferreting out the reason for the unexpected change of vote in the Finance Committee. The opposition senators, despite their political positions, were friends and displayed a warm and open courtesy to him. He was chagrined by their defection and believed it necessary to know what had prompted it after their initial understanding—at least they seemed to understand—of his testimony.

"They clobbered me, and I need to know what happened and why." The real reason did not appear at once. Only when he met with Senator Robert S. Kerr of Oklahoma in the Senate Dining Room for breakfast, to ask him point-blank what had caused all the reneging, did the true story emerge.

When he put the question to Senator Kerr, the senator said: "There's considerable sentiment in the Senate that they are being overlooked by the Executive with regard to patronage. If I can't get a marshal appointed in Tulsa, because Bobby

Kennedy thinks only Harvard graduates should be appointed, then the President is going to have trouble, and not only on the unemployment compensation bill, as we showed him, but on other bills. It's as simple as that."

Arthur himself, Bobby Kennedy, Larry O'Brien, and all the other people hovering around the President—and the President himself—all presumably men of experienced political intuition and knowledge, were given a deliberate lesson in the rudiments of American politics as it has always been practiced. Lyndon Johnson would have known earlier.

Without saying another word, Arthur phoned the President from the breakfast table to tell him. "Now I know why we're having this trouble. Here's Senator Kerr. He'll tell you."

The senator was laughing: "Mr. President, what would you have done in Massachusetts when you were the senator?"

ABC's Ed Morgan commented, "As spring arrived with a warm, sunny smile in Washington, the Kennedy administration began its third month in office, its hopes bursting like the magnolia buds, but its roots not down very far, and its accomplishments still pretty much unleafed on the naked branch. . . ." Then he changed to a "more sporting simile," quoting a story making the rounds. "The regime resembles the Harlem Globetrotters warming up before a game—plenty of fancy footwork and flashy passing, but nobody has scored a basket."

But two days before, on March 23, President Kennedy signed the Temporary Extended Unemployment Compensation Act and announced:

> This program will immediately provide economic help for some 700,000 jobless workers and their families whose rights to receive regular unemployment insurance benefits under state law are exhausted. Within the next year it will provide benefit payments to an additional two and a half million workers who are expected to exhaust their benefits. . . .
>
> This Act . . . is important also because it will add hard-working dollars to the nation's purchasing power. But important as it is, it is but a temporary measure to alleviate an immediate need. We must move forward with other and more permanent programs to invigorate our economy so that our free enterprise system can reach the level of production and employment which is its obligation and which its capacity and tradition promise.

So Arthur had scored the first basket of the administration. And that was not the only basket. There were victories to come in minimum wage protection; the Area Redevelopment Act; the Manpower Development and Training Act; the Public Works Acceleration Act; the Federal Labor-Management Program; the President's Committee on Equal Employment Opportunity; protection for minority groups; part-time jobs for married women; the Equal Pay Act; the creation of an Assistant Secretaryship; the President's Commission on the Status of Women; the Missile Sites Labor Commission; foreign trade; the creation of the Labor-Management Advisory Committee.*

In addition to legislative contributions, Art's work was a fusion of energy and morale for the Department of Labor. People were glad to say they worked there. Arthur was included in the President's small "kitchen cabinet," as it was sometimes called, on economic matters—Douglas Dillon of the Treasury, Walter Heller, chairman of the President's Commission on Economic Affairs, and Arthur. That gave the Labor Department a tremendous lift of spirit, that the smallest department was elevated to the highest council of the government. He was frequently called upon

*Here, briefly, is a description of some of the administration's achievements.

Minimum Wage Protection

The 1961 amendments to the Fair Labor Standards Act increased the minimum wage for workers already covered, and, for the first time in over twenty years, extended coverage to 3.6 million additional workers. Enforcement of minimum wage provisions reached record levels in the 1961–62 period: almost 3,000 cases were brought under the Davis-Bacon Act and related laws, and over half a million dollars in back wages were recovered. Not much in terms of the gross national product, but in human terms it meant a great deal to the Department and to the people—elementary justice.

Area Redevelopment Act

This Act authorized federal financing for training and retraining of the unemployed and provided federal loan assistance for purchase or development of land and facilities in local areas of persistent unemployment. It established a four-year program to be administered by the Department of Commerce, with the aid of the findings and special studies conducted by the Secretary of Labor and derived from his tours of the depressed areas.

Manpower Development and Training Act

New insights and purpose resulted in the Manpower Development and Training Act signed by the President on March 15, 1962, providing for the establish-

to speak for the administration in hearings on the Hill because of his popularity with Congress.

Perhaps more important than all of these tangible evidences of productive activity was that at the very outset of the administration—indeed, almost immediately—Arthur personally and on his own initiative went to states having areas of the greatest unemployment, bringing to them the message that the government was concerned about their welfare. He talked to labor, to management, and to public officials, but especially to the unemployed workers and their families.

He did not promise all of the unemployed jobs. He knew that would be an impossible promise to fulfill. He merely told them that the President cared, the government cared, and that their problems were to be given the highest priority, and they understood his remarks that way. Frequently, they said: "Politicians always come *before* elections. You're the first one we ever saw who came *after* an election." All he said was that the government was working on their problems and was trying to help.

Scotty Reston had cautioned the wives in the new administration not to proffer undue admiration to their Cabinet-officer husbands, lest they later get swellheaded and become ineffectual. Still,

---

ment, by the Secretary of Labor in 1963, of a centralized Manpower Administration, headed by the Secretary, and responsible for the administration of both the Manpower Development and Training Act and the Area Redevelopment Act. The Act provided for a nationwide training program for the large number of unemployed workers who lack the necessary technological skills to find employment. Institutional and on-the-job training programs were begun, and important research projects were commenced in the Department of Labor.

The Public Works Acceleration Act

The President was authorized by this Act to provide $900 million in federal assistance to aid the long-term unemployed by initiating and encouraging public works projects in eligible areas of local unemployment. The Public Works Bill gave opportunity for the unemployed at the very start of the Kennedy administration when the country was in a recession. At that time, there was 7.1 percent unemployment, so it was necessary to do something quickly to stimulate employment.

Federal Labor-Management Program

The Federal Labor-Management Program was created by an executive order on January 17, 1962, after a task force reported to the President on November 30, 1961. It gave all federal employees the right, finally, to engage in collective bargaining through unions of their own choosing.

the faces in the paper of the listening people and the faces of the quietly talking people who were speaking with Arthur made me temper my impatience at the frenetic pace and single-purposed drive.

That, of course, was a private-life consideration. From the public point of view, the Labor Department raised the economy from a steady decline to a gradual recovery in employment and in industrial production. The main factor was the raising of spirit, the recognition that the good of the country came before any special interest.

Charles Wilson, when he was president of General Motors, before he became Secretary of Defense in the Eisenhower administration, said that what was good for General Motors was good for the country. But Arthur said the opposite many times: "What's good for the country is good for the labor unions and everybody else."

Louis Brandeis' words were Art's own guidelines: "If we would guide by the light of reason, we must let our minds be bold."

The President asked Arthur once: "How do you do it? You moved in. I never gave you instructions and you've settled several strikes. Tell me what's the formula? Those strikes would have

---

The President's Committee on Equal Employment Opportunity
This committee was established by Executive Order 10925 on March 6, 1961. Although the Vice-President was named chairman, Arthur was the executive vice-chairman and he designated the director of the program, Hobart Taylor, who was followed by Stephen Shulman. Out of nearly a thousand cases of contract employment completely processed from 1961 to 1963, 72 percent resulted in corrective measures being taken to correct discrimination. Discrimination was found in over a third of the completed cases stemming from government employment. Some unions and large companies instituted special plans to insure equal opportunity in employment.

Protection for Minority Groups
Art took the initiative in his own department to recruit blacks and women to executive positions where they had been notably omitted before. On paper, the record of the Department listed in percentages for its nondiscrimination practices seemed satisfactory, but when Art looked about him in the main building, no signs were evident of these two much-discriminated-against groups. "Where are they?" he wanted to know and learned that the so-called favorable picture of the Labor Department in this respect was the result of its being in a completely segregated, very shabby building in downtown Washington where blacks were largely employed as clerks.

been injurious to the public and to me. As the new President, I'll have to do international negotiations of a delicate kind, and perhaps there are some principles that can be applied to both international and domestic negotiations."

"Mr. President, you cannot push the analogy between international and domestic labor negotiations too far. After all, whatever you say about our union movements and about our employers, they both operate within the system. A labor dispute is not designed to overthrow the system. Both parties are just seeking a bigger cut of the pie—the employers, more profits and less costs; the unions, a better shake, sometimes at the expense of profits and costs. And the unions never really object, except by words, to an employer's raising prices after a good wage settlement."

"Yes, but what about the public, doesn't it suffer the consequences through higher prices?"

"Well, Mr. President, that's where government enters. It has to be the watchdog to use its influence to see that settlements are not out of line, to see the public interest isn't prejudiced."

"But we don't have the tools to do this." The President meant the government did not have wage-price controls.

To which Art said, "Mr. President, don't underestimate the jawboning power of the President. Since management and labor

---

So, beginning with his choosing George Weaver as an Assistant Secretary in charge of international affairs, he began seeking out capable people for important work from the minority groups. Thus the capable services of Hobart Taylor and Howard Jenkins, and a series of economists, lawyers, and other professionally trained people were made more available to our government.

The Labor Department established the Office of Employee Utilization, which studied ways to maximize employee development for minority group members. The Bureau of Employment Security issued instructions to state employment security agencies prohibiting job referrals where the specifications were discriminatory and prohibiting the keeping of records with identifying information regarding an applicant's race, creed, color, or national origin. The Bureau of Apprenticeship and Training instituted a nondiscrimination clause in agreements with federal contractors.

Part-time Jobs for Married Women, Not much, but a beginning.

This innovative program, an obvious need if working women are to retain their skills during the child-rearing years for later reentry into the labor market, was included and enlarged in a recommendation made by the President's Commission on the Status of Women during Arthur's tenure. Unfortunately, it is not as yet accorded any significant consideration in the federal service.

operate withing the system, they don't like to collide with a President, even if his only power is to appeal over their heads to the public on television."

"Well, we're getting off the subject. The real question is: what's your formula for settling these complicated disputes?"

"Mr. President, effective mediation is more an art than a science, and my wife tells me an artist should not be called upon to explain a painting. It must talk for itself, but I'll let you in on a little secret I'm reluctant to divulge since it takes away from plaudits I thing I earned. The ultimate thing is for the mediator to be on hand and visible when the dispute is finally settled, and virtually every dispute is finally settled for good or bad. The same press and public that previously assailed the mediator for his failure to bring the parties to agreement at the time of settlement applaud him because people really want a settlement."

The President said, "You don't quite mean what you say, do you? Because you don't exactly sit around and let the thing settle itself."

Arthur said, "Well, to be serious, of course not. I try patiently,

---

Equal Pay Act

The Equal Pay Act prohibits sex discrimination in the payment of wages for the same job, and it covers all employees engaged in activities in interstate commerce.

Assistant Secretaryship

Legislation created a new Assistant Secretaryship in the Department of Labor, filled by Mrs. Esther Peterson, responsible for all Labor Department activities relating to women, as well as the functions of the Bureau of Labor Standards.

The President's Commission on the Status of Women

In December of 1961 the President established the Commission on the Status of Women, which studied the problems women face in employment and made a list of recommendations in its report to the President in 1963, suggesting programs and policies for the more equitable and efficient use of women in the labor force. Here were the roots of the growing movement for women's rights.

Missile Sites Labor Commission

The Missile Sites Labor Commission, effected with the cooperation of labor, management, and government, stopped strikes that had pyramided alarmingly in the missile plants.

Foreign Trade

The Trade Expansion Act of 1962, among other things, gave primary responsibility to the Secretary of Labor to provide assistance to those workers adversely

despite prior failure, to guide parties to agreement, but still, if you're around, whether you guide them or not, when you get a settlement, the press and public are more than likely to say, 'The President, or Secretary, successfully negotiated a settlement.' "

If Arthur had not been so surprisingly plunged into the midst of the center of power, if he had been a plain corporate lawyer, eager for clients and for problems on which to display his legal skill, I might have chosen the studio and my own work. True, it might have been more exciting if I had myself been at the center of power, free to respond to the needs of the country and to take some actions toward those ends. Those who want that should be free to make that choice and to enter politics in the hope of being appointed to high office, but I did not want that. It was not my work. What I liked in my own work was finding an ordering in the midst of a seemingly impossible art disorder that would "work." I suspected it might also be possible to approach community problems similarly—but not from the top down, rather from the bottom up—the volunteer in the locality. Now I found it more exciting to watch an event happening and was glad I was not in a work that would freeze me in one given problem.

Knowing the quality of his conscience and the way Arthur

---

affected by the increased foreign trade which the Act was expected to generate. Adjustment assistance was authorized by the Act in the form of weekly allowances, retraining, or relocation allowances. Further, the President assigned to Arthur, not the State Department, the proposals for a reasonable limitation, but not a prohibition, on textile imports from Japan, and with Mexico a reasonable limitation on the use of braceros, or wetbacks, as they were are unfortunately called.

The Creation of the Labor-Management Advisory Committee
    The committee was created by Executive Order in February 1961. Responsibility was shared by the Departments of Labor and Commerce in the task of advising the President on policy matters involving collective bargaining, wage and price standards, and other important economic questions. Though it did not reach its potential by the time Arthur left for the Supreme Court, it nonetheless provided a valuable example of the cooperation that is possible between labor, management, and government. The White House Conference on National Economic Issues in May 1962, involving representatives of labor, management, and the public, was initiated by Arthur. It is interesting to note that this type of summit conference was revived by President Ford as one of his first actions to combat inflation in September of 1974.

cared about injustices, for a man like that to have a chance to be in a position of power was something of a rarity and I wanted to see it happen, perhaps to share, perhaps to help—for better or worse. Why is it more valid for new feminists to support a man who stands for their issues as a candidate for public office than for his own wife to support him?

4

---◦∞◦---

Cabinet Wife

As time went by, the whirl did not slow, but I had somehow speeded up to meet it. My calendar for the first months of 1961 was crowded with entries of luncheons, teas, receptions, embassy dinners, meetings, speaking engagements, gallery openings, and appointments. After May 25, the pages were blissfully blank, providing a three-week island of time to be happily devoted to our daughter Barbara's wedding plans. The blank pages were soon lined with nonofficial happenings in Chicago.

Originally, Barbara had hoped to be married in our Washington home, but the guest list had grown too large for that. To avoid any possible guest-list complications in the new Washington milieu her father had entered as Labor Secretary, she decided to have the wedding in Chicago for family and friends. (That relieved me of the house-decorating situation, for the present. With Barbara married, however, and Bob at Amherst, we did not need the big house. We needed a one-floor house or at least one with a first-floor bedroom and bath for my mother who now had to climb too many steps. Thus, I was in the process of house hunting also. The painting needed when decorating was something I dreaded, but if we found a new house and then put the big one on the market, we would, of course, have to do some house improving first.)

Barbara and David Cramer had chosen June 11, 1961, as their wedding date. On June 10, they both were to be graduated with advanced degrees from the University of Chicago—Dave from the School of Medicine and Barbara from the School of Social Service Administration. (Arthur was asked to address Barbara's class and the gathered alumni and faculty members at her school on Friday, June 9. He made an important statement, which the press duly reported, about the United States' definite obligation to propagate the principles of its own revolution throughout the world. He was giving Barbara's school all the considered thoughtfulness of a major speech.)

Without my friend Janet Weinstein, our rabbi's wife, and our brother-in-law, Sheppard Lehnhoff, in Chicago, the event could not have been so joyful. In Washington, Frances Guilbert, my part-time social secretary, stood in for me when I was out of reach of Barbara's long-distance calls.

Janet had devised a time schedule for the various mother-of-the-bride details, which I was able to meet by spending several weekends in Chicago. Barbara fortunately knew exactly what was indicated: the once-in-a-lifetime plannings with her—the wedding gown, the photographer, the luncheons and teas given by the various aunts and dear friends. Some events, I could not possibly attend, but for the most part, I was there, though Art could come only for the wedding weekend.

Janet skillfully synchronized all the details, and Uncle Sheppard's contribution made the event truly unique. A professional violinist with the Chicago Symphony Orchestra, he had planned the wedding music with consummate care, and it was a distinguished string trio that played.

Arthur and I were elated that it still was possible to experience so important a moment of one's private family life so intimately. Despite all the fanfare attendant on his public office, none of it encroached on or diminished Barbara's and Dave's wedding day.

To travel as a Cabinet wife was an entirely new experience. A red carpet was unrolled, literally, extending from the bottom steps of the plane into the airport proper or to a dais where there was an earnest welcoming ceremony. There were television cameras, with portable ladders and cables, and equipment for broadcasting a supposedly eventful moment in history, and groups of solemn dignitaries and flowers for the official's wife. I liked that too.

In September 1961, we were invited to visit Sweden by Prime Minister Erlander, after his visit to our country in the spring of 1961. The President thought it would be an excellent way for the new administration to redress the slight to the Swedish people caused by President Eisenhower's unfortunate remark about Sweden being a nation of drunks and suicides. Of course, we were glad to go.

Arthur told me he had arranged for us to stop first in Amsterdam to see the home of Anne Frank and, by our official presence at a ceremony, to pay tribute to the Jews of Holocaust and our respects to those valiant Dutch people who had supported them.

Neither Arthur nor I were given to public display of religious observance and, indeed, in private life attended services mainly on the high holidays. He did believe, however, that for Jews in high office, there is an obligation to prevent the Holocaust from being stuffed into history's accumulated unremembered files. Holocaust was more than just another atrocity in a long line of tedious examples of man's inhumanity to man, and, whether or not we attended temple services as frequently in private life as other more observant Jews might have liked, public life had obligations also to a wider Jewish trust, transcending our particular private-life attitudes and practices.

A public official is in office only briefly, and his gestures before or after his tenure are of little import. He must, therefore, be mindful of his obligations to the immediate past and to the long historic chain of the past, even as he moves busily about his business in the present. Not that Art ever put it in so many words, but to me that was what the journey to Holland was all about, for there, and in Denmark, enlightened men and women had defended Jews and stood up to the evil. We had an opportunity to express gratitude.

The Hague, learning of our intention to visit the Anne Frank Foundation, invited us to the opening of the States General and to hear the queen's address. The *Algemeen Handelsblad* of September 21, 1961, reported:

This morning at a quarter past ten the American Secretary of Labor, Arthur J. Goldberg, arrived at Schiphol from London for a short visit to our country. Secretary Goldberg was welcomed by the American Ambassador to the Netherlands, Mr. John Price. The delegation was in a great hurry to go to The Hague, because the first point on the program of Secretary Goldberg was the attendance at the opening of the States General. But Secretary Goldberg still had time to issue a friendly and courteous statement to the press: "Yesterday I was with President Kennedy and he requested me to convey his personal greetings to the population and the government of this country with which we had so many good relations in the past and now. During the few days that I will be here I will have discussions amongst others with your Ministers of Social Affairs and Economic Affairs. We realize that we can still learn much about the manner in which, especially in Holland and in Scandinavia, labor peace is guaranteed through organizations such as for instance your Labor Foundation, the Social Economic Council [SER], the Government Mediators, etc., and . . . our experiments in this field are based partially on your experience. . . . [Then the real purpose, so far as I was concerned.] This afternoon at half past four I will lay a wreath in the Anne Frank House, at the request of President Kennedy, who also gave me a special letter for this event."

There was the house itself with all the rooms mentioned in Anne Frank's diary. We had to climb steep steps to the apartment where the Franks were hidden from the Nazis by brave Dutch friends. We saw the device for soundproofing the lock to the door behind the bookcase, and we also visited the room where Anne slept. We saw where her growth was measured on the wallpaper, and her drawings, and we peered from the same little window to glimpse the limited view of the street where others could walk in freedom, but not Jews.

From a community of 100,000 Jews only 6,000 remained. Frau Gertrud Wysmuller, a Christian who was one of the founders of the Anne Frank Foundation, and Mr. Endling, a director who worked with the chancellor of the university, showed us through the building. Frau Wysmuller wept as she pointed to a photograph of Jews awaiting shipment to a concentration camp. She herself had saved some 3,000 Jewish children. "They all went, and we remained." Her story was told in a broadcast, September 4, 1961, in a "Topical Talk" portrait of her on Radio Nederland (script by Bibeb): When the British government gave the British Jewish Committee permission to take in 10,000 children, Mrs. Wysmuller received the order to go to Vienna, to go to Eichmann. That was in December of 1938. In the streets of Vienna she saw how the police drove their automobiles right at Jews, purposely trying to crush them to death against the walls of the buildings. Whoever escaped was chased and beaten with rubber hoses. She had been told nothing about Eichmann. The house in which he was to be was no different from any of the others. It was large and stately, like all the houses in the neighborhood. An unusual adventure awaited her inside. She entered a room that was almost dark except for a small podium on which there stood a lamp. Under this burning lamp sat a man dressed in black; a large dog sat next to him. "I am not accustomed to negotiating with women," he said. But the power of Mrs. Wysmuller lies in the fact that she never lets herself be intimidated. She sat down and told him about the offer of the British government and of the Jewish Committee. She showed him letters which proved her words. At this point, Eichmann pushed a button and called out an order: "Send in the Jew Friedman." Turning to the man, he said, "Jew, do you know this woman?" and then, "Frau Wysmuller, do you know this Jew?" When both had answered that they did not know each other, Eichmann banged the table, laughed loudly, and said, "Now we are going to play a crazy joke [*Jetzt wollen wir ein toller machen*]. She will go back over the border tomorrow with six hundred children. . . ." He was convinced that these hundreds of children would never be welcome anywhere. She called the committee in Britain from her hotel and received the answer that she send five hundred children to them; she had to see to it that the other one hundred were sheltered in Holland.

When the Germans entered the Netherlands, she had to work even harder than before. If she had not been there, the children in the Amsterdam Jewish Orphanage would never have been able to flee to England. She continually brought small groups of children across the border, and many adults too. It will never be known how many were saved by Mrs. Wysmuller. She brought medicine to the chairman of the Netherlands Red Cross, Dr. Veldhuyzen, in unoccupied France to combat infectious diseases in the camps there. She had contact with Admiral Canaris, and took care of the transportation of Jews who paid a high price [50,000 Swiss gold francs per person] to leave the country. Her reward was that for each paid passage, one child was allowed to go along for nothing.

After we returned, Arthur's comments about how two can travel as cheaply as one hit the papers.

"The Secretary of Labor was striking a blow today for the portal-to-portal travel rights of the official wives of Washington. He will write a letter to the U.S. Controller General asking that government officials—'especially in the lower echelons of government service' be permitted to take their wives along to the four corners of the earth at Government expense.

" 'Wives make the best natural ambassadors this country had,' " he was quoted as saying.

"Secretary Goldberg has worked out a plan whereby two can travel for the price of one. He did it when he and Mrs. Goldberg made their recent trip to Scandinavia. He paid her way out of his own pocket, but both of them went economy class instead of deluxe. 'It cost no more for the two of us to go than if I had gone in luxury,' he said. 'And I felt no loss of prestige whatsoever. . . . We are failing to tap one of our greatest diplomatic resources when we do not permit wives to go along with their husbands unless they pay their own way,' he said. 'In most cases, especially in the lower ranks, where a man is sent overseas by his government for weeks and even months, the family can't afford to pay for their travel too.' "

What was left unsaid was our reception in Sweden, when the Prime Minister and Mrs. Erlander and other dignitaries, and a bevy of welcomers including Swedish and international press and TV representatives, waited bewildered at the first-class exit of our plane. After all had alighted except the Secretary of Labor of the United States and his wife, their expressions were really something to behold. That is, if we could have seen them from the distance when we emerged from second class, a block away. Then the entire entourage, with exclamations probably meaning, "There-they-are; there-they-are"— unless it meant in Swedish, "Hell and damnation"—had to scramble in astonishment to second class.

The Swedish Prime Minister was bemused, although he and his family lived in exceptional simplicity. When he rode in his official car escorted by a motorcycle policeman, the car ahead did not move out of the way and no automobile sirens sounded. We saw for ourselves how he asked the motorcycle policeman to please ask the motorist in front of us to permit our official cars to pass ahead of him. To that, the motorist replied that he himself was observing the speed limit and the Prime Minister and his party should do likewise. At that, Art said, "Then why, Mr. Prime Minister, are you surprised that we traveled second class?"

"But what office are you running for?" Mr. Erlander asked.

Later, Arthur said to me, "*You* are getting spoiled," when I demurred about returning second class, but his bag was not lost on arrival in New York; mine was. And I had to stay overnight at the Carlyle Hotel, without a toothbrush or nightgown, to await the arrival of the luggage in the morning.

"You should have packed better," he said as he went on to Washington. "That's what your little carry-on bag is for—not for all those notebooks and brochures."

If traveling was one of the pluses; speechmaking definitely was not.

Speechmaking was a ceremonial chore apparently expected of Cabinet wives. From the startling number of requests for appearances, it seemed to be taken for granted that a wife would be able to hold forth behind a lectern at least as well as her husband. I knew that congressional wives had active speechmaking clubs to polish the public speaking needed in support of their husbands' campaigns, or to address various constituencies at home. But would I merely be providing a passing diversion, an opportunity to appraise the wife of the Labor Secretary—her hair, her mannerisms, her way of speaking—a reassuring symbol of fluffy thinking even though she was precipitated willy-nilly by her husband's work into a status position? It would be a waste of my time. But yet, perhaps there was something I could say.

So, while I did not demur, I was not particularly enthusiastic when the requests stressed an art subject. It did not seem fair to me to be spreading art understanding like a Lady Bountiful when I had already established a fairly successful professional program for which subscribers paid. If there had been a pediatrician among the Cabinet wives, she surely would not have been asked to provide free advice about childhood allergies. Yet Arthur said a speaker's fee was out of the question and, of course, I would not have wanted to profit from his governmental status. But, as a painter, I had never given anything away and I felt a bit frustrated at having my skills summarily diminished.

I did not, however, feel secure enough in any field other than art to be able to stand before strangers in public halls to answer questions. It would be a challenge and perhaps fun. It turned out to be considerable work too.

The first request I accepted was from the Public Health Officers' Wives' Club in the Bethesda Naval Hospital. The subject I offered was "Tension In and Out of the Painting." The more inexperienced the public speaker, the longer the speech. I spoke two hours. The chairman apologized to me in her concluding remarks for two women who had had to leave before I had finished talking because of babysitters.

Arthur was appalled at dinner to learn I had delivered myself of a two-hour address. "Don't you know after all these years that a speech has to have a beginning and an end and in the middle make a few logical points? Never talk more than fifteen or twenty minutes—maybe a half hour, but no more than that."

"That's for you—for lawyers. My way is different. I need not go directly to the target. I edge up on it from side to side. Sometimes I hit the bull's-eye, sometimes I don't. So what? They all stayed."

"They're just too polite to walk out on you, that's what."

"Well, what should people expect for nothing?"

Several months later, at the Navy Doctors' Wives Club, my speech was only an hour and a half. Still, one woman cornered me as I was leaving to say somewhat superciliously that I had just rambled on. While I think my speech had virtually the same title, it was different from the previous speech because I was uncomfortable about repeating myself.

"Why not?" Art wanted to know. "It's a different crowd. All you need is one good speech—one good point in it. John Kennedy only made one speech, 'Let's get the country moving again,' and it went over big."

"But Adlai Stevenson was able to do better than that."

"So who do you think you are? Adlai Stevenson? No speech is worth all that agonizing."

Certainly, when the Navy Doctors' Wives sent me their November 1961 "Stethoscope" news bulletin later, I felt dismayed at the report of my spontaneous, unwritten speech as their reporter heard it:

'Tenshun! At ease, Ladies . . .

"Mosaics neatly assembled out of square cut tiles are very much in vogue right now—and I think them quite interesting; but I like those done out of fractured glass the best. These are exciting." Mrs. Arthur Goldberg spoke with a sparkle and a freshness which did convey excitement as she delved into her subject, "Tension in and out of the Canvas Space," to the group of 153 members and guests at the October Navy Doctors' Wives' Club luncheon. Certainly what she said came as music to the ears of those ladies who had long since despaired of ever running the perfectly organized house *à la* the *Ladies' Home Journal* or raising the model children of that bygone Victorian era.

"What you do with the fractured pieces of your day is what is important," Mrs. Goldberg said, "and it is the visual pieces that make up the whole picture on a canvas which determine its importance." She stated further that just as some brush strokes on a canvas are of more lasting value than others, so are the brush strokes that some of us make in life of greater import than others, but what is necessary is that we make a response to our tensions . . . in other words, CHALLENGE–RESPONSE. On the other hand we all need a place of refreshment when we sink into those inevitable valleys. We cannot remain on the peaks all the time. An artist might go to the zoo and sketch with absolutely no purpose other than to relax the best way he knows how, giving form to his skill which eventually will lead him back to the peaks. Women constantly have to rehabilitate and Mrs. Goldberg feels this is more true in our era than in any other. To her this accounts for much of the renaissance of the arts. The creative arts are a tremendous source of emotional and spiritual restoration, and she feels that we all have this ability in one form or another within us—that the Almighty has not been discriminatory in his gifts. To have a wholly free and creative way to respond to our challenges makes better wives and mothers of us all. The artist knows that everything is grist for his mill, even despair, which can be ultimately contained on the canvas, and the more self-contained the part the better the whole.

In a letter subsequently received from Mrs. Goldberg thanking the Navy Doctors' Wives' Club for the opportunity to speak, she again stressed a note of hope which she wanted to be sure the group realized: "Things do get better; demands become less; but even then we must be alert to our own personal growth despite our less fractured existence."

Mrs. Goldberg indeed had responded to a challenge in speaking to the Navy Doctors' Wives' Club. She had returned from Canada via New York early in the morning, and by an error in schedule was committed to a talk to the Women Democrats' League before coming to our luncheon at the C.O.M. . . .

After reading that report, I decided that every speech must be accompanied by at least some piece of paper to hold in my hand that could be given to a reporter. The reason I wrote a letter after my speech to include in their "Stethoscope" was that the chairman had introduced me and my accomplishments so glowingly that I squirmed—particularly when a young intern's wife turned out to know Barbara. I became uneasy lest she meet Barbara someday and communicate that exaggerated portrait of her mother being a paragon of virtues, when Barbara knew otherwise. So I added:

. . . for the benefit of those nineteen young internes' wives (one of whom may meet our daughter, also an intern's wife), this should be noted for the record: Mrs. G. has grown children. No sitter problems, croup, chicken-pox, etc. She has a full-time household-helper. Her husband has a devoted mother-in-law who makes him his special food delicacies. Mrs. G.'s good friend, Frances Guilbert, is a colonel's wife who is providing twelve hours secretarial service. Mrs. G. has a group of friends who volunteer to fill the commitments she can't keep, like helping at Sargent House, setting up a high school exhibit, taking her turn on Saturdays at the Gallery—even sharing the class presentations. . . .

Other speeches, more ceremonial, and more or less art substantive, but still needing some preparation, were made to a number of Jewish women's groups. They were so pleased that Arthur Goldberg was named to the Kennedy Cabinet that I felt obligated to accept because of their warm feeling for him. If he were too busy to accept, and most of the time he was, then I was glad to play second fiddle.

I began to be thoughtful about working on a single master speech that could be either cut or lengthened like the hem of a dress. Also, I learned not to be too influenced by Arthur's standards for his own speeches after a disastrous occurrence in Philadelphia.

I made the mistake of reading the first draft of my speech to

Arthur. After my tired voice had completed only twelve of the twenty-five pages I had written, he told me to stop worrying so much. "You fuss too much over a simple little speech. Just take my last speech. That's all you need. It sums up the campaign promises of the administration and shows what we've done so far to meet them and what we intend doing."

But his last speech had been to the Maintenance Workers and Janitors and Bartenders Union, and the women of the Philadelphia Branch of the National Women's League of the United Synagogues of America had asked me to speak on the theme of their forty-third Founder's Day celebration in honor of Mathilde Schechter, the revered wife of Solomon Schechter. The theme was to be: "And All Thy Children Shall Be Learned of the Lord."

The year was coming to an end and criticism of the administration, actual and implied, was blowing in the breeze. Chalmers M. Roberts, a cogent thinker whose comments I had learned to respect, had come out in the *Washington Post* of November 12 with a headline: "Lack of a 'Grand Design' Is Kennedy's Problem."

The next month, the *New York Times* featured several querulous cartoons. Herblock's, reprinted there, showed what was thought of the administration: a group of fat sailors in a small, storm-beset boat bellow directions to JFK struggling with the steering wheel. The Liberals shout: "Hard left"; the Conservatives: "Hard right"; the Birch Society: "Full astern"; the Americans for Democratic Action: "Full speed ahead"; and the Southern Democrats: "Slow down."

And an angry young comic, Dave Astor, was regaling patrons of the Blue Angel, a New York night club, with, among other comments, the following twitting of the President: "He told the NAM he would bring prices up and salaries down; he told the AFL-CIO he would bring salaries up and prices down; then he told Secretary Goldberg: 'Take care of it, kid.' "

The American Survey in *The Economist* of December 30 wrote of the New Frontier as if it were receding into the past; only one year had elapsed. It was like reading a dissertation on eighteenth-century Whigs *vs.* Tories:

The Democrats lack the cultural and social homogeneity of the Republicans, who remain for the most part a minority party of business executives, professional men, merchants and farmers, primarily of native or early immigrant stock. Apart from the nearly autonomous Southern wing, the Democratic Party consists of reformers and other political amateurs, big-city machines led by professional politicians, ethnic and racial groups, liberal intellectuals, trade union leaders and organizations of left-wing farmers—a conglomeration almost certain to generate internal friction. . . . Although most of the big machines were effective in getting out the votes for Mr. Kennedy's paper-thin triumph last year, the party's reform element believes that the urban bosses could do the Democrats more harm than good in the long run. . . . Surprisingly narrow Democratic victories in Philadelphia two months ago indicated growing public resentment against the supposedly invincible Philadelphia city machine of Mr. William Green, who lives a dual life as Congressman and big city boss. . . .

I was becoming less detached and more protective of the New Frontier image, trying to remind my listeners, whenever I was called upon to make remarks, that the New Frontier was, after all, an experimental attempt. My clipping file enlarged to include background material for speeches, such as two sentences that I liked from a *Washington Post* editorial when Congress opened in January 1962:

It has been a frankly experimental attempt to make a free market system work without many of the motivating forces of blind economic coercion that many at first thought an indispensable ingredient of the system. . . . The genius of the compromise between necessity and humanity is that the economic system has been made to work better at the same time that it has been made to work more humanely. . . .

5

·——————·◦◦◦·——————·

Widening Horizons

So much had changed after a year of being the wife of the Secretary of Labor. The morning of Thursday, January 11, 1962, the opening day of Congress, of the second year of the New Frontier, the temperature was six degrees above zero. I shivered doubly when I thought of the schedule of the day ahead and of the next day, when we would be hosts at a formal dinner party in honor of Vice-President and Mrs. Johnson. I shivered not because of the still-unplanned seating arrangement, and not because of the many other incomplete details for both days, but to impress upon Art that everyone would be shivering worse the following day.

All the women in flimsy clothing arriving in Conference Room B of the Labor Department would have to walk down the passageway to the Departmental Auditorium that on normal days funneled strong winds between the two buildings. With the weather near zero, the cold would be unendurable. With all their New Frontierish bravado about pretending to be oblivious to cold, and the older ones not wearing thermal underwear, half the government would come down with pneumonia.

"Nobody will thank you for this."

"Nonsense. They'll love it. It'll be different from all those dinners we go to all the time. There's a corner fireplace. They can warm up there."

At least I tried. But Arthur was anticipating a great time and planned for cocktails to be served before a lively fire in the smaller conference room adjoining his own private office. Then all the guests would march east nearly a mile to Conference Room B to finally find their places at round tables for eight.

They would certainly work up an appetite. Art said it was unnecessary for them to drag their coats and furs along once they had checked them for the reception in the upstairs office.

"You mean they have to go mountain-climbing all the way back?"

"Why not?"

So I began shivering as we bent over the dining table after breakfast to arrange the place cards at imaginary tables for ninety-six guests.

The decision, Art's, finally was to have two tables of twelve and others of ten, or however it would work out. But he would not wait for me to make a list because he said people spent too much time making lists instead of moving ahead into the work itself. "Don't waste time organizing things to get ready to work. Just do it."

So the morning of the opening of Congress, I confronted the ninety-six little place cards. After they were appropriately arranged in circles, I carefully stacked them in order and put them in envelopes for Arthur to bring to his secretary, who would place them on the proper tables.

All this nonsense would have made a Benjamin Franklin's hair stand on end, and it did that to mine too, but that was our life. None of us had any protocol experience, and Art would not let me call Letitia Baldridge, Jackie's social secretary, who would have gladly arranged the cards in no time. "She doesn't know the Labor setup," he said, and he was right. One had to know who was on speaking terms with whom.

At noon I drove to the opening of Congress ceremonies. You could tell the White House cars because they were parked in No Parking places in the Mall area.

I entered the executive gallery to find virtually everyone there. Ethel Kennedy, Jane Freeman, and Lee Udall looked fresh in brilliant crimson suits.

The opening of Congress is a thrilling, majestic spectacle, but the gymnastics of rising and sitting down, and rising and sitting again, and trying to applaud with an armful of coat got a bit taxing, but no one told me where to check it, assuming, I suppose, that I attended frequently enough to know—although the only time I had been there previously was to the same event the year before. Mrs. Kennedy arrived looking beautifully uncluttered in a black beret and white wool coat. Everyone rose for her. Lynda Bird used her mother's tan silk scarf to sit on the gallery steps to see better.

Lady Bird had invited a group of visiting Texas ladies to luncheon in the Senate Dining Room afterward, and I had accepted her invitation to join them, as had Ruth Ribicoff and Virginia Rusk. But Jane Freeman had also invited me to luncheon at the same time to get publicity for the Democratic fund-raising dinner for the President. She was not sure that Mrs. Kennedy would come and hoped that as many Cabinet wives as possible would accept. Jane was the Cabinet wife with the political flair.

The President's earnestness came through in his speech. The Supreme Court was not there because, as Mrs. Warren informed me, their work came first; Court was in session and could not stop just for the opening of a new Congress. The Cabinet clapped enthusiastically for the President; therefore, there was no reason for the ladylike restraint on the part of the Cabinet wives. I had thought, on other occasions, when their husbands were main speakers at some event, that perhaps their restraint was caused by one's not wanting to applaud one's own family. But I always applauded when Arthur was applauded, regarding myself in public as a citizen paying honor to the one being honored—therefore, I applauded vigorously, and particularly for the President's stand on the United Nations. Mrs. Warren and Ruth Ribicoff said it seemed strange not to see Sam Rayburn, who had died November 16, 1961. The Republicans seated on the floor below us clapped only when the President said that a strong defense was necessary.

After the speech, I went with Lady Bird to the Vice-President's office—my first visit there. He had a Brumidi painting all over two ceilings. Sherry, Dubonnet, wine, and tomato juice were served until the Vice-President entered to shake everyone's hand. Then, all of us looked at a portrait of Sam Rayburn on a small table.

After that, we went to the new dining room with its very shiny new stainless steel knives and forks; Mrs. Johnson said she liked the old dining room better. The chandelier was her idea. Apparently, it had come from the Vice-President's office. She had suggested to him that it ought to be where many more people could enjoy it; besides, it was just too overpowering for an office.

Thus, the new dining room did have a part of the old Capitol within it. I sat across from Senator Jackson's bride, and while Mrs. Johnson told her who all the people were, I listened also. To my right was Mrs. Hale Boggs. Mrs. Johnson said it would be all right for me to leave after thirty minutes. I decided she knew better than I how long Jane's affair was to last, and she proved right.

At the Senate Office Building, I ran along the hall until I noticed that the crowd in the middle of the distant bank of elevators was made up of Secret Service, policemen, and photographers. I walked more sedately then and pressed for the second-floor elevator, but then I noticed 219-G was right there and exclaimed, "Well, this is it." (That Alice-in-Wonderland exclamation brought a man—not a white rabbit—who looked at me suspiciously.) "Your name?"

"Goldberg."

He continued appraising me dubiously and said, "But it's halfway over."

"I know, but I had to go to Mrs. Johnson's first."

He looked even more dubious, and I thought, why on earth do I have to tell him, and walked in.

Jane Freeman was talking and said, "And here is Mrs. Goldberg." I sat down quickly and listened to Jane telling about the dinner. Mrs. Kennedy was listening dutifully, occasionally smiling, and the strong lights of the photographers were focused fully on her. Jane was saying that Mrs. Kennedy had promised to be at the big dinner and so had all the Cabinet and their wives and that was nice, because they did love having Mrs. Kennedy at the President's side. The President felt better when she was there and so did everybody else.

All of us rose as Mrs. Kennedy prepared to leave, and there was an embarrassing silence. First she said, "Oh, my goodness," then, "I know it's going to be successful and I hope everything will work out well." Another pause, then Carrie Davis, wife of congressman

Clifford Davis of Tennessee, started to clap, and everyone else joined in the applause. All the newspaper women flocked out to watch Mrs. Kennedy leave and then returned. Lady Bird Johnson entered then with Mary Louise Day, Ruth Ribicoff, and Mrs. Hale Boggs, and again everyone applauded. Then Jane said, "And Mrs. Goldberg, too." So I was politely applauded.

Then the old pros like Mrs. Fred Vinson and Mrs. Davis suggested what should be done that had not been done last year. One woman said, "At least, could someone see that everyone gets something to eat," and suggested that there be a troubleshooter the waiters could go to when no one had anything to eat after paying $100 a plate. Margaret Price, vice-chairperson of the Democratic National Committee, whose husband was Assistant Secretary of Commerce for Domestic Affairs, rose to say that the dinner was free; those who contributed $100 to the Democratic Party would be invited for nothing.

More pictures were taken. Jane thanked everyone and I left for the Labor Department while the talking continued.

Art's staff was desperately engaged in arranging little cards around imaginary tables. "What happened to Arthur's lists—the cards clipped together in envelopes?" Apparently they did not know he had arranged the seating plan himself; they had erased the cards and had changed them according to the Green Book, which sets forth State Department protocol, instead of Labor protocol. Only Art knew who among the big-wigs was not on speaking terms with whom.

The florist came in then to look at the room where the dinner would be held, and I walked the mile of floor with him until we came to Conference Room B. The fireplace there had never been used and I couldn't see any chimney. I asked the florist if he would mind looking into the fireplace. He said that there did seem to be some kind of an opening there, so I was hopeful the Department of Labor would not be in flames when the Secretary of Labor and Mrs. Goldberg gave a dinner in honor of the Vice-President and Mrs. Lyndon Johnson.

I returned to the office where the struggle of table arranging was in process, while wondering if the John Birchers would clamp on to *Goldberg Does Big Partying at Government Offices.* Arthur, of course, paid all bills personally, and when an eager journalist asked the caterer, he replied, "The Goldbergs always pay their own bills." Then, when the journalist asked Art to show him the check stubs too, that was promptly done. First, I fumed at the arrogance, then I realized that in a free society such irreverence is a vital component of citizenship. Now Art was merely on the other side of the taxpayer-versus-government fence.

The menu, after John Leslie of Public Relations consulted with proper authorities, had an interesting Mexican-Texas flare. The Mexican Ambassador, Antonio Carrillo Flores, was bringing in a bank of singing musicians, Los Delfines, for his own musicale on Saturday afternoon at the Mexican Embassy, and he had arranged for them to come to our party the evening before, which was quite a coup. I had found a cookbook with a "celebrity" section in it and there was a recipe called Noches Specials, signed by Mrs. Lyndon Johnson. When the menu for the dinner was printed, it read, "Nottes—Lady Bird Johnson," and when I pointed out the error, John Leslie said, "Dorothy, that's your mistake, not ours."

"How come?"

"Well, I've consulted Spanish-speaking authorities, and they say 'noches' isn't right."

"But that's what Mrs. Johnson called it in this recipe."

"But how do you think it'll sound," he said. " 'Noches, Lady Bird Johnson' means 'Nights with Lady Bird Johnson.' " So we changed it to "Noches Special (Tortillas) Lady Bird Johnson," which parenthetically saved that critical situation.

By the second year, I was beginning to feel less of a hostess-wife responsibility for official dinners such as the one for the Johnsons, since Cabinet wives were not expected to reciprocate.

The Johnsons did, however, invite us to their home on several occasions when they lived at The Elms. Mrs. Johnson's menus were skillfully planned to comply with her husband's weight-reducing needs and were appetizingly prepared.

She showed me the long corridor hung with pictures of the two of them photographed with the world's great. I liked the picture gallery idea, and, when later we were at the Waldorf Towers during the United Nations period of our lives, remembered to use it, although we used only photographs of Art's trips to deprived areas and current cartoons of him. With each move after the UN period (to the Pierre Hotel in 1968, and returning to Washington permanently later) we divested ourselves of more and more of those images of public life, until now there are only two we keep in Arthur's study. One is of President Kennedy; the other is of the opening of the joint session of Congress where the President is addressing that body and the members of his Cabinet are listening intently.

If 1961, was full of "firsts" for me, 1962 was filled with even more and newer experiences. I already had learned what the role of "public wife" required—largely the ceremonial presence of consort status. I accepted ceremony, and liked it, as a necessary element of the interaction between government and citizen, but people in crowds tend to merge into a faceless mass, difficult to accept.

Often, all I would know before accompanying Art would be a calendar notation: dinner at—— for—— on——. Helen May, Arthur's secretary at the Department, would clear the dates with Fran Guilbert, my secretary, and Fran would note the engagement on my schedule. Thus, I would frequently attend a meeting feeling quite unprepared.

By the second year, this no longer troubled me so much. For State dinners, Virginia Rusk would send a short briefing for me by messenger; my being a conscientious newspaper reader also helped.

I had learned not to say to my dinner partner, "Please tell me a little about yourself," lest he reply, "I'm your host"; or, "What, may I ask, is your particular discipline?" lest he reply, "Haven't any"; or, "Do you have children?" "No." That would end talk unless one of us burst into laughter at the attempt to meet the proprieties, since each knew neither cared about the other's progeny. Sometimes I would care very much. It would be interesting to know whether the celebrities I was meeting so frequently wanted their sons and daughters to be similarly engrossed in their spheres of public life. And the young ones—did they want as much for themselves? And were they politically inclined, and if so, were they of the same political party? Were they protesters on university campuses? It was not necessary to ask questions of a personal nature, but, frequently, explanations would be forthcoming as a result of some nonpersonal observation.

The second year of public life presented the sameness of public dinners, but the game had expanded. The game was to ask a question about that particular moment, that particular group, that would interest another enough to encourage him to be more forthcoming. I had a genuine interest, but as everyone knows, if one is interested in everything, it means being interested in nothing. By the second year, my interests had become channeled into a concern of my own with groups that meant a great deal to me— people working for the public schools of the inner-city.

An art project for the schools seemed a logical beginning. Dr. Carl Hansen, the superintendent of schools, suggested that I meet with Ben Henley, the assistant superintendent.

When I met with Mr. Henley, he gave me the first issue of the *Urban Service Corpsman,* a newsletter describing the school needs and particularly stressing the need to recruit volunteers. Agnes Meyer, widow of the publisher of the *Washington Post,* who had founded the Urban Service Corps through the Meyer Foundation, had written a column stressing the urgency of employing youth, hoping that the public school system could train youngsters, particularly dropouts, for various service jobs.

Under the mantle of the Urban Service Corps, there would, at the least, be justification for my seeking Labor Department support for whatever school projects I might undertake. The Labor Department was concerned about training programs and fostering upward mobility.

Arthur was chairman of the President's Committee on Youth Employment, which had been established in November of 1961 because more than a million young people between the ages of sixteen and twenty-one were out of school and out of work. The Youth Employment Committee had lofty goals but, unfortunately, they outlined hopes more than they developed actualities.

Without knowing where I personally could begin to make a contribution, and having professional training only in my own discipline, I had suggested to Dr. Hansen that a seminar for high school teachers on the value of arts in the school curriculum might be a valid beginning. (It would also give me time to better understand the local school situation before concentrating in a given direction.) I reasoned that whatever funds were available to the public schools were being directed largely toward the science department. James Jones, the art supervisor, had no office help, whereas the science supervisor, I was told, had three to help him.

The art department was still short of supplies, and the prevailing attitude seemed to be that art was a frill. I had already learned how readily a position near the center of power could be put to use. Arthur's name worked magic, and the magic worked even when prefaced by the "Mrs." Like waving a wand or murmuring an incantation, an important authority would respond to a telephone call instead of his secretary replying that he was in conference. None of that now. Instead, instant contact.

The idea of a seminar for high school teachers on the value of the arts in the school curriculum appealed to me. It was a challenge because in the District schools, as those in other cities of the country ever since sputnik, whatever funds were available were being poured into the science departments. Office volunteers were not acceptable to the school administration to help Mr. Jones, but at least I could find him someone to effect liaison immediately with the National Gallery of Arts docent program for public school youngsters. That project was a long-established Junior League concern, but there was no Junior Leaguer at that particular time who cared to do the very necessary clerical coordination. Fran Guilbert agreed to assume responsibility for coordinating that program with the public schools. So my first volunteer was already recruited.

The graphics department was nil—equipment and supplies were virtually nonexistent. Some teachers, poorly paid as they were, provided their own materials. The attitude that art was not an educational need touched a raw nerve within me; it was for that very reason that art had been completely dropped from the curriculum of the Chicago public schools and those, like myself, who were prepared to enter teaching, were advised to renounce that work.

Now it occurred to me that with Arthur in high office I had a chance to help the art teachers. The magic of Arthur's name, the instant communication with authorities that it made possible, meant that it no longer mattered whether or not I would be enjoying doing volunteer work for the public schools as a temporary diversion from my own work, although I had fully expected to find it a worthwhile activity.

Another factor had entered, separate and apart from my willing it. The ease with which I was able to effect communication and recruit support of various high officials meant that I really could not consider a negative response in good conscience. What was important was my using or failing to use an instrument for service that, without my really asking for it, had fallen into my hands.

I was glad I was free to choose to use it—though I recognized I had to be careful not to rub Aladdin's lamp the wrong way—to deliberately try to achieve what I could for the time being, however tenuous or fragile the result. So I decided that I would paint at some other time. Now there was this moment, and this extraordinary willingness of strangers to cooperate—an incredible situation. I was expected to do something. Why? Because I was an artist? No. Simply because I was Arthur's wife and the Labor Department had been charged by the President to do something about the school dropouts. But that was Arthur's work, not mine. Right. Except there was that astounding respect for him, for everything he did, for the people who worked with him, for those near him, and so that benevolent mantle had similarly fallen upon his wife.

Then I began the practice of first submitting a short statement to the person whose help was being sought—sometimes not so short—outlining the purpose of my call and the time when I would make it. That gave the other person an opportunity to provide an alternative suggestion or to prepare for another meeting or to suggest another helpful resource. The people I contacted invariably responded with enthusiasm, and the first project, a meeting and seminar for the high school teachers of the District, was planned in the Roosevelt High School auditorium for 3:30 P.M., March 30.

The meeting and seminar was greeted by the superintendent of schools, who introduced me as the chairman. The moderator was Dr. Ralph Beelker, executive secretary of the National Art Education Association (NEA). For the panel we had Mr. Jones; Babette Kasmir, art teacher at the Georgetown Day School, who also taught a class for parents at our Associated Artists Gallery on Creativity for Children and Parents through Art; Dr. Harry Kelly, associate director (Education and International Activities), National Science Foundation; Eugenia C. Nowlin, associate professor, George Washington University School of Education; Jack Perlmutter, artist, former Senior Fulbright Professor at Tokyo University of Art, faculty, Corcoran School of Art, professor of art at the D.C. Teachers College; and Mr. James Porter, head of the art department at Howard University.

Perhaps the most important proposition was the responsibility of a free society for the art education in its public schools. The health of a free society is endangered if public schools do not discharge their obligation to all citizens and students at every level. Such failures are invariably reflected by an ugly public life. Community leaders, parents, artists, and other public and private groups must assist, stimulate, support, and cooperate with the schools in this area.

A list of goals and objectives was developed, but one in particular I liked very much: the need for appropriate and proportionate stress on the arts, as well as on science, in our pursuit of excellence and as the mark of our greatness as a nation.

Coincidentally, at about the same time, I met Mrs. Arthur Sulzberger, Jr., of New York. Her husband, "Punch," and Arthur were attending the men-only Gridiron Club party where leading journalists, editors, and publishers present musical skits satirizing that particular political period. The women were all dressed in their finery with no place to go.

Some wives of Washington journalists had arranged for private dinners in their homes. At one such dinner, about a week before the planned seminar for the high school teachers, Mrs. Sulzberger told me of the New York School Volunteer Program—an activity that interested her also—and she very kindly arranged for T. Margaret Jamer, the director of that program, to send me pertinent material about it a day or two later.

In New York, the seven-year-old program emphasized primarily the development of reading skills, which are, of course, fundamental to all learning.

There was no question about reading being fundamental to any educational progress or job opportunities. There was no question, either, from what all the magazines and media were publishing, based on professional educational research, that public education had failed the children who most needed it. For me to enter the educational scene—even at the local level with a plea to extend assistance for the arts—would be regarded as a diversion from the main thrust of professional educational authorities. But school officials would be less likely to regard volunteers in the arts with as much hostility and suspicion as volunteers in "fundamentals." It presented less of a threat to their own professionalism, particularly when in a letter to Superintendent Hansen, on April 13, I stressed: "To be sure, higher appropriations would solve everything, but realistically, perhaps, we had better first create the climate for bringing that about. There are several ways the community can help in terms of resource people to provide workshops and resource people to come into the classroom at the teacher's request only to provide demonstrations in various art forms."

However, before even waiting for a reply to my letter from Dr. Hansen, I had already secured Conference Room B in the Labor Department for a meeting place for the recruitment of volunteers. Thus, on March 28, the first of three orientation workshops had already begun on behalf of the professional counselors who needed aides, i.e., people to settle playground disputes or to telephone parents from the nurse's office or to follow through on referrals to various clinics, or whatever did not require trained professionalism, but would relieve pressure on staff. These workshops were under the sponsorship of several Kennedy Cabinet wives: Margaret McNamara, Ethel Kennedy, Anne Celebrezze (Health, Education and Welfare), and Jane Wirtz, wife of the Undersecretary of Labor.

Among the first group of active non-administration volunteer planners I recruited for working with the Urban Service were Mary Frances Pearson, an associate in the art orientation series of the Associated Artists Gallery; Eleanor Smollar, a private professional teacher in remedial education; and Patricia Schiller, a former public school teacher and counselor who had taught our children, temporarily on leave before returning to professional work at American University.

Eleanor Smollar and Patricia Schiller could be relied on to work cooperatively with the public school officials in providing a summer training program for school volunteers for the following September opening of school. Then, Mary Frances Pearson and I began working on an art orientations program for would-be volunteers in April. After that, we hoped to be able to move into the

World of Work program for junior high and senior high school students—a primary objective of the Department of Labor's Youth Employment responsibility. Most of the major government bureaus and agencies under the sponsorship and with the active working help of the wife of an Undersecretary or Assistant Secretary, also set up at least three programs for the youth on tour. I was rueful about how much actual good was accomplished by the spring art seminar other than alerting the administrative and teaching staffs to the value of art—as well as science. But now, finally, some action was resulting—not much, but a beginning.

Then, in April and May, a series of "workshops" for volunteers was also started to recruit volunteers and also to start women thinking about areas in the school system that were badly understaffed, e.g., only 87 counselors were then serving 133,000 children. Counselors' aides were needed, but even more desperate was the need for remedial-education aides. Thus, women were offered an option of either volunteering and being trained and supervised as aides, or exploring several areas as possible jobs for themselves when they were ready to reenter the labor market. The publicity also alerted the public to the inadequacies of the school system.

The Labor Department bureaucracy evinced some bafflement about an all-day "Enrichment" program for arts and crafts, but they were reminded of the Youth Employment objective. The use of that handsome Conference Room B for art purposes could be further justified as a valid Labor Department activity because of the postretirement possibilities an "Enrichment" program offered to disengaged workers who might be at a loss for the use of leisure time. The Department of Labor owed it to them, I said. Besides, retirees too might become school volunteers.

Thus, Conference Room B held demonstrations by Jay Anderson in weaving; silk-screen printing by Ruth Barnet; rug hooking by Leila Fleisher; contemporary stitchery by Maurine Gilbert; ceramics by Edna Lee; mosaics by Laura Popenoe—to provide volunteers with an opportunity to explore a variety of art experiences and learn what materials, techniques, temperament are required and where training was available for those interested.

When Department of Labor officials looked dubious about what these activities might do to their attractive rug, I suggested drop cloths. The event, cheerfully publicized, brought many new recruits. We were reluctant to drop the momentum of interest and outpouring of volunteer help by signing off for the summer, since we could be in town, and suggested a summer program to the school officials. There were only two weeks before the closing of school, however, and there was no time for adequate preparation of schedules and transportation or even to properly alert the young people. School officials were busy completing their records and they had too many meetings of their own. Next summer would be better, they said.

But we hoped to set up a summer project that would provide young people with an opportunity for obtaining adult approbation. They could not find jobs. They needed some form of reference that could be used after graduation on a job or college application, that would offset their natural frustration and prevent dropouts in September.

That was our basic objective—certainly it was more than the easy-to-ridicule goal of art museum tours for the impoverished. But I thought it was also an outrage that poor children living within two blocks of the Smithsonian knew nothing of it or of any of the other buildings in the Capital that out-of-town tourists visited daily.

But the basic objective was defeated by school officials, because they would not bother with the added clerical work of listing on a student's record some acknowledgment of his or her not having wasted the summer. For a volunteer to do that, the officials said, would violate the confidentiality of school records.

But we tried—thirty-five of us—to open up the resources of the nation's Capital for youth living in Washington. It was a hastily improvised program and served only 135 young people that first summer; but we kept a record of what was wrong and that helped us to grow.

By 1964 the program grew to serve 2,500 students. Funds were raised from the community to provide transportation for young people who could not otherwise participate. In April 1973, the Widening Horizons program was awarded a Gold Medallion for excellence among federally funded programs.

This is not the place for a detailed history (and I regret the many names that are omitted) but the much needed work still continues. Among the women who gave virtually full-time, devoted work to the project, women whose husbands were in high office, was Gay Vance, wife of Cyrus Vance, who assumed the directorship after Margaret McNamara. Mrs. McNamara was director after Jane Wirtz, who followed my term. But others, such as my friends Anita Lyons, Peggy Harris, Joan Benesch, Barbara Luchs, and now Mary Brown have given the kind of service that the community cannot buy with money.

During the Kennedy-Johnson years, every Cabinet agency and many other federal and local public and private institutions opened their doors for the first time to the young people of the District of Columbia. During the Nixon administration, many wives of high officials maintained an interest and involvement, particularly Maria Hodges, wife of the first Labor Secretary.

What started out as a purely volunteer project had, by 1965, a full-time, year-round staff under the United Planning Organization. When the UPO grant ceased in 1967, Widening Horizons became a part of the D.C. schools' Title One Program under Mrs. Marguerite Selden, assistant superintendent for Adult Education, Summer Schools and Urban Service Corps.

In 1968, a youth sports project became a joint effort with members of the business community who acted as mentors for students interested in various areas of the business world.

In 1970, Widening Horizons launched a presummer job orientation program which then became the Career Orientation Program in three junior high schools, with many city, federal, and private enterprises donating their resources.

In 1972, Widening Horizons became a part of the Career Development Programs of the D.C. Board of Education, and expanded its services to eleven junior high schools.

It has never had an advisory board. All volunteers have been active participants.

Babette Kasmir coordinated the summer tours at the National Gallery of Art, and Mildred Granatir coordinated the Smithsonian tours. Even at the very beginning, we moved into the World of Work program for junior high and senior high school students—limited as it was. A beginning was made with six programs arranged by Herbert Salinger at the Department of Labor for the Career Planning Series in the interdepartmental auditorium. Also, with Mary Frances Pearson's help and that of the women's board at George Washington University Hospital, of which she was a member, a series of eight programs was set up to acquaint District youth with various job possibilities offered by hospital work, depending on how much education they were willing to work for by staying in school. Every department and division of the hospital responded.

6

The Steel Crisis

The public relations office was keeping a clipping file of news events and I was glad to be relieved of the chore. Besides, I was preoccupied with speaking engagements and the volunteering activities. If I had not felt the necessity of maintaining a fairly informed communication with Bob at Amherst, I might have been tempted not to take notes on the steel situation.

Ordinarily, my letters to our children were filled with breezy details about the family, with bits of newsworthy items happening to us, but on March 4, 1962, an item appeared in the *Evening Star,* not about Arthur but about our son, and it made me more thoughtful about letter writing. The clipping reminded me that Bob had become managing editor of the Amherst college newspaper and was also working on the college radio station. If he was seriously interested in newspaper work, then I thought we really owed him more news on a different level. Arthur, through the years, had explained about labor conflicts to him, but now he had no time for correspondence.

When Bob was eight years old he knew, according to Edith Cohen, our neighbor on Albemarle Street, what steelworkers were being paid. She told us what had happened when Robert brought her a crudely fashioned doghouse he had put together from an old box. She told us that when she had offered him a fifty-cent piece, Bob had pulled back saying, "Mrs. Cohen, I did this for Spot, I didn't ask you to pay me, but if you want to pay me, I think you ought to know a steelworker gets $1.67 1/2 an hour and I worked all day."

Edith said, "Bob, I think you'd better learn the facts of life, then, just like the steelworkers have to learn—if you don't like what I'm giving you, then you don't get anything." Art didn't laugh; he was sympathetic and gravely explained that the steelworkers' wages were not exactly applicable.

When wage-policy board meetings or conventions were held in Atlantic City, whenever possible we took the children. During his labor lawyer strike-ridden years when Art often had to be away, I studied the issues between steel management and labor, partly to explain satisfactorily to the children about his absence. I made a scrapbook for them with simplifications about the issues, and illustrated it with newspaper photographs and drawings, trying to dramatize the events in the news for them.

I did this to prevent the children from misunderstanding and resenting Art's absence. When Bob was very young and Art was off on some labor business and I was going out too, Bob had been furious. I tried to explain about the poor little children whose daddies couldn't buy them shoes. They couldn't go to school and had no warm sweaters or coats or enough food and their houses were cold. Their daddies were on strike to earn enough to take care of their little children, and some of these children were even sick in bed. Bobbie would have none of it. He was heartless even when I dramatized the police going after the poor strikers; he shouted with venom: "Nasty old strikers; police ought to come and shoot 'em all dead." That horrified me, but as further proof that a mother's early fears are groundless, Robert is now practicing labor law in Alaska with the same dedication his father gave to the labor movement.

Now, on January 8, 1962, Eddie Lahey was headlining his report: "Hope Grows on Steel Wage Pact—Administration Confident of 'Honorable Contract.'"

Of one thing Mr. Kennedy and Goldberg are certain—the steelworkers don't want to strike. Since January 1959 they have lost more than one-third of their normal work time, partly because of recession and automation layoffs. . . . But the steel workers would strike if anything were forced down their throats. . . . Anyone who knows Roger M. Blough, chairman of U.S. Steel and chief spokesman for the industry, can sense his almost fanatic determination to resist the upward pressure on employment costs in 1962. He and other leaders of the industry believe that productivity per man-hour has lagged behind increases in wage costs.

On January 9, in the *Evening Star,* Norman Walker headlined his report "Goldberg Moves to Avoid Steel Strike," and there was a flood of articles in the various journals about how Arthur had confidently predicted, at the beginning of the year, that this time there would be better relations between management and industry.

For months, he had been arguing for wage restraint and price restraint on the part of the unions and business, but neither liked the idea. The unions thought collective bargaining should prevail as usual with no government interference, and management always has a horror of government interference—any attempt to put any restraint on private enterprise was inimical to our system. What worried them was the speech (thirteen pages, double space, pica type, a serious dissertation) Art had made in Chicago on February 23 before the officers and directors of the Executives' Club.

He told them that the nation simply couldn't afford a repetition of the 1959 strike. This had to be averted, and the President was calling on the parties to measure up to their plain responsibility to the nation not to start a wage-spiraling that would send the whole economy into a dizzy downspin.

He said that the country had learned a lesson from that steel strike, and things looked much better now, because 1961 marked the greatest period of industrial peace in the country since the end of World War II.

"The 3,300 work stoppages recorded in 1961 was the smallest number since the war. Man-days lost because of these strikes dropped from 19.1 million in the previous year to 16.5 million, a low mark for the postwar period. Total strike idleness amounted to 0.15 percent of the estimated working time during the year, making 1961 the most peaceful year in recent history. . . ."

Then he went on to say that what we do at home is related to our foreign affairs, and we can't be isolated from the rest of the world. "Such issues as price stability, balance of payments and international trade are directly involved with labor-management decisions at home affecting wages, workday standards, and profit margins."

Then he spoke about the influence of the President's Advisory Committee on Labor-Management Policy—nothing very dramatic to report but at least they were still meeting and talking. I, myself, remembered how funereal Art was in 1959 when Roger Blough just sat through negotiations saying nothing, looking glum. The purpose of the committee was not to pass resolutions but to get to talking with one another and to "articulate a consensus of these views."

Arthur told them that the country was getting lots of extra dividends from those dialogues: local committees were also meeting and there were even international implications. Great Britain followed suit and developed a commission of its own called the National Economic Development Council. "It was reported that the one factor leading to the participation by the British Trade Union Congress on the council was the participation by American labor on the President's committee."

He kept talking, and it all led up to the fact that labor "must now look beyond the councils of their tradition and out into the broad fields of modern economic realities, both at home and abroad. . . ."

No wonder the unions did not like it. He said it may be fine to save a job but it may not be so fine if the precedent of that action endangers many other jobs over a period of time. Then he told management that it too "must stop its blind resistance to change," specifically damning their almost automatic stand against improving the unemployment insurance system and medical care for the aged.

Poor Art. I shivered a bit at his recklessness.

The word that made both labor and management see red: "Today, in the light of our nation's commitments both at home and abroad, government and private mediators must increasingly provide guidelines [that was the word] to the parties to insure that the settlements reached are right settlements that are not only in the interest of the parties themselves but which also take into account the public interest."

Guidelines? They wanted no guidelines, and George Meany

exploded to reporters that Goldberg had overstepped proper bounds, that Arthur's position was "infringing on the rights of a free people and a free society."

To labor, "guidelines" meant a ceiling on wage increases in the series of contracts that were coming up.

This was not particularly upsetting to Art, who had been speaking to large audiences all over the country about the need for a public-interest committee that would avoid these clashes and about his hopes that the Labor-Management Committee would avoid the clashes that enter when a strike is threatened. He kept insisting that our country could not afford to let big business and big labor make whatever decisions they chose. They simply had to consider the rest of the country too—the public.

The labor grumbling was getting so loud that in Pittsburgh just before the new steel contract was initiated on March 31, a United Steelworkers man grumbled: "I sure wish Kennedy had put Goldberg on the court instead of White." They felt that Art was leaning over backward to show how nonpartisan he was, and that labor would get the worse of the settlement.

On April 10, labor, though grumbling and irritated with Arthur, agreed to a moderate steel settlement—for the first time in eight years without first calling a strike. It was less than labor would otherwise have accepted, because of the basic assumption that the steel companies would not raise prices.

That day, chairman of the board of U.S. Steel, and a spokesman for the steel companies, Roger Blough, announced matter-of-factly that U.S. Steel would have to raise prices; five other companies followed suit.

That evening, we were supposed to go black tie at 9:30 to the White House for the reception for Congress. Arthur phoned me on the White House phone at 7:30 to say that he was still at the White House and that I should pack his things and leave earlier for the Department; he would dress there. I couldn't imagine what on earth was up, thinking it was the maritime situation in Hawaii. I wore my white dress with its own short coat and red beaded bag, because there would be at least a thousand people and a long chiffon would just get all messed up, and my red satin and ice-blue satin needed putting away.

The news broadcast had already gone off the car radio and Mr.

Johnson, the chauffeur, said he hadn't heard anything about any strike when the news was on. He kept searching the stations for me, but no news. At the Department, he opened the little side door to Arthur's private elevator. (The brass had been shining beautifully since one of the janitors had been told to pay attention to it. I marveled at Arthur having time to point that out.) The elevator downstairs meant that Arthur hadn't come in yet. That meant he was still at the White House and I couldn't imagine why.

Upstairs, I began putting the black studs in his shirt. Mr. Johnson took the newly pressed dinner jacket out of the plastic bag. Art had said he wanted his Rogers Peet one but I couldn't find the label so I had brought both. Mr. Johnson knew to look in the pocket, where men put labels so no one can see—really better than the women's designers who put them where no one can fail to see. (They sewed the union label in my things most conspicuously too, but that was a small accommodation to all the people in the garment industry who were so fond of him and who called me the First Lady of Labor and who took such pains that I might wear the best of Seventh Avenue.)

After puttering about, I sat down to wait and read the newspaper. Art swung in around 8:30 or 9:00 and his face was full of exploding weather: the industry raised prices five dollars a ton, the s.o.b.'s. Then he started writing the statement for the President. Walter Heller and others were already working on one too in the Executive Offices. Arthur wrote furiously, breaking in once to say, "Get me Herblock." I never could figure out the buttons on his dial phone and tried every one of them. None worked, then PL, the private line, did. Then I went to the White House phone and asked the operator for Mr. Herbert Block. After a few minutes, she located Herblock and I put Arthur on.

"Herb? Do you know what those s.o.b.'s in the steel industry did?" Then, "I've got a caption for your cartoon for tomorrow— Big Steal! How's that?"

Then, Art was on the phone to someone and learned that it wasn't five dollars a ton increase, but six.

Peter Henley, one of the Labor Department economists, and a colleague came up and started pouring over books of figures. Art read them a statement and they said they wouldn't be on firm-enough ground until they had more April figures to examine.

Art checked every little thing carefully, calling Marv Miller and Dave McDonald to check further, lest the President be put on a spot that would not be verifiable. Before Mr. Henley had come in earlier, Art had shaken his head. I asked what was the matter now. He said, "I just wonder if the union figures are all okay too. I'm not going to use one thing that won't stand up."

Then he said, "One thing I told the President and the others around [he meant Ted Sorensen] anyway: I'm not the indispensable man. This proves the Secretary of Labor is not indispensable."

Arthur told me too that he wasn't going to be the kind of Secretary of Labor who appeared at union conventions to say what a nice union they had and what a grand job they were doing and what a wonderful president they had. He had nine union conventions coming up in May and he said, "I'm not just going up there and tell them to hold the line. My usefulness really is over. There's nothing else to say. What am I going to do with it, just be a bureaucrat? Maybe they didn't like what I had to say before, but it was something that had to be said. Now, the policy is a failure."

At a meeting with the President the day after the industry announced they were not keeping their agreement, the Vice-President, who was in the room, made a move to go when Arthur entered but Art said, no; what he had to say could be heard by both. Then he said he could no longer keep the office. The President brushed that aside and said, "You and I are in this fight together." But Art said, "No, one can't accept plaudits one week and not bear the responsibility the next. This was my counsel, my planning, and the administration does not need to bear the brunt of it."

The night before this meeting, the President had telephoned us out of sleep at 1:30; it was something about their having to have on hand a bill that would be all ready, or some practical measures, to deal with the steel price increase and Art was saying, "Listen, that's right. We don't want to sweep them out of court. They're going to have to be lived with after this, but right now, let 'em have it."

The next day, before he left for work, Arthur telephoned Charles Bartlett, a great friend of Kennedy's, who apparently had a friend in the steel industry to whom he confided Arthur's conversation with the President. The story jolted the industry.

I thought his intuition and sense of timing were operating. It would really have killed the industry—psychologically anyway—if he had resigned because the whole country knew that his feeling for the public position was his basic motivation, and it would have implied that all he had tried to do had been betrayed. Arthur said, "I almost feel sorry for the industry. Wait till they see what all hell is going to break loose." He told me that when he was speaking with the President, he had said, "Mr. President, this industry cannot be tamed, they rule this country, and even Mr. Truman couldn't take them on." That quieted the President and he said, "My father always said too that they were a bunch of skunks." He added the further comment, now well known, that his father characterized them as a bunch of bastards, a remark which leaked not from Arthur but from others in the White House—a leak that caused Kennedy much embarrassment and trouble with the business community at large. Art said, to me, "I don't care what people have said about the older Kennedy—he's okay. He knows a skunk when he sees one."

On Friday, the price increase was rescinded. The press, the TV, the radio people were hounding Arthur's office. Speaking to one newsman on the telephone, he said, "No, I can't say. The President's is the only statement and it still speaks for all of us." He kept insisting that if the President had not acted like a President, the price rescinding would not have happened. "I will give you a phrase though, but don't quote me—when everybody said that this was like another Cuba, my thought is that it is a domestic West Virginia."

At dinner he was in high spirits: "Never, never, did I expect anything like this."

The next day he brought me Murray Kempton's article saying, "When Murray Kempton gets through with anyone, they're mashed." Kempton wrote:

The historians of whatever America survives this century will probably know the names of the men who decided to raise the price of steel on Tuesday, April 10, and, if they do, we can be sure that these men will have a unique and special place in their books. For those men, whoever they are, may have altered for all time the history of American Industry. They have aroused a young President, who until now had a proper respect for businessmen, to a point of wrath which only their punishment can appease.

Clark Clifford phoned to say, call off the subpoenas on Walker, Sentner, and Tyson. Steve Shulman phoned and said it made him feel good to be working for the government. I felt that perhaps the sense of dedication and immediacy of New Deal days was swinging in again.

Art spoke to the Attorney General: "Hello, Bobby, fine, never felt better in my life. Say, your FBI men have served subpoenas on Tyson, Sentner, and Walker of U.S. Steel to appear on Monday morning . . . You already subpoenaed their records for Friday, so suppose we do it on the basis that you want to look at the records first . . . I think it would be vindictive for us right after the announcement to haul them before the grand jury. I wouldn't make any public announcement of it; I'd say you want to look at the records . . . As far as I'm concerned, you can put 'em in jail for a million years . . . We have no commitment on timing, so therefore we have to keep watch on these fellows, but now that we're on top, we can't put the screws on them and get the rest of the business world upset, so that they think we're going after business . . . This is what happened: after Bethlehem announced that they had rescinded the price increase and the call came through to me at the Carlyle, Blough was talking to me at lunch and I said there was no use talking further, the party's over—they better start moving with the rest. He tried to remark that the President had been too strong, I said, 'The President let you off easy. What I would have said, and what I'm saying now—and I'm saying it to your face—is that you're using double-crossing s.o.b. cheap shyster tactics. If you had guts, you would have stood up like a man that time when David McDonald had had his say. You should have said, "Mr. President, we're not going along no matter what the union does," but you kept silent, and silence is consent. One thing you owe a President is candor.'

"I think Blough's dumb. You see, they talked out this tactic before. Tyson let it out. They had agreed they wouldn't say anything on price and they thought that that meant they weren't committed. Yes . . . I can blueprint what must have happened.

Under this fellow's tutelage, they made up that I had good credentials with the union and the union wouldn't let us down, so they would lead us down the path, even though we continually said to them that the whole purpose is price stability. The reason they didn't say anything is that they were afraid we'd do something, and we would have. I don't think they let in more than a few—four or five: the chairmen of the boards of Republic, Bethlehem, Jones and Laughlin, and U.S. Steel. No, they didn't talk to Joe Block [President of Inland Steel] because they know he's close to me. . . . But before that, Doug Dillon and the President had Clark Clifford and Charlie Bartlett and they had made some statements, and I don't want the steel crowd to say the President is a double-crosser.

"It took guts and a lot of determination to do it. He really acted like a President. I think this is going to be the high point of his administration . . . Edgar Kaiser immediately made a commitment not to make a move, at least for the time being, and Joe Block directly through his brother, Phil. Joe is a member of our Labor-Management Committee and he's supported the type of policy we're trying to do. [Block was the only one among the industrial group who had come out in support of Art's Chicago speech.] Yes, I called; Gudeman called; several called. His brothers had been in touch with him in Japan. Just good newspaper enterprise—*Chicago Daily News*—Dillon was calling, everyone went to work here. That afternoon I met with Tyson to call it off, not to compromise. Then I met with the whole group up in New York . . . Tyson and Worthington. We have to revive our relationships now. The one thing I wouldn't want is any vindictiveness. There are no deals. It has to be considered on the merits.

"We better find out what they said. Clark Clifford tried to negotiate yesterday. Blough said he wanted to talk to the President and explain what could be done now, and I said, 'Nothing doing. He's not going to talk to you, now or ever.' Then he said something about wanting their tax problems to get consideration, and I said that the tax problems are for the Congress, but I'm sure Doug and Charlie Bartlett have said something. I tried to say to Doug and everybody that we can't commit ourselves not to let the law operate, but still I think don't let's put the thumb into them Monday . . . Good, that's terrific."

Art told me later that they were going to be indicted on a

separate price-fixing charge. I learned from listening. He kept brushing me out of the way.

"Sure, I'm in agreement with that, but I would say first you want to get the records and then work out an orderly way . . . I agree . . . You can't make it look like there's a deal and you have gotta go after them, but you better check if any agents of his [the President's] have made statements to them. We better find out what it is . . ."

These one-sided fragments of conversations were mystifying to me, but I scribbled away, hoping to understand later when the jigsaw pieces of references would fall into place. At this point, Art was already trying to anticipate ways for closing the rift between industry and government while letting the processes of law take their due course.

The background is as follows: At the time of the settlement of the steel case in New York, Roger Blough asked Art whether the government would prosecute them unfairly under the antitrust laws. Art said, "No deal. If you're guilty of antitrust violations or other violations you'll be prosecuted, and if not, you won't be. If what you're asking is whether the President will be vindictive and go after the industry unfairly, I shall say to the President that there should be no vindictiveness and that the industry should be treated like any other person, prosecuted with the full vigor of the law if prosecution is justified and not prosecuted if not justified."

The following conversations that are here reported are, of course, only one side of the wire and they relate to the fact that there were grand jury proceedings pending involving alleged violations of the antitrust laws by U.S. Steel and perhaps some other companys. U.S. Steel had been subpoenaed by the government and ordered to produce certain records within a very short time.

This subpoena was issued while the price dispute was going on. John Tennant, counsel for U.S. Steel, called Art and said he felt that the shortness of time to respond to the subpoena was vindictive since they normally would be given a reasonable time to produce their records. Art said to Tennant, "Jack, Roger will tell you that I made it clear there was no deal with respect to antitrust or any other cases. However, it seems to me that normal professional courtesy warrants granting you a reasonable time to produce your records and that I'd recommend that."

Then Arthur telephoned President Kennedy on Saturday. The President was in Florida and Arthur said to him, "You'll recall, Mr. President, that when I telephoned you yesterday and reported that U.S. Steel had withdrawn its price increase I further had said that I told Blough there would be no deal on antitrust violations but also that no vindictiveness would be shown to the industry." Then he told the President about Tennant's call and said that it did look vindictive not to give them a reasonable time to produce their records. According to normal procedures, ten days or so would have been reasonable, but Bobby had been demanding them "forthwith." (My own sympathies were with Bobby's actions, but when Art explained he said that a reasonable time is a normal professional courtesy arranged between the prosecution and the defense.)

The President agreed and said for Art to call Bobby and say he agreed. To that, Art replied: "That's not my job. I made the agreement about no vindictiveness on your behalf. You confirmed it when I reported it, and I think you're the one to take the proper steps to see the commitment is kept." The President agreed.

Then Art called Leo Levinger, the Assistant Attorney General in charge of the Federal Trust Division: "I do think that we have to strike the right note, that the processes of the law are not influenced by political pressures. No, no, no. None. No deal! The President had Clark Clifford come up with me. The spirit of our conversation was we can't have a war with them . . . John Tennant, the counsel of U.S. Steel, called him. The request ought to be to you by anyone who wants to do this. If you do it for U.S. Steel, you got to let Bethlehem and the others too. You can give him ice water for all I care. That's all they deserve, but after all, there is such a thing as lawyers' courtesy."

Then, to me, in between calls while his soup got cold and the decorator and the cabinet repairmen were prowling around taking measurements and both doors were closed: "I don't see why the hell I should be doing this for that crowd. It burns me up. Well, I'm doing it for the President." Then, in the middle of everything, the washing machine repair people were on the phone to say the man would come out with the necessary parts on Monday.

Then Art was on the phone to Clark Clifford. "Clark? I didn't know what I was taking on when I said I'd try to pacify things with the Kennedys. D'you know that Bobby's had two hundred FBI men talking to each steel executive? And d'you know what John Tennant told the FBI? He said they were too busy that week to talk to any government people. The President saw it in a report this morning and split his guts . . . They had an anonymous conversation of a meeting between the top executives last Saturday. Apparently, someone has filled them in and they're going after them. My own feeling is everybody better cool off a bit . . . They asked for a meeting yesterday. They're an arrogant crowd. When you're representing a client and protecting his interests, do you tell an FBI man you haven't time to talk to him? Leo Levinger said he'll give 'em only normal courtesies. I would think, Clark, that it's advisable for you to call Tennant and tell him to call Levinger to work out that arrangement for this week, following which we'll talk to the President."

The next call was to Walter Heller: "Congratulations to you! We won a great victory, but we must watch out that it doesn't become political retribution in people's minds. They asked for a meeting yesterday; I said later. I wouldn't let Roger. I wouldn't have him rehabilitated. That's right. I do too. So I turned him down on a meeting . . . I said, later. The President would be glad to meet with a representative business group but I don't think it should be Roger's crowd. . . . They shouldn't be made to feel that this terrific power of the Presidency will be brought to bear in every situation. Bobbie really has thrown out a dragnet second to none. That's right . . . He assigned over two hundred FBI men to this investigation. I'm afraid there'll be a turn of opinion if we push our advantage too hard. Yeah. Right. Right. That's right. We've made no deal. We must not make it even appear that there was one. There is no deal. Not a damn thing. I was in no mood to make any commitment. I don't understand. Sure. Everybody. . . . The essential difference between now and then: then it was a travesty. Truman acted strong and Charlie Sawyer [Secretary of Commerce] acted weak. Here the whole administration acted together and Bob was wonderful, and Luther. Everybody wonders why Bethlehem. They're in the shipyards. Bethlehem has the closest relationship to the government of all the steel companies. Then Bobby raided them with the FBI. We were in bad shape with our policies for a while, but it worked out fine. Yeah . . . No. I think my judgment is that on the top level, about five or six top executives. Homer knew but Martin didn't. Sheer economics. Though Joe Block, he's on our Labor Management Committee. Anyone who doubts if it's worth anything can see now. It's some medium of communication and education. He believes in it. Now we gotta coast a little easy, guard against any appearance that the President will take on every business move with this same vigor."

Then, to Charles Bartlett: "Congratulations. You're the man behind the scenes here. Well, I think it's the President too. He's entitled to the whole credit. They were ready to cave in. They wanted to negotiate but we had them licked. See, they couldn't take it when the little ones started going. The real hero in the industry in all this is Joe Block, isn't he? Yeh . . . it sure was. Oh, yes, we're back in business now. We're very strong with the labor people. You see, they'd rather have a President act like a President than get a dollar increase, and Joe Block has subscribed to the view we're developing in that committee. Yes, that's where we got him. He's the fellow who came out in support of my speech defining the President's policy in Chicago, and before that too. I think we now ought to move into the area of discussing rationally problems like this."

Then he spoke to our son Bob, who had called twice before on other days when Art couldn't take time to talk. In this conversation, I felt free to be on the extension:

ART: You got a real President, my friend.

BOB: I think so. Now the program's a success, isn't it?

ART: I don't know, but right now, from the ruins, we've constructed a fine building.

BOB: Did you hear about my telegram?

ART: Good for you.

BOB: We sent one to Blough first: "The President is not alone in his surprise and dismay, our good faith has been shattered," etc. We got about one hundred and fifteen names at Amherst to sign. Then one to the President: "We share your surprise and dismay and encourage continued action." Then one to Mr. Block at Inland Steel congratulating them.

ART: Very good. Well, it was quite dramatic, Bobby. It started to cave in yesterday.

BOB: Is that when he got served?

ART: No, while I was meeting with him, Tyson.

BOB: Say, the President, his popularity must be ninety-two percent. I must say Block is a good man. You found out about it at five forty-five in the afternoon?

ART: I let go for him, then and today. I gave Roger Blough the dressing down of his life. You know what, Bob, it's this: When you're dealing with the President of the United States, you owe him at the very least candor. I told Blough the same I did at the White House: "You should have said, 'Mr. President, no matter what the union does, we have to raise prices.' " He tried to say the President made a mistake. I said, "He was acting like a President, *I* made the mistake. I presented you to him as a man of honor." Blough said, "I'm sorry you feel that I'm not." I said, "I'm telling it to your face, you were playing games. You don't play games with a President. If nothing else you owe him candor." Confidentially, Bob, the secret weapon was I tendered my resignation. They heard about it and they were afraid it would create an uproar.

BOB: Anyone know about that?

ART: Just the President.

BOB: That press conference, was it ever terrific. Wow!

ME: [*Here I feel free to be on the extension.*] Tell him what you said about Krushchev.

ART: I told him, "You acted exactly like Krushchev did. While he was negotiating for a test ban, he was making secret arrangements to blow the bomb, and you, while you were negotiating for noninflationary agreement, you were making secret arrangements to do the same thing to the public interest." Well, he turned white. I said, "I don't see the difference. In that White House, where George Washington and Abraham Lincoln had been, you were standing like a shyster, using the President of the United States as a lackey for your labor relations with the union. For your private interests, you used the President of the United States. It was a shabby performance, Roger." And I was calm and not angry, just letting the words sink in one by one, in a quiet voice, slowly.

BOB: The President really showed his stuff. Wow! He really came through. What a guy!

To me, it was worth everything to hear Robert's reaction, that of his Amherst co-signers, and Steve Shulman's, the son of Harry Shulman of Yale Law School, and then an aide in the Labor Department—their excitement and enthusiasm. And if this were so, then how many other young people there must be who also shared that exhilaration that government service was in the public interest after all. We were proud of our President, of our government in a critical moment. And our family was so proud of Arthur for having shown what moral conviction exacts of a leader through his choice of action.

7

Mr. Justice Goldberg

On Wednesday, August 29, 1962, President Kennedy announced he had received on the previous day Justice Felix Frankfurter's letter of resignation from the Supreme Court. The President was quoted in the *Washington Post:* "I decided after I received the Justice's letter that I would appoint Secretary Goldberg and discussed it with him on that occasion."

The President certainly gave no one a chance to suggest another name. His was the right to appoint, and he did so with no uncertainty. In Philadelphia, the *Evening Bulletin* informed its readers on August 30 that "Goldberg will be the fourth Jewish member of the Supreme Court. The others were Justice Frankfurter and Justices Louis D. Brandeis and Benjamin N. Cardozo." On that day and for the next several days the newspapers were filled with retrospective material about Arthur as a labor lawyer, as Secretary of Labor, and as Justice-designate. The telephone rang constantly.

On August 28, Arthur had phoned at 8:00 P.M. to say that the trip we were planning, to attend the inauguration of the Honorable Mr. Eric Williams as Prime Minister of Trinidad, was off. Instead, there was something very important he had to tell me. He would be going to Chicago to attempt to mediate the railroad

strike once more, but that was not what was so important now—
something else, and it was a favorable thing. He asked me to save
something for dinner.

At 8:45 we gave up waiting and started dinner. Then Art came
in and the telephone started ringing again about the strike. When
he sat down, he told us that the President had set an appointment
with him for five o'clock to discuss the impending strike. He had
phoned Arthur to come in earlier but Art could not leave because
of strike developments and asked if he could come in at the appointed hour. "Sure, anytime." Art said he should have known
then that "anytime" gave it away, that something extraordinary
was brewing, because Presidents are not usually so deferential in
allowing Cabinet officers to fix the time of meetings with them. He
came in prepared to plunge into the railroad strike, but the President said, "Wait, I want to talk to you first," and he told Arthur
about Mr. Justice Frankfurter's resignation.

He said, "I can't in good conscience not consider you, because
these opportunities are rare and I think it should be you. But who
would we get for Labor?"

Art said, "Bill Wirtz." The President wondered if Bill would be
acceptable to Mr. Meany. Art said he'd call him. He said again
that Bill was extremely capable.

The President said, "But do you think he's colorful enough?"

And Art said, "The opportunities on a job are what makes a
man colorful or colorless. I think Bill would be fine."

That evening George Meany came to talk. I sat in my attic
studio-office, thankful that such an honor had come to our family
through Art. But I roused Bob to wrath because I kept pointing
out that even being considered was enough, because the opposition
would be bitter and might be terrible.

Bob walked into my office beaming again, "Isn't it great,
Mom?"

I said, "Look, you're the one who's going to make it terribly
hard for Dad if it doesn't come about. He'll think he's disappointing you if it doesn't happen."

"No. It's got to be joyous *now*. Whatever happens later, *this* is
a joyous moment and everyone should be joyous now. Later is
time enough for it if it won't be." He had already figured out where
Art would work at home. "You can put all his books in my room,

Mother. That can be his study and I'll move into the guest room."

Arthur told George Meany that he himself felt an obligation to see to it that his successor was acceptable to the labor movement and to business and the general public. Kennedy was not enthusiastic about Bill Wirtz and had said, "Hell, I went along with you to have him made Undersecretary, but now you're asking me to make one of those last-stand guys for Stevenson at Los Angeles Secretary. Even though we had the votes, he was emotional and prejudiced us against the Stevenson voters when we needed them."

Art said, "Mr. President, remember what I told you then. You're President of all the American people, and prenomination hatchets need to be buried. It's doubly true now. You've been President almost two years, and Wirtz has been a loyal member of the administration."

Then he told the President that, in a sense, Bill Wirtz was even more loyal than Arthur himself: "Let me tell you something. When I walked into the Department of Labor, every office had your picture filling up the blank spots of the day before where Eisenhower's picture was. I called the Department together. 'We're not Russia; we don't need the leader's picture in every office. We'll have one official portrait at the entrance. That's appropriate—but not more. Of course, if anyone has an autographed picture showing a personal relationship, not just official, okay, hang it.'"

But Art had made one exception and told that to the President. Bill Wirtz, in light of all his Stevenson advocacy, had asked if he couldn't hang one even without the autograph. "So there you are, he's loyal."

Then Art added, "By the way, I heard through the grapevine that some of your personal aides took a dim view of my order against exhibiting your face in every single office. I disregarded that, but now I want to put a question to you: Do you really like this Russian-style personality-cult business?"

The President was thoughtful. "I guess you're right, though I react like every President, and I like having the bureaucracy know that I'm President."

Shortly after, the President accepted Bill Wirtz as Arthur's successor and said, "Well, if you think it's all right, you handle it and sound out the proper persons."

Thus, Arthur asked George Meany to come to the house. He also telephoned business leaders and some public personalities who were familiar with the labor scene, and also leaders in Congress as well as some press people. Everyone agreed that Bill Wirtz would be a good appointment.

But Meany was somewhat doubtful, so Art said, "George, if you start fooling around trying to recommend a labor man, you'll have twenty candidates and that'll mean trouble for you as well as the President—politics, disappointments—aren't you better off saying, 'Well, he's been the deputy, he's been fair?' " So Meany agreed. Walter Reuther was a little more ready than George Meany to accept Bill.

Arthur was in Chicago the day after the President talked to him about the Supreme Court, and the day the appointment was announced, he was in Chicago too.

Mother and I met him at Andrews Air Field and there was a sweet, unposed picture of us embracing each other. I learned the sequence of events. He had been up all night trying to settle the train strike, and he thought the announcement could have waited until he had returned to Washington, but around noon, he had received a call from the President. "I'm going to have a press conference and if it's all right with Dorothy and you, I'm going to announce."

Art said, "What about the American Bar Association?"

The President said, "[Expletive deleted] the Bar Association! How can they oppose your appointment?" Then he reeled off Art's credentials: "First in your class at law school with a record still unequaled, editor-in-chief of the Law Review, a practice of more than thirty years, and before the CIO you practiced from 1929 to 1948 in almost every field of the law, a great Supreme Court advocate, moral character beyond reproach. I'm going to announce at three o'clock."

We learned later that the Attorney General, brother Bob, had cleared Art's appointment with the appropriate committee of the Bar Association.

All the papers expected an early Senate confirmation. George Meany made a statement lauding the appointment, saying that Art "has been a capable, able, and dedicated public servant during his term as Secretary of Labor, just as he was a resourceful, capable, and hard-working advocate of the ideals for which the organized labor movement stands." David S. Broder, writing in the *Washington Post,* went on to say that "Mr. Meany said those who have worked with Mr. Goldberg are sure he will serve the nation in his new role with exactly the same sense of dedication to the public welfare." He said Mr. Goldberg "fully deserves this honor."

As Art returned calls to various friends and acquaintances, I continued to make notes, harvesting some satisfying time in between his calls to ask questions, and also jotting down some of my own reflections. The noting and the writing was an anchor that enabled me to keep in balance all the changes once again taking place in our lives.

I still did not know to what end all the note-taking. Most likely for family archives, I thought. But there is no question about the value of such a record, particularly for the older, long-married wife of a high public official. It helps one detect any still-remaining tendencies—if any there be—to self-pity and self-centeredness and to go about one's own business should the stand-by situation become overly constraining.

But I had been learning so much from all the note-taking. Government relationships, for instance, became evident, and I could ask questions where I was puzzled, but I still was reluctant to start concentrating on my own painting. I also enjoyed the perspective the notes provided, as in a space-concept painting deep within the center of an ever-moving environment—a viewpoint from within and without at the same time in relation to no fixed flat ground, but as if traveling within the orbit of a comet, carried along in its wake. I liked that.

I knew very well I was "minding" Art's business more than my own, but I found it sheer fascination to watch what I romantically thought was a destiny unfolding. His destiny, to be sure, not mine, but it was so altogether amazing to me and so surprisingly contrary to all the usual cynicism about government and people in high office and the American Dream. I knew better than to be overly effusive about that, and yet to my dismay, despite my best intentions, my joy would overflow, and in more than one interview I blurted: "It means there really is an American Dream, and it still does come true—once in a while." But reading it in print, I would feel a hollow between the lines, a chill unspoken reminder to me: "What about the kids in the inner city right now?"

Yet, I could not bear to miss a part of any of the moments leading up to his ascension to the Court and found it difficult to accept it as merely another honor happening to a deserving individual. It should have happened to a Learned Hand and didn't. It should have happened to others similarly worthy and didn't. I could not curb the wonder of it.

The *Wall Street Journal* thought the President had downgraded the Court by his two appointments—Byron White's and Arthur's. David Lawrence, the conservative columnist, took a dim view, of course. Art was speaking to Nathan Feisinger, an arbitrator, and a professor at the University of Wisconsin Law School:

"You know, we've come a long way from Brandeis' day. Even though Brandeis was a conservative lawyer, he handled a few cases for the Consumers' League, and nine Bar Association presidents all came out against him. And the Bar Association in 1933 said the whole New Deal was communistic, and the Social Security Act would just take care of a bunch of bums.

"My nomination went up Friday. I have said that once the nomination goes to the Senate, I will not act as Secretary of Labor, though the President has asked me not to resign. I'll help Bill out.

"It lays over until a week. It may be Friday. Then I spoke to the Chief Justice yesterday, and they want me sworn in right away . . ."

Then I heard Art tell someone else about certiorari:

"Lawyers think that all the petitions are thrown up to the ceiling and those that don't stick are the ones that are denied. That's the way I always thought too."

To Mr. Justice Black: "Mr. Justice? I must have disturbed you in one of your tennis games. I would like to drive out and have you give me a drink tomorrow afternoon." (Art wanted to get started on his reading, and Mr. Justice Black would give him the books to be read while preparing for the deluge of opinions.)

The Black's daughter, Jo-Jo, came to the phone to congratulate Art. Art asked her for the number of young Hugo, who had written him a sweet note telling what it was like to be the son of a Justice.

For the first time in many years, I again recalled their mother,

Josephine Foster Black, with whom I had painted every day for two years. I remembered how careful I had been always to call her Mrs. Black, and not just because she was the wife of a Supreme Court Justice and Arthur was counsel for the CIO and Steelworkers, but because she was an older woman. For a fleeting moment I realized that new people I had been meeting, however friendly we were becoming, continued to say "Mrs. Goldberg," not "Dorothy," and there was no question that I warranted it because of age —all those many new lines in my face produced by the stress of meeting deadlines. "Is it worth it," I asked myself, "to age so fast?" And my answer was a hasty, "Yes."

Now he was speaking to Elizabeth, Justice Black's second wife: "Elizabeth, we've invited ourselves for dinner, as you probably heard from the judge. No, I won't let the judge take me on at tennis. I want to be sworn in first. You remember what Alexander Woollcott said about exercise? He said, 'Pardon me, I've got to get out of these wet clothes and into a dry martini.' "

Then to me: "Three thirty at the Blacks'—dinner. And I'm going to call Buddy Cooper, too. [Jerome Cooper was the outstanding labor lawyer in the South.] Why wouldn't Buddy make a good Undersecretary or an Assistant Secretary?"

Bob and I were enthusiastic, but, "You can't tell Bill what to do."

Bob: "But all Daddy would have had to tell the President is no about Mr. Wirtz."

Bill Wirtz had vetoed Franklin Roosevelt, Jr., when the President had suggested him as undersecretary. Bill wanted someone less colorful, I think. The new Labor Department complexion was to be more scholarly, evidently, no longer with Art's dash and bustle.

Art said, "Deciding doesn't bother me two minutes." What Justice Whitaker was bothered by—that necessity to decide—he wasn't.

He phoned Bill Wirtz about Buddy Cooper: "He's very dedicated to the labor cause. He's not a zealot, but he has good judgment . . .

"My hearing is announced—September 11. It depends on Lister Hill. You've been nominated and can go ahead. Congratulations on your new secretary. She's going to stay with you. I'd prefer to bring her over, very frankly. It'd be a lot easier for me. But I thought about it; she is an asset in the Department, and it is a more lively place, and I think she reacts to it, and I have no right. She has a right to a career of her own, and she's accustomed to working under pressure. She knows everybody in the area. So you got yourself a real asset." (Helen May was married not long afterward to Assistant Secretary of Labor James J. Reynolds and remained secretary to Bill Wirtz for a long time.)

"I talked to the Chief. He wants me to get started right away on my certiorari."

There was a deluge of news analyses by the various correspondents about what it all might signify—Frankfurter had been a conservative; Arthur was a liberal. The Doris Fleeson column was captioned with a query wondering why the President would agree to let Art go. She said that it had long been one of the nicer ironies of Washington that Frankfurter, the Harvard Law School luminary, a feared radical when named to the court by Franklin Roosevelt, had been the judicial voice of opposition to the New Deal philosophy. She went on: "The Supreme Court today is the most dynamic force in our national life. Conservatives in Congress are preventing the President from following through on his program, and the legislative output is at best a compromise on every problem it touches. Most problems Congress prefers not to touch if it can avoid it, especially in the realm of planning for change."

James F. Clayton of the *Washington Post* wrote: "When a man steps through that velvet curtain behind the bench of the Supreme Court, the world he faces is totally different from any he has faced before. Of course, what he will say and how he will vote bears some resemblance to what he has said and done before. But only the few who know fully his philosophical approach to law and life can predict what his views will be—and often their predictions go askew. . . ." He said that Justices Clark, Stewart, and White were unpredictable.

"After three years no one can predict with any certainty how Justice Potter Stewart will vote on any particular case. And, in his first major dissent, Justice Byron R. White voted in June against the 'liberals' he was said to be joining on the Court.

"Not so long ago, Justice Douglas said that it takes years for a Justice to go around the track just once. Until he has made that circuit and faced all the issues that come to the Court, predicting how he will vote is just guesswork."

I took a deep breath and began making clippings from other newspapers, trying to understand better all the issues that had everybody speculating about which side Art would be on. Privately, I wondered if the President might have thought Byron White would be his conservative appointment and Arthur would be his liberal one—except I knew that Art would not be typed.

I wished that I had not skipped news of the Court so blithely and regretted having ignored all those rows of books on our shelves about the various Justices, but it had seemed such a waste of time for two in one family to concentrate attention on the same interest. I had skipped the articles about law and the courts because it was so much simpler to ask Art for a quick précis.

Art brought me two helpful little books by Professor Paul Freund of Harvard and Professor Charles Black of Yale. Professor Freund's book, he said, was all one needed to read about the scholastic view of the Court, and Professor Black's was about a more activist approach. Arthur said he was neither of the one school nor the other. He believed the function of the Supreme Court was to apply the Constitution without worrying about whether or not it would be received with popular acclaim.

The picture was becoming clearer. The excitement in the country was caused by the realization of all those decisions waiting to be made until the ninth man arrived. The ninth man would be the "swing man"; the Court had become divided four to four.

Arthur and Justice Frankfurter were at opposite poles in their thinking. Once Art had told him privately that he thought his position on the death penalty was incomprehensible and shocking. That angered the Justice and he snapped: "You do know that I testified in England before a parliamentary committee that I was utterly opposed to the death penalty."

"That's precisely the point, but as a judge you upheld the death penalty under the most inhuman and cruel circumstances."

It was the case of the man who was put in the electric chair; after they had shocked him terribly and he still was not dead, because the chair was not functioning properly; they unstrapped him, and after a period of time he was again sentenced to be electrocuted. His case was appealed to the Supreme Court on the grounds that under those circumstances it certainly was cruel and inhuman punishment. Justice Frankfurter, along with the majority of the court, rejected that appeal, and the man, who had already experienced that barbaric punishment, was electrocuted again.

Then Justice Frankfurter began to lecture Arthur about his not knowing the difference between being a judge and a legislator. Art told him that judges were sworn to uphold the Constitution, and that it was "utterly incomprehensible [to him] how any judge worth his salt could hold that the death penalty under those circumstances was constitutional in light of the plain language prohibiting cruel and inhuman punishment."

A month by present considerations is a short period of time to await confirmation of a high-level government appointment; but, in those days, a month was regarded, at least by Art, as a tediously long wait. The Judiciary Committee conducted a full-field FBI investigation, examining every detail about Arthur from the time he was a child until the appointment, consulting with almost everybody who had ever known him—our friends, acquaintances, neighbors, relatives.

I remembered that when Art had been admitted to practice before the Supreme Court, it had seemed to me to be the acme of everything important for a lawyer; I thought he should be quite content with that honor for a lasting remembrance. I did not dream that one day Art would be on that bench and I, sitting in the family pews, would be looking at other young wives in the audience sharing the glow of a similar ceremony.

By August of 1962 I was already working on my first book. It was the result of my having prepared what I hoped would be a security-blanket speech to cover all contingencies, should I again be called upon unexpectedly. I broke it into sections to interest various groups but directed it particularly to the women with young children who were always asking questions about how does one have time.

The "elastic" speech had sections on art as a serious work interest; on art background for understanding the contemporary period; on the options available to women at home in community work, in preparation for academic certification for possible later return to the labor market, or just learning for its own sake.

In the fall, we met Robert Luce, the publisher, at the home of friends, Leila Fleisher, an artist, and Henry Fleisher, a public relations executive for public-interest causes. During Arthur's years as counsel for the labor movement, Henry was the editor of its newspaper. I had compiled enough speech material to be able to answer, "Yes," when Bob Luce, who had read quotes from press-reported speeches I had made, asked if I would have time to work on a book.

Using the speech as a skeleton, I added more substantive material from the gallery lectures I had been making. Then, using only material that I could handle readily, researching little since the book would be based largely on personal experience, I did have a work of my own in progress—*The Creative Woman,* Bob Luce's title, not mine. Since I enjoyed watching the changes taking place in Arthur's career, to meet the book deadline I had to drive myself during the last month to use every available moment—while traveling on planes, under dryers at the hairdresser's, while waiting for him when he was late.

After the appointment was submitted, Art had to testify before the Judiciary Committee. Senator Eastland put Estes Kefauver in the chair instead of presiding himself. Although Eastland voted for Arthur, Art's civil rights background over many years might have caused Eastland political problems.

The courtroom was jammed with people—most of them strangers, and all were sympathetic to Arthur. In the light of Senator Sam Ervin's recent flowering as a liberal constitutionalist (except for his position on civil rights), it is interesting to recall that Senator Ervin was Art's principal interrogator.

The month's delay seemed interminable, though in comparison with other nominations, such as Brandeis', or more recently Stewart's, Arthur's confirmation was fairly rapid. It was a source of great satisfaction to us when the liberals and the conservatives, the Democrats and the Republicans, voted for him unanimously—a far cry from the later Carswell nomination. The committee's unanimous report for confirmation was reported to the Senate by Everett Dirksen of Illinois at Arthur's request.

Although Art differed with Senator Dirksen on many legislative matters (the senator, after all, was the Republican leader), nonetheless they were friends.

There is a role for an opposition in a democratic society. It makes for a healthy democracy. Although Everett Dirksen was a strong oppositionist, he had no malice in his heart. He was a political "pro" to whom Art always could turn for a candid statement of the Republican position.

We asked a real estate man to look for a new house for us where Arthur could have more room for study and which would also have space for a clerk to work. Our present house had no privacy for that, nor room in the den for the many books that a Justice needs at home.

Bob and I speculated about what outlets there would be for Arthur's dynamic energy. Mr. Justice Black had his tennis; Mr. Justice Douglas wrote books and marched on the canal trail. Art said Douglas was assigned when he was young and his boundless energies overflowed. But Art said that for him the Court would be the only effort now—no more speeches, no more public appearances, no more dashing about. All his energies were to be concentrated on scholarship. Bob and I wondered if maybe he was having second thoughts.

Bob said to me, "Oh, I understand. It's like me wanting to be on Student Council so much. Then when I was elected, I wondered why had I wanted it. Maybe he's getting nervous, but he can do it if anybody can."

A few days after the announcement of Arthur's appointment to the High Court, a messenger rang our doorbell as we were at the breakfast table to bring us an official envelope from the President. Arthur, very surprised that it was not addressed to him but to me, said, "Open it," and, looking quickly at the signature after I had torn the envelope, he said, "That's it; it's his signature, not Ted Sorensen's."

"It's in answer to the letter I mailed him yesterday."

"Yesterday? Who'd you send it down with?"

"Nobody. I mailed it—at the mailbox on the corner."

To be certain the President saw them, people sent their missives by messenger or delivered them themselves, yet mine had cut through all the load of incoming mail to the White House and had received as much attention. I had merely written: To the President, The White House, fully expecting that it would be delivered promptly, and it was.

I had written by hand to say that I was grateful, not only as

Arthur's wife for the honor that had come to our family, because I knew that Arthur warranted receiving it on the merits, but for what he had done as President in appointing such a man. As a citizen I thanked him.

The President acknowledged it and added, "I gave away my right arm."

THE WHITE HOUSE
Washington

September 28, 1962

Dear Mrs. Goldberg:

Many thanks for your kind letter.

Appointing Arthur to the Supreme Court was a most generous act on my part as I gave away my right arm. However, I know you will both continue to serve our country.

Sincerely,

(signed) John Kennedy

Mrs. Arthur Goldberg
2811 Albemarle Street, N.W.
Washington 8, D.C.

That letter made Arthur reflective about perhaps having failed the President.

"I could have waited," Art said to me, "but I never knew that to Kennedy what I was doing was more than just . . ." He searched for the word and then said, "I guess I never did understand the President's personality and now I never will."

I myself think that had the President ever shared the slightest warmth, had he ever invited him to lunch or to dinner—there were plenty of times when he was undoubtedly eating alone—to just talk, so that a Cabinet member would feel that he was more than a fixture, Art would not have put his own Court ambition first and accepted with such alacrity. Because, while it was a dream come true, he did not want it if the President had a sense of having been left in the lurch. Bill Wirtz after all, had capacity for the job of Secretary.

I reminded him Doris Fleeson's column had said that in our society now, the dynamic force is the Court. He could serve the country there.

A friend reported that the President had tears in his eyes, had smashed his fist into his hand with a bang and had said: "Dammit! *Why* did he want it?"

The clouded confusion between the public and the private life is troublesome. There had been friendship in a removed way, and yet the President gave to Arthur the highest office he could award to anyone—except that of the Chief Justice, and in his position, the Chief is still one man among nine equals. And yet, perhaps he had hoped that Arthur might not accept?

It bothered Arthur. Despite all the news profiles and plaudits, he had not thought of himself as "indispensable." The President himself had never given him to believe that. If one regards another as indispensable, somehow one makes it known. Besides, Arthur felt that maybe the time had come when he was becoming less useful. The press had begun murmuring objections about his being here, there, everywhere and not being able to talk with him when they called. A *New York Times* man had sent him a wire the week before: "I've tried to get you for two days and can't." Arthur couldn't resist replying that "Like all newspapermen, you apparently do not read your own newspaper or you would have seen where I was."

Then there had been comments about his being a publicity hound. In fact, he had just tried to make up for that to a certain periodical when they wanted to get a recent interview. After such an intimation, Art had replied, "No, I think I'll follow your suggestion and curtail my press interviews."

And there were innuendoes in one or two places about "flamboyancy." In all, there had been an overexposure by the news and Art felt he really should no longer be so much to the fore, but if he were to be more retiring and of less service, he might as well be on the Court. It is every lawyer's dream, of course, but he was troubled and reflective about whether he was leaving the Labor Department short—except that he knew Bill had learned much since they had worked together.

It made me a little exasperated. He had wanted, wanted, *wanted* this, and now he was having second thoughts. "Make no mistake about it," I said, "the President would drop you like a hot potato if you were no longer politically useful."

"No," Art said. "It isn't that. It's just that I think I did not know his attitudes well enough to make the right judgment on the acceptance. If he had said to me that I was his right arm, I wouldn't have cut it off. I could have waited, if it served the country better, but he never gave the slightest indication, and I can serve the country too on the Court."

Besides, how did he know yet? "That's just it," Art had said to Bob. "You must not expect that I will be a great judge. I don't know. Look, ten men. I'll be the tenth in that seat, and I only know one other, Story—besides Holmes, Cardozo, and Frankfurter. And the decisions go down in history and I really do not know if I will be a liberal judge." This was because Bob had said, "You better be a liberal."

"And what's more," Art said to both of us, "you cannot put even a hint of a pressure on me to be liberal or vote with Mr. Justice Black or Justice Douglas and the Chief Justice. I'm not sure I will. Now I have to study. I'll have to dig in and grit—and I haven't done that for fifteen years."

On Friday, September 7, Arthur gave awards to his assistants, and there were tears. I heard later that close to two thousand people had filed through the Conference Room at the open house.

Bill and Jane Wirtz, Arthur and I were in the receiving line and I was touched by the good wishes. First, the Department had hoped to have a testimonial in a hotel, or some big splash, but Art said no—the Conference Room or nothing. There never had been time, much as he had hoped, for an open house before. There was cold punch for everyone and cookies, and the warmth of the handclasps and the fervent good wishes made me want to weep.

The judicial robe was hanging on the hall hook near the stairwell where the battered little bluebird of happiness minus half a wing and brightness of hue had been dangling for ten years—battered because that's where clothes to be cleaned were also hung. Arthur said the robe was ironed plenty good enough—no one would see any wrinkles. Mother asserted some prerogative or other and insisted on ironing it the night before, after the family and close friends we had invited to a small reception had left on the dot of nine.

The robe was of an excellent quality, given to him by Jack Potofsky, president of the Amalgamated Clothing Workers of America, and David Dubinsky, president of the International Ladies Garment Workers Union; it had two union labels.

Bob dawdled over getting dressed, vexing me because his radio was tuned to the Ole Miss, and he kept relaying bulletins to us. He was on time, however, and so were Barbara and Dave. Barbara looked radiant.

When we came to the Court, we went to the chambers to show them to mother and the children. The rooms looked as if he had been in them for a long time. The plants I had bought were in place.

We were hurried to the conference room for photographs. "Gentlemen, good morning. This is my family. My wife, you know; my mother, Mrs. Kurgans; my daughter, Barbara, who is married to Dr. David Cramer; my son, Bob, a senior at Amherst." When he had finished with the introductions, he explained that Mrs. Kurgans was my mother.

What everybody particularly noticed at the historic swearing in of the newest junior Justice was the absolute disregard of the administration's executive branch. We should have expected it, of course. Everybody took the separation of powers for granted, but after the years of adulation of the Kennedy family, to have them regarded with such cool disinterest by the judges, was like a dash of cold water flung into our dreaming faces.

They all were there: the President arrived about four minutes to ten. He looked at the clock anxiously; he was on time. The clerk banged a gavel without comment. Everybody rose, and sat down. No announcements were made to the audience, no "Ladies and gentlemen, the President of the United States." None of that, and the Vice-President was there too, sitting near the President and near the Speaker who was seated in front of us. The Court wives were in the last row of the family section, and in front of them were Arthur's sisters.

My mother wept later when she told me how happy she was that he had introduced her as his mother. And on Sunday, a friend said that the only quotable quote he was taking away from our little celebration gathering was mother's remark in response to his question about how she herself had reacted to the news, "Wasn't it wonderful about Arthur?"

"Wonderful? Yes," she said, "but who cares about Arthur? Everybody knows something like this could happen to him, but that it should happen to *me,* that's more wonderful. That I'm the mother-in-law of a Supreme Court Justice!"

In the Court, when Arthur's voice sounded so firm and so clear, I thought that all who heard must know that we were witnessing an unusual happening, that of a man responding to a calling. Every Supreme Court wife probably feels that same sentimentality. Of all the millions of Americans in our country, only nine men are chosen for that High Court. Naturally, there is pride. But I realized that I was trembling. One doesn't tremble with pride ordinarily. I wasn't apprehensive about his capacity to fulfill the duties of that high office. I knew very well that it would not be difficult for a man of his talents, nor would it strain him unduly. Then why was I trembling?

It was altogether unreal to me. It was altogether remote from anything we ever had thought might happen in our lives—to other people possibly, yes, but not to us. Mother's remark notwithstanding, though all who knew him believed something great *should* happen to him, we never gave thought to the possibility that it would.

Arthur had arrived at that station by doing everything the wrong way. What, then, is the right way? When Joseph Kraft, the columnist, wrote in *Harper's* in June 1963 about Douglas Dillon, the Secretary of the Treasury, he pointed out:

> He came from the right background (son of a Wall Street ty-coon). He underwent the right schooling (Groton and Harvard). He made the right marriage (to a Boston debutante). He chose the right jobs (partner in the family firm of Dillon, Read; ambassador in Paris; Undersecretary of State). He favored the right hobbies

(golf and the collection of French paintings and fine china). He accumulated the right properties (an apartment on Fifth Avenue in New York and houses in Washington; Hobe Sound, Florida; Dark Harbor, Maine; Far Hills, New Jersey; and Versailles, France). He supported the right causes (Groton, Harvard, the New York Hospital, and the Metropolitan Museum of Art). He wore the right clothes (dark suits with vests over finely striped shirts and figured ties). He was blessed by the right looks (tall and lean with a well-shaped head and good features). And he conducted himself in the right manner (reserved with strangers and crowds; engaging with friends).

But Arthur had none of these reinforcements. He had not sought the appointment. He had not done one thing to gain it. He was not the product of any Ivy League School. He had no influential family. He certainly had no money put away for our future and had only begun to realize the kind of income any management lawyer long ago would have enjoyed. He was not a politician. He had never been part of a regular political party and was instead involved in the reform movement in Illinois. He had represented labor, not management.

Arthur had represented the fledgling newspaper guild against the powerful chain of newspaper publishers, a formidable non-ally, if not foe. He was in all the liberal causes long before it was popular to be liberal. He was in the civil liberties fight. As a labor lawyer he stood for all the unpopular causes. When he said union halls had to be desegregated, voices rose up among the members crying, "Impeach him, impeach him."

As for his wife, she never could help him in his own field, and her artist friends were "way out" of his field, although they were also his friends. His wife brought him no wealth and no social connections.

Later Arthur heard through the grapevine that Kennedy had felt somewhat taken aback by the Court's apparent disregard of his presence as the President of the country.

It still seems incredible, it still seems unreal. It still seems as if strangers, not ourselves, were acting out a mystery. The *New York Times* said that the Cabinet turned out to show their respect for the law and the judiciary, but I think they came as a tribute to a member of the Cabinet.

But no one paid them attention. As soon as Arthur was sworn in and had taken his place in the junior seat near the family box, the Chief Justice, on behalf of the Court, admitted the lawyers whose admission was moved by various senators, congressmen, and barristers. Then business went on as usual in the midst of the most glamorous group of administration celebrities ever under that roof. The President arose, shook hands with Arthur and left. Then the Vice-President and the Attorney General left. Then some of the senators.

When Court was adjourned, Lady Bird Johnson waved a greeting and shook my hand and so did Ethel Kennedy, and suddenly, there I was holding an impromptu receiving line over the wooden gate-divider.

8

Judges, and the
Women They Married
When They Were
Young

The next day, I paid a formal call on Nina Warren, wife of the Chief Justice. I brought her a charcoal-colored ceramic bowl of gracefully arranged white and pink carnations to thank her for standing with the Chief Justice and us for a time on Sunday to receive our guests. She had her notes all written, with points to call to my attention.

She asked me if I had Carolyn Hagner Shaw's book, adding that *Modern Manners* was the very best for Washington situations, and presented me with a copy. I said I was very glad to have it. She said it might be marked inside; I said that I didn't mind. Mrs. Warren told me that the book presented social problems in question and answer form, like the ever-present glove issue—to wear or not to wear in a receiving line. I said I had a *Congressional Club Cookbook,* and it said one need follow no rule. Mrs. Warren told me very firmly that the *Congressional Club Cookbook* was all wrong. I didn't pursue any reservations I had further, relegating the matter to the usual controversies about the separation of powers. Mrs. Warren lived the role of the wife of a Chief Justice with whole-hearted dedication, as one filling the highest calling herself.

She then proceeded to tell me about how she kept social engagements untangled. Mrs. McHugh, who was the Chief Justice's secretary, would make her three copies of a week's events, which she kept in strategic places to make it impossible for her to overlook or to forget.

Then she discussed the mail—one does not open crank letters, one learns to recognize them on the outside. She told me her means of recognition—among others, the attempted disguise of handwriting. Arthur said that the FBI prefers a minimum of handling of such letters so that they can check for fingerprints.

Mrs. Warren baked an angel food cake with chocolate icing for us. Apparently this was a tradition too. She wrapped it expertly in a cake carton specially prepared for her, so that they could be given away for bazaars and for presentation to the Justices on their respective birthdays.

Formal social life on the Court was quieter than on the Cabinet. Justices and their wives are not expected to reciprocate invitations extended to them by others, nor do they very often accept invitations other than from their private friends. We had, however, become friendly with some of the ambassadors, and we continued to receive invitations from them and from some members of the Cabinet. We rarely accepted Thursday evening invitations, however—conference was on Friday; and we declined others if they brought the total number of our evenings out to more than one or two a week.

The speaking engagements continued for me. The many Jewish women's organizations expect the wife of a Jewish high official to let herself be used for ceremonial functions, particularly if she has been among their membership. Since so few have been in such a position who are willing to let themselves be so exploited, I felt I had to comply for national events, at least. It was a physical impossibility to accept the many local requests.

If one's husband is a Cabinet officer, one can look forward to a time when the administration leaves, but a Justice has life tenure, and I knew that at some point I would have to say no to all the requests for being seated on the dais.

Responsibilities did not noticeably lessen.

Between October 1 and October 3, we were at the University of North Carolina, where Arthur was giving a series of lectures and I was scheduled, as well, for several speeches. On my return, I found the following memo from Fran Guilbert about calls during my absence; it was fairly typical of what the period demanded of me.

To: DKG

1. Mrs. Nam (in Mr. Mortimer Lebowitz's office) wants to talk to you about Equal Opportunity Day.
2. Call Barbara Dubivsky. She is with the *New York Times* and wants to talk to you about Art Work at Blair House.
3. Mrs. Frank Siscoe. Called re you attending the Book Fair given by Scholarship Fund for Children of Foreign Service. She hopes you will be there on the 14th of October around the noon hour. I told her you planned to be there. She wanted you to bring some of your books to be sold there and autographed by you, with the proceeds going only to you, not anyone else. I told her that this I could not promise, and that you would let her know.
4. Mrs. George Wortheim. She is with Georgetown University Law Wives and is pleased that you might consider talking to one of their luncheons. Was interested in a date in November and would like to know your schedule in hopes of working out something for that month.
5. Mrs. McNamara called to say that Princess Ruth-Desta of Ethiopia wanted very much to have a copy of your book. Mrs. McNamara felt that you would want her to have an autographed copy so it would be even more meaningful to her.

   We left it that Mrs. McNamara would tell the Princess that one would be mailed to her. If you send one, we can call the State Dept. for exact title and address, etc.
6. Mrs. Gladys Edmonson (Howard University, Assoc. Dean of Students) would like you to call her.
7. INVITATION: Doris Fleeson called inviting you and the Justice to a light supper around 7 P.M. the eve of the UN benefit on Monday, October 21.

   ALSO, she would like to have you as her guest (and the Justice if he could make it) at a luncheon at Womens Press Club the day Madame Nhu is there. She said, "regardless of our feelings re this woman it might be an interesting experience— like going to the zoo."
8. INVITE: The Justice accepted (on an if possible basis) to attend private showing of documentary film *A Lover's Quarrel with the World—Robert Frost.* Hosts to the Frost documentary are Secy.

Udall and Senator Aiken. It will be held in New Senate Office
Bldg. (Room G-308). Invite is attached.

NOTE: Invitations went out for Brunch for law clerks for 12
noon, Sunday, October 20th. I will send list of names to house.
Including clerks and wives and press people the list will be close
to 50 people (a few under that figure.)

I did maintain my interest in volunteer projects. The numerous
volunteer recruits of Widening Horizons, who then turned to
Urban Service, were learning that many truly deprived young
people were not being reached by the schools, nor by Urban
Service and, of course, not by Widening Horizons itself.

Whatever good the volunteers were doing was desperately
needed, but it was obviously most inadequate, and without wider
community concern and involvement not much more would result. Agnes Meyer's far-visioned planning had seen that earlier,
and the Meyer Foundation, which had initially subsidized Urban
Service within the school system to work with volunteers, was also
concentrating on problems of school financing through the National Committee for Support of the Public Schools. But before
school budgets and financing could be practically expanded, the
community needed facts, and there had to be a way of stimulating
interest.

A new organization was needed, and in October of 1962 some
volunteers approached Charles Horsky, the White House Advisor
for the District of Columbia. He initiated a series of meetings with
a wider representation of citizens to explore the ground needing
to be covered. They groped and struggled until May of 1964 to
avoid duplication with existing organizations and with the new
Washington Project for Youth, then just being launched.

Finally, on May 15, 1964, D.C. Citizens for Better Public Education was formally announced. Its "moving spirits," in addition to
Charles Horsky, were: Flaxie Pinkett, who had been closely associated with Bobby Kennedy; Margaret McNamara; Eleanor
Smollar; George E. C. Hayes; Belford Lawson; and Nancy Harrison. Although I had started the DCCB, it was Nancy Harrison's
dedicated concern and support that was most responsible for its
growth and continuity.

According to its current literature, DCCB is the only city-wide
agency giving full-time attention to local public school problems.

It works closely with other organizations whose goals include improving public education. It early recognized the need for informed citizen participation in civic and school affairs and provided it by alerting the community to the needs of the schools through research projects, special reports, and public meetings. DCCB works for "realistic budgeting and community information on school finance." It regularly attends and reports on board of education meetings.

DCCB started RIF (Reading Is FUNdamental), which distributed thousands of paperback books to D.C. children and has since become a separate continuing organization under Mrs. McNamara and Mrs. Smollar, and grown much beyond its earliest hopes.

The Supreme Court is the only place in the government where wives and family are accorded a special courtesy and regarded as a group. Of course, it is easier when only nine persons are involved. The Congress has a wives' gallery, to be sure, and the President's family has the first row in the family section on opening of Congress occasions, but the Executive, to my knowledge, makes no provision for the inclusion of family during work hours and probably would prefer that wives remain at home, to emerge for picture-taking purposes only. Early in the Nixon administration, there was an effort to show how wives were included in a briefing with their husbands, but that laudable effort seemed to collapse almost immediately.

On the Court, whenever a case is being argued, there is always room for Court wives in the family pews. There is also a dining room where they may gather for luncheons, though officially it is a place for entertaining visiting foreign jurists or for intimate ceremonial events, such as the presentation of a portrait by members of a Judge's family.

I had not known about the family pews and was surprised to learn from Nina Warren that a wife was expected to be there when her husband delivered an important opinion. Perhaps only Nina expected that. "Dorothy, we haven't been seeing you lately." When I looked as puzzled as I felt, she explained that the wives often appeared for Monday morning opinions, particularly if their husbands were making important contributions. I had thought that Arthur could surely deliver himself of an opinion without my presence. I had never been essential previously, though I had always been present at his steel hearings, and at conventions and various meetings, but that was because he invited me, not because I was expected.

It occurred to me that Court wives were more like the wives of executives in the labor movement—not exactly camp followers but present and supportive in a quiet way. In the labor movement, though, however solid the husband-wife relationships may have been, the men observed *machismo* with a capital M. Wives were to be seen and not heard. If May Reuther and Walter had more than the usual rapport and companionship, May was careful not to flaunt it and often sat apart at conventions in a first row balcony seat. True, at the Atlantic City meetings, at the informal parties of Steelworkers or other CIO gatherings, the wives were there listening with amusement to the post-mortem stories and occasionally contributing anecdotes, but I do not recall any special courtesies accorded to them as a group. Union wives were supposed to regard themselves as lucky to have a vacation while the men worked.

Labor movement wives may be said to be more like congressional wives in one respect, because Court wives see more of their husbands. Even though the long Court recesses are not really vacations, since a Justice has much work to do, at least his physical being is present, even if his thoughts are wrapped in certiorari.

Perhaps a Justice has arrived at a later stage in his career, being provided with life tenure, whereas men in other branches of the government, who do not have the luxury of such security, must scurry and scratch for a living.

Whatever the reason, there is a courtliness in their bearing toward their wives, an observance of old-fashioned manners, at least in their publicly visible relationships. One almost never sees a Justice walking several feet ahead of a wife who is breathlessly trying to walk alongside him as he rushes to talk to another Justice or lawyer. Only rarely does one see a Justice skillfully ignoring a wife or another Justice's wife after the first routine arrival kiss.

I saw the Justices and their wives through rose-colored glasses, I suppose, glimpsing only affection, devotion, loving kindness, with everyone trying to avoid the slightest bit of gossip.

The relations among the members of the Court were, in general, marked by a civilized atmosphere of respect for each other's opinion and a genuine attempt to be friendly. The sociability had a purpose.

Once, Winifred Reed, wife of retired Justice Stanley F. Reed, looked at me with dry amusement at one of the early dinners given in our honor. When everyone arrived with such an abundance of friendliness, careful not to overlook anyone and dutifully greeting each other with the light kiss on the cheek, she said, "Did you ever see so much kissing as goes on around here?"

The very real friendliness reflected a transcendent bond among the "brethren"—their respect and love for the Constitution, however much they differed about its interpretation. Indeed, the very term "brethren"—"My brother Harlan," "My brother Douglas" —a quaint, old-fashioned word imparting a family tie, still keeps popping up in opinions and oral interpolations, often before their clobbering of each other, with the Constitution as a weapon.

But all unquestionably were committed to the rule of law. Every day in the robing room before the opening of Court, they would perform a solemn ceremony. Before the red velvet curtains parted and the "Oyez, oyez, oyez" announced their presence, each Justice would shake hands with all the others. A few minutes later they might be castigating one another bitterly and publicly because of deep-rooted differences, but whatever their public antagonisms, each member of the Court treated every other with respect and friendliness that, in a few instances, verged on affection.

I liked that and could understand the underlying significance. It never is an empty form. It is what the artist Braque meant when he wrote in his *Notebooks,* "I love the rule that corrects the emotion."

Similarly with the Harlans, who were the first to entertain for us at a dinner party, even though Arthur and Justice Harlan disagreed more often than they agreed. And when Arthur and Hugo Black differed, not as often as Arthur and John Harlan but sometimes very sharply, Art could chide Hugo with "departing from the true faith." But all would be resolved by dinner time if a party occurred on the same day, and laughter and song would not be diminished by the morning's differences. The evening of the day on which Art's opinion in *Griswold* was attacked bitterly in Court by Justice Black, we were at the Blacks for dinner. The evening was made lively by the way that Hugo and Art jousted with each other about the morning's events.

Art said: "Hugo, despite your long service on the bench, you're still an Alabama jury lawyer who can't resist playing to the galleries."

Hugo, in his dry, good-humored way said: "It'd be awfully dull at the Court if every now and then we didn't enliven proceedings with the forensic display, Clay County style."

Unlike the Cabinet wives, the Court wives were not involved in many outside-the-home activities, were never in any political work, and were careful about the organizations to which they might lend their names as sponsors, lest a case arise that might require a husband to disqualify himself. Some of them were active supporters of Goodwill Industries, the Salvation Army, and various other projects sponsored by churches and other worthy organizations.

Their presence or patronage of a given event is all that is really expected of them on such occasions, though many contribute time and effort to noncontroversial projects, having private interest in them. In the larger community, it is a ceremonial role that is required of them, and they fulfill it dutifully and sometimes with enjoyment. They would attend, for example, the breakfast in honor of the First Lady, given annually by the congressional wives in the spring.

Nina Warren reminded Court wives, for instance, about the annual Salvation Army Benefit, so that we could sit as a group at one table, but Nina's interests were almost entirely wrapped up in the welfare of her husband and family.

The Warrens were, of course, an exceptional couple. Nina was content merely to be in the Chief's presence. At any gathering— and they were, of course, invited to so many—where crowds of people elbowed their way to talk to the Chief, Nina could usually be found nearby, smiling and watching the others press toward him. She was an extremely self-reliant person, ready for any exigency or emergency.

If, at a large buffet dinner, the Chief's arm was inadvertently brushed by a passer-by, causing something to spill on his jacket, Nina, noticing it immediately, would dart from across the room to relieve him of his plate and matter-of-factly remove the stain at once with a napkin dipped in sparkling water, while the Chief continued talking.

When they traveled, she had a packing list that insured his readiness for every possible situation. She kept it pasted in his closet, and she also had a similar list for herself. When we were invited to Asian universities and high courts, Nina showed me her lists; one item was an American Legion cap for the Chief. That made me remember the little yarmulke that must be worn in orthodox synagogues, yet I was not thoughtful enough, because when Art needed it, I had forgotten to pack it, and he had to borrow one.

If Arthur's black bow tie at dinner came unhooked, Nina would be able to find a tiny black lingerie clasp that would save that sartorial situation. If Adlai Stevenson, traveling with Mrs. Agnes Meyer, the Drew Pearsons, and the Warrens on a yacht in foreign waters, became afflicted with a painful toothache, it would be only Nina who would not have forgotten to pack oil of cloves and would be able to relieve the ache.

Both Warrens had exceptional energy and traveled constantly. Their life was very private, their family very close-knit. Nina was observant of all the obligations of the old-fashioned commitment to wifehood, motherhood, grandmotherhood. The Chief's endearing look at her, the way he tenderly drew her near to him to include her in a conversation if she were standing outside the circle of discussion, attested to their relationship.

On occasions when we were in a car with them and Nina felt freer to comment about a matter Arthur and the Chief were discussing, the Chief would interrupt his conversation to explain fully to her what he had meant, according her the same courtesy he would extend to one better versed in the law. I, too, was glad of the explanation, usually reserving my own queries for Arthur when we were home. Behind the circumspect, noncommittal attitude of Court wives, I think there is more knowingness and strong-mindedness than people may think, and it is to the credit of the men that they do take time to explain.

The Salvation Army was Nina's particular project. But there were numerous requests for her to stand in receiving lines, to give an item for auction or sale to benefit a charity, to sponsor worthy causes as a patron, and with all of these she conscientiously tried to comply.

The Warrens lived at a large hotel, but we were not entertained there by them. On occasion, they would entertain at the Congressional Country Club. John and Virginia Warren Daly entertained for them on the Chief's birthdays, beginning with his seventy-fifth for us. At that time he said, "I always feel sorry for those who feel sorry about growing old and I say to them, 'Think of how many friends never get to this age.'"

Upon the death of the Chief, Nina said to me, "Every moment was beautiful. The young people who don't know what a real marriage is miss so much."

I had had occasion to meet Selma Burton, wife of Justice Harold Burton, early in the Kennedy administration. I liked Mrs. Burton for her independence of spirit, for her not caring whether others thought it singular or odd that she wore only one shoulder-length pendant earring at a time. When it was pointed out to her that she must have lost one, she merely smiled and continued talking. I thought that perhaps she was keeping a silent tally of the busybodies who felt impelled to advise her. She stubbornly set her own pattern for nonconformity.

Selma Burton had an infectious laugh and also a genuine young-heartedness. On April Fool's Day, I received a mystifying little card from "Guess who?" and did not learn it was she until sometime afterward. Nor did anyone I know ever send greeting cards on Halloween except Selma, and she also remembered to send greetings on Valentine's Day.

Justice Burton suffered from Parkinson's Disease, and when I met them together he was already deteriorating noticeably; but I never will forget the fortitude and courage he displayed, supported by his wife, who refused to let it deter them from participating in reciprocal hospitality until it became altogether impossible. Several times they entertained great numbers of friends, from many different fields, taking over the entire large hall of the Congressional Club. At these parties, Mrs. Burton provided corsages for all Court wives and lapel posies for the Justices.

Upon our arrival at the Court, the Burtons gave a large party for us, and we were asked to stand in the receiving line with them and the Chief Justice and Nina. Justice Burton, slight, frail at the time, but smiling and alert, greeted guests with no evidence of his ailment until, to my horror, he quietly crumpled to the floor. Mrs. Burton lost no poise while Arthur and a passing clerk quickly assisted him to an upright position and he continued as graciously as before, though after a few moments the receiving line broke to allow him to be seated.

On several other occasions at private dinners, where just the Court and wives were gathered, Mrs. Burton had no hesitancy about feeding the Justice, who no longer was able to raise his fork to his mouth or drink from a glass without spilling. Yet both of them evinced such quiet stoicism and acceptance of that humiliating disability that I only could admire the affirmation of life that was implied thereby. It was an example to all of us, particularly to those who became uneasy at seeing the inroads and ravages the advancing years wreak upon the physique of a person whose mind is still perceptive.

The Bill Douglases entertained on occasion at the Court and several times at their home. Friends were glad to see them at the Brennans, the Bazelons, and other places including the White House. Arthur and Justice Douglas were friends of long standing, and Arthur was asked to be chairman of the dinner to honor Douglas on the occasion of his having served longer on the Court than any other Justice.

We were closest, however, to the Hugo Blacks. I had known his late wife, Josephine, for many years. Their son was a labor lawyer in Birmingham. We were so glad when the lonely years ended for Hugo upon his marriage to Elizabeth Seay, a Birmingham woman who became my good friend. Elizabeth enjoyed all the ambiance of Washington life and provided the Justice with great happiness and contentment in his later years. They were a most popular couple, invited frequently to embassy and White House functions, and were especially good hosts. They entertained formally in the beautifully proportioned rooms of their eighteenth-century house, with Josephine Foster Black's paintings still glowing above the dining room mantel and elsewhere—and they also entertained more informally on the terrace adjoining the rose garden and tennis court, where the Justice skillfully presided over the barbecue grill after a brisk game. Their home was filled with the sounds of life, the ever-coming-and-going of children and grandchildren.

Best of all were the small dinners exchanged with the Blacks and the Skelly Wrights. Judge Wright was on the U.S. Court of Appeals and his wife, Helen, who, notwithstanding her time-consuming commitment as an officer (and later president) of the National Association of Mental Health, is a splendid cook. After dinner, we sang old songs, and Hugo recalled some very old Clay County ballads. Only Bill Douglas could exceed Hugo in this talent. Bill Brennan liked to sing, too, but his singing, unlike his opinions, was usually very much off-key. I noticed that when they attended our seder.

While Arthur was on the Court, Justice Tom Clark and Mary entertained once or twice at their Connecticut Avenue apartment, though I remember best the receptions they gave after-hours in the Court itself on the occasion of a special anniversary or birthday.

A home-oriented person, Mary Clark always had a special concern and interest in projects having to do with the rehabilitation of deaf children, and her name appeared on the patronage lists of worthy causes and charities. Both Clarks showed the warmth and affability typical of Texans, and Mary Clark is still the picture of a Southern gentlewoman. Ultrafeminine, outward-going, dressed with chic, she fluttered with goodwill and a verve for life.

The Harlans were among the first to entertain us in their home at a dinner. There was a strong sense of form in Ethel's household, as indeed in the houses of all the Justices. When the Harlans entertained for us in their Georgetown house, with its high-walled garden that she tended, it was memorable.

The Harlan house held another aura in the very name of Justice Harlan's grandfather, John Marshall Harlan, who sat on the Court between 1877 and 1911. He was the great post–Civil War Justice who was the single dissenter in the famous case of *Plessy* v. *Ferguson,* in which the Court adopted the separate-but-equal doctrine.

So, long after he forecast exactly what would happen to our country in race relations, his grandson had the unprecedented opportunity of participating in a judicial decision that vindicated his grandfather's vision. Arthur, who liked the grandson too, although they frequently took opposing views, often said that the first Justice Harlan was his greatest hero among all the Justices of the Supreme Court.

Retired Justice Stanley Reed and Mrs. Reed early entertained for us in their suite at the Mayflower Hotel. As the Solicitor-General, Stanley Reed had presented Arthur to the Court many years ago, and we had always felt warmly toward them because of that. Winifred Reed carried herself regally and looked, because of her bearing, the picture of what a Court wife must have been in an earlier age. She was dressed as contemporaneously as any of us, but there was a certain old-fashioned elegance in her well-coiffed long hair, her erect carriage, her polished speech.

When I was organizing the Friends of the Juvenile Court (now an adjunct of the present Superior Court), Miriam Ottenberg, a Washington newspaper woman, told me that her mother had been among the founders of a similar project years before, and from her mother I learned that Winifred Reed had been among the active leaders at that time. Thus, I invited both of them to attend some of the early meetings, and both spoke of the hopes and objectives and the work of that earlier time to the new group, which included my friend Val Davis, wife of John F. Davis, Clerk of the Court.

It was a pleasure to ask Winifred for her support of the fledgling project, not only because I knew she understood the import of the work, not only because she would be agreeable about the public relations aspect of her patronage, but because as she sat there pouring tea, evincing a smiling interest in the committee, she looked every inch of what she was—a noble spirit.

Bill and Marjorie Brennan invited us often to their Georgetown home, with its lovely garden, and included as well non-Court friends, such as the Richard Harknesses, who shared a party wall with them. They annually celebrated Bill Douglas's birthday because it coincided with an anniversary of their own.

Marjorie never seemed overtaxed by such efforts, claiming that she merely tried not to let her work get ahead of her. That meant having a systematic approach and adhering to it, because her home sparkled, and she did too.

Despite a frailty of physique in her own feminine self, Marjorie Brennan communicates a quality of courage and inner strength when confronted by crisis that is more often associated with male heroism. Still, Agnes Fahy (wife of retired Judge Charles Fahy, U.S. Court of Appeals) has that same courage.

Both Brennans are hospitable, warm-hearted people, the Justice enveloping his women guests with an effusive exclamation of delight and a smacking kiss on both cheeks. Marjorie, somewhat more reserved, carefully refrained from expressing herself on Court issues, once telling me, "Nothing people may ask me about the Court, particularly the press, is for my personal opinion. They merely want to know what Bill is thinking through me, and I'm not going to tell them."

Their home, like that of all of the Justices, was run on a modest scale. We liked that about the Court. If our country has suffered from a near-monarchical Presidency, this surely can not be said of the Supreme Court.

Andy Stewart, wife of Justice Potter Stewart, and Marian White, wife of Justice Byron White, were also basically home-oriented in their interests. They too, while chic and modern in outlook, nonetheless comported themselves with dignity. They too supported only such causes or organizations that could not possibly cause their husbands to disqualify themselves in matters before the Court. I was grateful to Andy for accepting the leadership of the project I was leaving, the Friends of the Juvenile Court, when we left Washington for the United States mission to the UN.

Cecilia Marshall's (Mrs. Thurgood Marshall) natural, unaffected dignity and poise, coupled with a quiet reserve, bespeaks self-sufficiency balanced by wit and a sense of humor. All of which I suspect she needs to juggle the double-ceremonial demands possibly being made on her as had been made on me.

Except for Cathy Douglas, who is now a member of the District Bar and a practicing lawyer, the Supreme Court wives, so far as I know—and so far as the public knows—find self-fulfillment in home and a private life. Public notice is to be avoided as much as possible, so that the name of a Court wife might be in the papers only on the occasion of a wedding in the family, as a White House guest, or as a patron of an event to raise funds for an old, established charity. If she actively supports other projects, she keeps her name, as circumspectly as her person, relatively in the background.

Thus, none can be categorized as a "public wife." They eschew labels and cherish their own privacy, having their own coterie of loyal friends apart from the Court. This extends to wives of judges on other high courts. Only Helen Wright, I think, among High

Court wives, has achieved demonstrable success in a work of her own and as a full-time volunteer.

My friend Miriam (Mickey) Bazelon is an admirable example of a Court wife who develops interests of her own in the public sphere. Mickey is the wife of the chief judge of the court of appeals, David Bazelon, and they are among our earliest friends, dating back to Chicago days. Her organizational talents and executive ability were first devoted to volunteering. In the 1950s, she became the first woman president of the Jewish Social Service Agency. She served three terms and was also active in the city-wide planning organization of the Health and Welfare Council in the Family and Child Welfare Section. She was the only woman invited by the D.C. Board of Commissioners to serve for city-wide planning. From volunteer work for the Peace Corps she went to VISTA (Volunteers in Service to America) to help set up the concept and structure of using volunteers in a domestic peace corps.

It is to the credit of the Civil Service Administration that they provided a classification that includes all the security benefits of government employment to people having qualifications of "lived life" experience. Thus, Mickey was able to leave volunteer work and enter the paid labor market, working full time in OEO from VISTA to Headstart to the Community Action Program on a professional basis. Recently, she has been studying in the Graduate Program of Science, Technology and Public Policy at George Washington University.

Alice Edgerton, wife of the late Judge Henry Edgerton of the court of appeals, was first to challenge the political status of Court wives by joining the Women's National Democratic Club in 1952 when "I just decided I could no longer accept not being a participant as a citizen." She was assuredly ahead of her time in her attitudes about women's rights, having written many articles on the subject as early as 1917 and also articles on current affairs for *The Nation* and *The New Republic*. But the demands of child-rearing, education, managing a home without help, and the early attitude toward women on college faculties prevented her from working in her own field of interest—mathematics.

Mercedes Douglas, while still Mrs. William O. Douglas, was the next to follow suit about political club membership, but no other Court wives, to my knowledge, have been so venturesome. Art told me, "Listen, Do, when I took the oath of office, whether you know it or not, you did too. Get it?" I got it, though I had not known that I too had made a vow to be politically neutral. The day will come when a Judge's wife will have the same right to participate, as every citizen should, in taking a stand on issues that she thinks are important.

The code was brought home to me personally in November 1962, on the occasion of the Thanksgiving Day football match between a predominantly black Washington high school and a predominantly white school. A fracas ensued that went beyond any usual team competitiveness and was the first of the bitter racial clashes erupting publicly; It was, at least, the first of which I was aware. I thought it important to call Charles Horsky, Presidential Assistant for the District of Columbia, to tell him that it was a sign that something had better be done quickly to alleviate rising tensions. He agreed. It occurred to me to invite the high school superintendent, the administrative staff, and Mr. Henley of the Urban Service, the newly funded school-volunteer program, to meet with Mr. Horsky and the others to discuss what the schools could do to avoid similar situations and what the private sector and government might do to help. I unthinkingly sent out invitations to a meeting in the wives' dining room of the Court, since I had always had full permission from Arthur to do so in the Department of Labor.

When I phoned Nina Warren to invite her, she said, "Have you talked with Mrs. McHugh?" (Mrs. Margaret K. McHugh was secretary to the Chief.) I said no, I hadn't thought to invite her. Nina said nothing further, but that evening, at a dinner at the embassy of Israel, the Chief came up to me and said earnestly, while wagging his index finger, "Dorothy, Mrs. McHugh tells me you're planning on inviting school officials to the Court. That is impermissible. Arthur would have to disqualify himself if a case arose involving the schools."

I was vexed with my obtuseness at having to learn the hard way all the fundamental facts of everyday life. A person of my age should not have been that naïve, I realized, and now again I was marching into new areas without first having thought to ask about directions.

The invitations were already out. Jane Wirtz and Margie McNamara were also involved. I suggested to Jane that she ask Bill about using his conference room, but Bill had an event already scheduled. I called Charlie Horsky to ask about the Executive Office Building, and he said, "What about the State Department?"

The State Department? That would mean the Thomas Jefferson Room or the Benjamin Franklin Room, two elegant reception rooms used ordinarily for visiting dignitaries.

"Why not?" Charlie asked. "Nothing's too good for the schools."

Another instance where I unwittingly overstepped the unwritten code was a luncheon I gave at the Court to honor Elizabeth Chrisman, the former executive director of the National Women's Trade Union League. Elisabeth was close to eighty, and I had regretted Arthur's failure to acknowledge her work publicly when he was Secretary of Labor, as he had that of Mary Anderson, the first head of the Women's Bureau.

I invited Esther Peterson, head of the Women's Bureau, Mary Switzer, head of vocational rehabilitation at Health, Education and Welfare, and friends from various volunteer groups, art interests, and the labor movement to honor her. Arthur entered while Elisabeth was talking about marching "picket" for the old Gloveworkers Union. He said a few pleasant words and left.

Afterward, he said to me: "Well now, do you think the Supreme Court is the place for all this talk?"

Again, I had had to be told. The Court is sacrosanct.

The perquisites of Court life differed from those of the Cabinet. On the Court, only the Chief Justice has a car and chauffeur. In the Cabinet, all the members enjoyed that luxury. The Justices do, however, enjoy the services of a messenger. When Arthur was on the Court, only one secretary was available to him, and thus his messenger helped with Xeroxing and secured and returned whatever books were required from the Library of Congress. If a Justice was lucky and his messenger was able to drive, his services could be used, if he were agreeable, as a chauffeur, but those services were paid for. As for Arthur's messenger, Robert Suttice, his salary was supplemented in this and many other ways.

The messengers also served lunch to the Justices, bringing it upstairs from the basement cafeteria, the menu being the same as that being served to everyone and, of course, paid for by the Justices. The Justice's messenger was also available after his own lunch was served to assist in the wives' dining room if a Court wife were entertaining. The food was the same as that being served in the regular cafeteria at the same prices.

No liquor was served, except for an occasional surreptitious sherry, a far cry from the fifth of bourbon that was served the Justices every third day in the time of the first Justice Harlan. Arthur saw that item in the Court Archives in Harlan's own handwriting. In the old days, the Justices were what Arthur called "two-fisted drinkers," and he would regale listeners with an anecdote that used to circulate among the Justices. The story was about the original John Marshall's Court at the beginning of the Republic. At that time, the Justices maintained their residences in their own hometowns. There was not too much Court business, and their wives were not present, so they were not averse to a bit of liquor. One day, Justice Marshall said, "We're hitting the bottle too hard. Let's unanimously agree we'll confine our drinking to rainy days." The next day was a bright, sunshiny day, but as they began eating their dinner, Marshall brought out the bourbon. Justice Story said, "Chief Justice, it's a bright sunshiny day today, and have you forgotten our agreement about drinking only on rainy days?" Marshall replied, "Mr. Justice, you forget we are the Supreme Court of the United States. Our jurisdiction covers the whole country, and surely it's raining somewhere in the country today." If that perquisite of office no longer applies, quill pens are still provided. A craftsman in Williamsburg supplies the Court.

During Arthur's time, each Justice had two law clerks and one secretary. Now each has two secretaries and three clerks; the Chief has five law clerks. The Justices have no entertainment allowance; neither, for that matter, do the Cabinet members, save for the Secretary of State.

The greatest perquisites, of course, are life tenure and the $10,000 pension to which their widows are entitled.

Cabinet members had available to them, depending on the President, the use of the yachts, the *Patrick J.* and the *Sequoia*, for entertaining dignitaries from foreign countries, and the use of

Camp David. The Supreme Court Justices did not have this per-quisite; on one occasion, when Arthur was entertaining the Chief Justice of India at the request of the Secretary of State, the *Sequoia* was made available to us, and we invited the Court; it was the first such sail for many of them.

A Cabinet officer has his portrait painted at government ex-pense for hanging in his department upon his leaving office, but a Justice's portrait must be paid for by his family and presented by them. Both a Justice and a Cabinet officer may, for $100, purchase his chair. (Arthur had enough chairs, certainly. He gave the Secretary of Labor Cabinet Room chair to our son, Robert; the United Nations Cabinet Chair to our daughter, Barbara; and the seat that he used on the Bench is on our farm. A rocking chair that he used at his office at the United States Mission to the UN was bought by his staff from the government, inscribed, and pre-sented to him. And that is on the farm in the small living room.)

In both the Cabinet and on the Court, one is provided with official stationery, of course, and free postage, but only for official business. A Cabinet officer is reimbursed for his official travel expenses—$25 a day plus his airplane ticket. A Justice does virtu-ally no traveling except to infrequent judicial conferences, and these are mostly academic in nature.

Each Justice is assigned to a circuit. From Justice Frankfurter, Arthur inherited the First Circuit—the New England Circuit, whose conference is in Boston. The custom is for the members of the conference to invite the Circuit Justice, as he is called, to dinner. But before he went to Boston, Arthur, at the invitation of Justice Clark, was invited to give an address at the Midwest Seventh Circuit Conference in Chicago.

It was a typically gregarious event sponsored by the Circuit Lawyers' Bar Association. We were met at the plane by a delega-tion and a chauffered limousine and escorted to the Ambassador East Hotel. There we were ensconced in a luxurious suite with a handsome cloth-covered sideboard on which were set cheese, fruit, and liquor. I was presented with the usual orchid corsage. We really were very handsomely fêted.

In Boston, wives were not invited, but Arthur gave me a report of the dinner. It was a little different from the Chicago conference. First, no one met him at the airport. He had to take a taxi, for which, of course, he paid. Then, they had reserved for him what he believed to be the smallest room in the Sheraton Hotel—no fruit, no flowers, no liquor, nothing. Then he had to find his own way in the morning to where the conference was held. There, of course, he was most courteously and deferentially welcomed by the judges and the lawyers. Unlike Chicago, however, where the judicial conference was open to about a thousand lawyers—making it reminiscent of the old CIO conventions—the First Circuit Conference in Boston was a very exclusive affair confined to the presidents of the local bar associations (but not the women's bar association), the deans of the local law schools, and the local federal judges.

Art was told by the Chief Justice of the First Circuit, Bailey Aldrich, that that evening there would be a dinner in his honor —a stag dinner—at the staid Parker House. The dinner itself was convivial enough, though limited to the same group as the conference. The food was good, the liquor good; in general, a most agreeable evening. Arthur was expected to make an after-dinner speech, and he did—a short talk in which he tried to portray how the Supreme Court was "doing." The dinner came to an end at a very early hour—also unlike the Chicago dinner, where the Seventh Circuit, in festive black tie, was able to dance to the music of a good orchestra later.

As Arthur was preparing to leave the Boston dinner, after thanking his hosts for a pleasant evening, the clerk of the court discreetly told him, "Mr. Justice, the cost of the dinner for each participant is $7.50—either pay me now or in the morning, since our dinners are Dutch treat." I laughed. Art's only comment, as he shook his head in wonder, was, "My circuit is a Yankee circuit, that's all, and New England is New England."

There were one or two other perquisites—if they may be called such on the Court—"customs" may perhaps be a more apt term. The Justice could be served lunch in his chambers if he cared to eat privately. In Art's time, lunch during arguments was only one-half hour, so he usually ate with the other Justices, but if mother and I were in the Court, he would invite us to eat in his chambers. His messenger would bring us a fruit salad and cottage cheese plate from the downstairs cafeteria, but Fran Guilbert, once again his secretary, not mine, would have set a sweet little table with a white cloth for us in his paneled chambers before his fireplace where a fire was always burning in the cold months.

There was a robing-room attendant to assist the Justices in the room directly beyond the red velvet draperies. Their robes would be carefully pressed and hung there in lockers. And there was also the convenience of a barber in the Court building, who was, of course, paid by the individual Justices. The fact that the clerks, and even the lawyers and others of the general public, could avail themselves of his services, led to a small discomfort. When Arthur entered, the barber would evict whomever was in the chair, his hair half cut. Art would protest and insist that he did not mind waiting his turn so that some unfortunate would not be left with a suspended haircut, but the barber would hear none of that.

Coming from the labor movement, and the Labor Department, Art thought the price the barber charged was too small and gave a somewhat generous tip. A few days after the first time he did this, one of his colleagues commented at lunch, before all the others, that Arthur was undermining the tradition that limited tips to a quarter. Art answered that the tradition that he would maintain was the tradition of the Supreme Court—a nine-man Court with each Justice sitting on the Bench having an equal voice and vote, and that the same tradition applied when he was sitting in the barber's chair.

At the time of the Cuban missile crisis, the Justices received a notice from the President that arrangements had been made to evacuate the Supreme Court to a safe place.

Arthur called the President and said, "I don't know what's going on and perhaps I don't need to be told."

"Nobody told you?"

"No." That surprised the President.

"I'll send a briefing officer to brief you and whoever else of the Court who wants to know."

Art said he'd appreciate that very much but that was not the purpose of his call. "It doesn't say Dorothy will be evacuated, so I have a question to ask you. You'll have to be evacuated in the event of a nuclear attack. Wouldn't Jackie go with you?"

Art thought the President fumbled a bit. He answered: "You

know, don't you, that arrangements are made by the Office of Preparedness?"

"Well, Mr. President, I can't answer for others, but for number one, I wouldn't leave by myself, and number two, what the hell difference would it make if there's going to be a nuclear attack on our country if I tell you I don't go without Dorothy. If there's going to be a nuclear attack on our country, there won't be any cases to hear and no need to worry about the members of the Supreme Court, but you can still send over a briefing officer, because I'd like to hear what's happening."

The other Justices were going to meet in conference, and Hugo Black objected to being briefed: "We can't get mixed up in the Executive branch of the government."

Art said, "Nonsense. I'm not being briefed in order to advise the President. I'm being briefed as a member of the Court, which is being told that measures are being taken to evacuate us. I've already made up my own mind because they're not evacuating the wives. But that is a matter for each member of the Court to determine for himself. But in any event I'm not asking that it be put to a vote. I'm merely advising you that I will be briefed."

Then considerable discussion ensued, whether to hear the briefing or not, some being with Hugo, some with Arthur. The President sent a colonel to the Court, who for the next several days, until the crisis was resolved, briefed Arthur in his chambers. Every member of the Court, including Justice Black, came to Art to ask him privately about what he had learned.

Preparations, of course, have to be made for the unthinkable becoming a reality. In the event of crisis such as that horrifying possibility, I wondered—as he told me the story of the evacuation plans—how would Arthur have been able to find me. Unless a wife carried a walkie-talkie, her husband would be hardly likely to reach her in time; and what wife would carry an appliance that —Doomsday or not—has the connotation of a chastity belt. Moreover, I would not have agreed to be evacuated without mother or our housekeeper, Lillian, and Lillian would not have agreed to be evacuated without her children and grandchildren.

Nonetheless, it was reassuring, and I would make an effort to remember the great loving-kindness of it when for long periods I would see only the back of the newest Justice's head in study.

Poring over a huge book, surrounded by papers, barricaded by a rolling trough-table filled with other relevant books, he would respond with a grunt to a question; it had to be repeated at least three times to catch his attention; often, I had to stamp and shout an *"ARTHURRRR!"* Then would follow the cold look that asked: Are such hysterics really necessary?

Marriage to an Associate Justice of the Supreme Court is better if the wife is not short-tempered. But the prodigious amount of self-restraint involved was more heroic than I could muster constantly; it helped to be outright explosive on occasion.

9

---◦◦◦◦---

The Warren Era

Ethel Harlan told me that she called the day before conference day "Bloody Thursday." I reflected that probably none of the Court wives ever indulged herself with foot-stamping shouts to get her husband to listen to the news that something was happening to the basement drain and water was coming in fast. (Arthur finally came down, and the two of us emptied water into dishpans and soup pots.) And if I heard noise at night, I hesitated to shake him on the shoulder; I knew how much he needed his sleep if he was to be alert to the decision-making process the next day. (He would raise himself to listen for a minute, and if I repeated my whispered concern, "Art, it sounds like someone is trying to get in the front door," he'd say testily, "So what do you want me to do—go down and shake hands with the burglar?" and go back to sleep.)

Now that he was a Supreme Court Justice, presumably no burglar would dare to enter. I speculated that, in any case, Arthur would probably sit down and tell the intruder that such behavior, regrettably, called for police attention. But before calling the police he'd advise him not to answer any questions unless he had a lawyer.

Such short-tempered thoughts on my part were as transitory as the wind rattling through the house's old casements. If one is married to a man who genuinely believes in equal justice before the law and needs his sleep in order to judge coolly and dispassionately, one just tiptoes downstairs in the middle of the night to greet the nonexistent burglar oneself, particularly if it's on "Bloody Thursday."

Once, when commiserating with Elizabeth Black about parking problems and how careful I was to avoid receiving a police ticket, she said, "I know just how you feel. If I ever got a ticket, I'm sure Hugo'd let me rot in jail." So would Arthur, for that matter, but at least he wouldn't let me burn in a nuclear-bomb hell all alone.

On such little things does a person set the pattern for his or her relationship to that vague abstraction called society, and Judges (and their wives) who might be inclined to challenge the "expired" meter flash were expected to be punctilious about every little thing if it happened to be the law, lest by their behavior they demean the Court and the law itself.

I thought Art carried propriety to unnecessary lengths at times when the law was not even involved—merely the question of an appearance of an impropriety. An innocent little Fruit-of-the-Month Club basket arrived from one of his admirers—such well-packed, ripe, delicious-looking plums. But not one bite for us. Off it went to Children's Hospital by a personal messenger, who even had to wait for a receipt; a letter was sent to the donor advising him to stop future fruits.

"It's not so ridiculous if that fellow has a case coming up before the Court."

"But he doesn't."

"But he might—in six months, six years—and I'd have to disqualify myself."

"But don't you remember Paul Douglas [the former senator from Illinois] saying you can accept gifts from constituents so long as they're not worth more than the price of a ten-pound ham."

"Maybe for politicos—legislators. Judges can't."

I asked, "Who would be silly enough to consider that a bribe?"

"No. Judges can't accept gifts except from their own family or long-time family friends, and he's neither."

On the Court, there was no stretching of a point. At home, notwithstanding Art's rejection of any gift, however insignificant in value, the fruit kept coming each month, and each month Arthur sent it to the Children's Hospital and had his messenger wait for the receipt.

Scholars have pointed out that the Warren Court really became a Warren Court, rather than a Frankfurter Court, upon Arthur's ascension. When Arthur came, he provided, in many cases, the necessary fifth vote to change the previous dissents of Justices Warren, Black, Douglas, and Brennan into an affirmative majority.

Art's position was that he believed in facing up to the facts and not becoming mired in legal fictions or abstractions. Justice Black, one of our closest friends on the Court and one of its great minds, charged that Arthur, in several opinions, confused law and morality and was a proponent of natural law.

Art said, "I don't know what natural law means, not being a natural law philosopher, but I do know this: the founders of the Constitution believed there was a moral basis for the Constitution they were writing. If you want to call that natural law, call it that. I'm not frightened by labels."

It seems that for Justices Holmes and Frankfurter, and Judge Learned Hand, the definition of the law was based on what the Courts will do, that is, on what the Courts will enforce—and nothing else. It was Judge Hand who had said natural law made him puke. Art believed that the Constitution was a moral document, and that it was the great function of the Court to give moral leadership to the nation, because the Constitution means more to our country than a series of rules on how to set up a government. To Arthur, it was more than a political instrument; it was a moral document.

The relationship between Justice and clerk is, of course, beyond that of teacher and student, rather more like that of a senior partner in a law firm working in a common enterprise with a gifted new associate. How lucky such young people are to have ready access for so many hours of the day—I almost envied them—to the practical experience, the wisdom and breadth of vision of the Justices; and how equally fortunate the Justice who has such loyalty and concern as Arthur's clerks showed for him.

Arthur's clerks—Peter Edelman, David Filvaroff, Alan Der-
showitz, Lee McTurnan, Stephen Breyer, Stephen Goldstein, Dan
Levitt, and John Griffiths—all became our friends. When a clerk
argued with him, as all of them often did, it usually was because
of loyalty and his really wanting to protect Arthur from making
what he thought would be a mistake. Sometimes Arthur would tell
me in the evening with considerable pleasure and regard of his
clerks' sincerity, as well as their ability (but ability was taken for
granted), about their worries on his behalf. Still, there was such
respect and courteousness in his chambers that one would have
thought the period was not the 1960s but several decades earlier;
and I liked it.

Several incidents illustrate the relationship and also what I call
the whodunit in reverse of constitutional problems, as tackled by
Arthur and his clerks. Some Florida legislators had begun investigating the National Association for the Advancement of Colored
People on the ground that their leaders were Communists. The
lower courts held the NAACP in contempt because it refused to
turn over its membership lists. Arthur thought the courts had no
right to do that because there were not sufficient grounds for
Florida to start such an investigation.

The NAACP is a respected, patriotic group of people that also
happened to be the most effective group in the early organizing of
the civil rights movement in the South. So Art said that it was a
"smoke screen." "The realities are that they just want to kick out
the NAACP, but this is an outstanding and responsible organization and is protected by the first amendment in their rights of
association." Still, the clerk who was assigned to that case was
worried lest Art "not be able to write a tenable opinion to carry
his swing vote," and he said as much.

"We'll write it." And Arthur outlined the theory.

I think it says much for the integrity of the clerk—and Arthur,
of course, recognized that quality in him—that although he argued his point vigorously and balked with considerable obstinacy,
he nonetheless loyally cooperated in assisting with research and
suggestions.

The clerks were always worried, too, about the legal academic
minds and how they would react. Later, after that particular clerk
in the case *(Gibson* v. *Florida Legislative Investigating Committee,*

372 U.S. 539 [1963], when Arthur delivered the opinion of the Court) had developed the argument step by step, he took pride in how often that opinion was and is cited as an example of appropriately safeguarding the right of association and privacy.

Until then (before Arthur—with the "liberals" dissenting), the Court held that a congressional investigating committee might lawfully ask an organization and its officials about Communist Party membership. After Arthur, that was changed. If a congressional committee wanted to ask a private organization about Communist Party participation, the investigators would have to show good reason for asking. They could not just pull in the membership at large for questioning and, by their questioning, impugn the members loyalty and thus adversely affect a legitimate organization.

I began to understand why lawyers like "whodunits" so much —all those murder mysteries with garish covers that Art would read for relaxation. The Constitution is the rock and the strength of the people; it prevents the rights of Americans from being assailed by those in power, but discerning its true meaning needs a detective-like patience in ferreting out clues.

In considering the influence of clerks on their Justice, Art thought that every Justice made up his own mind. He has said to able clerks, "If you are capable, you may very well have an opportunity to be an influence, but I would like to caution you about remembering that you can be an influence only so long as that Justice chooses to be so influenced."

Once, after a brunch in the garden on Albemarle Street, he told a group of clerks a story about Justice Holmes. It seems that in the middle of an argument, where a rather pompous, self-important lawyer had been belaboring the Court with the obvious, Justice Holmes interrupted: "May I ask if you ever read French novels?"

The lawyer was mystified. No, he was not in the habit of reading French novels. Then the Justice said, "Counsel, I think perhaps you ought to do that. There are many good ones in translation." And it was left at that, to the complete bafflement of those who heard the exchange. Later, when friends of the Justice asked him what he had meant by interjecting so apparently irrelevant a question, Holmes said: "I was trying to help the lawyer by pointing out that the Supreme Court cannot be raped, but it can be seduced, and what better teaching is there in the art of seduction than reading French novels."

Both Art and I enjoyed the several events held in the garden for the clerks. The first was at the beginning of the new term, when they and Arthur were beginning the year on the Court. We gathered for a Sunday brunch at small tables outdoors.

On a tree in the garden I posted a welcome verse—mine. It was a convenient piece and had to do with lawyers and judges. I used it for the first time as a New Year's card when Arthur was involved with the 1959 steel arguments:

> Oyez, oyez, oyez
> Loudly for all to hear
> The Honorable Supreme Court
> Will now attempt to steer
> Clear of all the issues
> That obfuscate the year.
>
> Oyez, oyez, oyez
> Decisions rendered here
> By time that great Chief Justice
> Eternally appear,
> Based on the merits solely
> Of facts that we revere,
>
> So, to *unum y pluribus,*
> Good luck from both of us,
> And a wish for health and happiness
> In the coming new year.

After coffee, I would welcome them briefly, then Arthur would toast them and make some pertinent but light comments about what lay ahead.

Afterward, they would talk and exchange observations. Art always showed respect for their thinking but was careful, of course, never to infringe on the confidentiality and loyalty of each clerk to his respective Justice. He enjoyed hearing their fresh reactions, not that he adopted their views any more than those of his own law clerks, but he regarded such an outward-goingness as being a part of the necessary open-mindedness for decision-making.

The young women present, some of them lawyers (none, as yet, at that time, a clerk), all the clerks' wives or friends, would inquire of me about Washington, if they were new to the city. The young wives were, for the most part, remarkably capable, coordinating their marketing and the laundry with being au courant about the Court and current Washington politics. The couples with small children were usually living in the less expensive suburbs, which meant considerable traveling if they were to participate in the so-called Washington whirl, and sitters were also a problem. Not that the so-called Washington whirl of cocktail parties usually included them, nor did many of the publicized events. I wondered how much of a social life they had among themselves and felt a pang on their behalf when some of the young women asked me how I managed to find time to be involved in all my projects.

I sensed, too, that the young mothers, particularly, must have been having second thoughts about their own lives as their husbands were advancing. At the time, I was still brimming full of *The Creative Woman,* and tried to tell them that everything need not be done at once, at one time. I said then, and I still think it true, that growth in a marriage should allow for the wife as well as the husband, but growth can be a staggered affair—first the one, then the other should be given an opportunity to develop his or her potential. If the family has had to move to Washington for a year or two because of the husband's work, then an agreed-upon period following should be accorded for the wives professional development.

The young men were so filled with energy and vitality that in some instances it was reflected in the attitude of the young women. I resisted the impulse to make mother-noises at the ones whose eyes showed a certain hollowness.

Arthur's law clerks were always conscientious and devoted to arguments about why a case should go one way or another. They would arrive with him on a Thursday evening, sagging under heavy loads of books, briefs, and papers. Across the hall, I could sometimes hear the tones, if not the substance, of their discussions. Arthur invited them to air their differences with his position, but they learned early that he could not be unduly influenced in decision-making. His vote was his alone and law clerks learned how he voted at conference after his vote was cast.

In only one instance did a clerk pursue an argument particularly vigorously. It was a tax case, and he, motivated by devotion to Arthur, was concerned lest, in that specialized field, Art might allow his instincts against permitting any subterfuge tax evasion to overcome the orthodox view of the difference between tax evasion and avoidance. To engage in avoidance was permissible, according to some Harvard teachings, provided the so-called avoiders thought what they were doing was within the law.

Arthur listened attentively but voted the other way. Then he called for the clerk and said: "Now I'll let you help with the dissent even though I know your personal views are otherwise." And the clerk helped very conscientiously. Art personally dictated his own views in the matter, but the law clerk was called upon to research the supporting legal decisions. At the end of the long process, when the dissent was filed, he came to Art to say that upon more mature reflection and after having worked with Arthur and becoming more understanding of his analysis, he was convinced that Arthur was right and that he had been wrong. And that dissent has since been acclaimed in academic circles. Later, when Congress plugged the particular loopholes that Art had characterized as fraud, it was a satisfaction to Arthur and to his clerk.

There was much of interest for me to learn. Evidently, it was an illusion that because the clerks were young, enthusiastic, and filled with the vitality of their work in the law that they were great liberals and influenced the Justices in a liberal way. In Arthur's chambers, at least, the opposite was sometimes true. If the "boys," as he called them, were from Harvard, they would have been taught that "sanction" means "criminal sanction," but Art did not agree. In one case, for example, he regarded the stripping of citizenship from a person as a very grave penalty. He quoted Shakespeare, that putting a man in exile is worse than death. That was the Mendoza decision (*Kennedy* v. *Mendoza,* 372 U.S. 144), where Arthur wrote for the Court one of those five-to-four decisions.

In the *Mendoza* opinion, Arthur's was the "swing" vote. His majority decision held that it is unconstitutional to take away a man's citizenship without a hearing. Again, Arthur followed the same practice of having the clerk, also a Harvard Law School graduate, work on the majority opinion, although initially the clerk did not believe that a sound majority opinion could be written for Art's point of view.

Arthur's approach was that of a patient teacher. Although he may not have agreed with a clerk, he still provided him with an opportunity to work out for himself the points of the opposition. He always discouraged them from "straining after technicalities." He would say that the Supreme Court is the least technical court in the whole country, and that was the way it should be, because it was concerned with such grave constitutional matters.

The Court, since *Mendoza,* has gone further and has said that a person's citizenship cannot be taken from him unless it is expressly renounced by him. By the time the *Mendoza* opinion was written, the clerk who had originally opposed Arthur's point of view had already changed his own mind.

To me it was all fascinating.

The young lawyers, the young people in any field, are engaged in creating their mature selves even as they become absorbed in their vocation. It is not much different from the artist in search of his or her authentic signature.

Then there was the Case of the Missing Footnote. That involved a very important antitrust decision, in which it was decided that a footnote in Arthur's opinion, which had already gone to the printers, should be deleted. The change was made but the clerk, by mistake, distributed the first printing to the lawyers in the case with the footnote still included.

After Court had already convened, he sent Arthur a frantic note: "Mr. Justice, something terrible has happened. I must see you immediately." Art sent him a note: "What? Anything happen to my family?" The clerk sent another note: "No, but I must see you immediately." (The way they worry about mistakes on the Court, the clerk should have written, "No—worse.") Since arguments were being heard, Art wrote back, "I'll see you at lunchtime."

The poor clerk was ashen and extremely agitated. The incident occurred during the early days of his clerkship so that he did not know Arthur very well, and he was apprehensive that Art might say that he could not have a clerk who made such errors. Art was also feeling hollow about it, to be sure, "but if it happened, it happened and was past." They would take necessary steps to correct the error, and he was sure, he told the clerk, that the other Justices would be similarly understanding.

A few weeks later, when Art was talking on a general subject to the Antitrust Bar (a group of lawyers who specialize in that branch of the law), there was much speculation and mention made by others about the "missing footnote." He could not, of course, tell them what had happened, but he told the group: "I promise you, gentlemen, that in my will I shall leave complete details of what happened in the Case of the Missing Footnote."

I hope to see the day when a woman will sit on that Court, too, because of her acknowledged merit. I hope she, too, will be able to find some cause for momentary laughter in a confusion of abstract complexity and not let the tragic sense of life in the individual instances that come before the Court prevent her from at least sharing with others a brief chuckle. I suspect the tragic sense will be dominant if she has to hurry home to prepare dinner for the family.

The years were significant both for the Court and for Arthur. For the first time since the appointment of Earl Warren as Chief Justice there was a majority for a constitutional approach that gave full meaning to the great rights safeguarded by the Bill of Rights.

The majority consisted of the Chief Justice and Justices Black, Douglas and Brennan, and Arthur. On some occasions, although not often, one or more of the Warren majority dissented from his colleagues. One example of this was Justice Black's consistent failure to give full recognition to the protections afforded by the Fourth Amendment's prohibitions against unreasonable searches and seizures.

Fortunately, however, Justice Harlan, who was called a "constitutional conservative" on most issues, believed in the Fourth Amendment as the "judicial activists" did, which insured a constitutional construction of the Fourth Amendment. It claims too much to say that in all regards the Court changed when Arthur supplied the necessary fifth vote, although in civil libertarian matters it was basically true.

From 1954 on, and even until recently with the Nixon appointees, the Court was unanimous in holding that state-sanctioned discrimination on the basis of race was unconstitutional under the Fourteenth Amendment. The lode-star case, of course, was *Brown* v. *Board of Education,* where Chief Justice Warren, speaking for the Court as a whole, overruled *Plessy* v. *Ferguson* (the post–Civil War case that sanctioned the separate-but-equal doctrine in education and public facilities). The Chief Justice said, "Separate cannot be equal," and this is how it has remained.

But in the field of safeguarding the rights of the accused in criminal cases, the rights of political dissenters, checks on unbridled legislative trials (as in the McCarthy hearings), protection of the right to an equal vote, and a good many other issues that may loosely be called civil libertarian, a majority of the Court, until Arthur was appointed, followed, for the most part, Justice Frankfurter's lead.

Although political dissent is an important part of our democratic rights, for Justice Frankfurter, the right to speak freely was not an absolute right despite the absolute language of the First Amendmant. He believed in "balancing" the right to speak freely and the right of the legislature—federal or state—to modify this freedom in the interest of "national security." (But we have learned to be suspicious of the loose use of that term in recent days.)

For Justice Frankfurter, the rights of the accused were to be respected, but the Constitution did not require a poor person, who was accused and charged with a felony, to be provided with counsel for his own defense. The Fourteenth Amendment guaranteed equal protection, but for him this did not mean that the government had to eliminate or to minimize the economic handicaps that prevented poor people from obtaining justice. "Egalitarianism" in the provision of justice was a bad word. Thus, a poor defendant convicted of a crime had the "right" to appeal, but the state was not obligated to provide him with a transcript to make his appeal effective.

Evidence obtained by the police illegally was called "tainted," but the remedy, for Justice Frankfurter and others, was to punish the policeman—which, of course, never happened—rather than to exclude the evidence itself.

The Constitution makes no distinction between native-born and naturalized citizens—except that the latter may not run for the Presidency—but Congress, in its wisdom, is not to be questioned by the courts even if it imposes a variety of special restrictions upon the travel and foreign residency of naturalized citizens.

The dual sovereignty of nation and state made it possible to re-try in a state court, and conceivably jail, a person acquitted in a federal court, and vice-versa. This is not looked upon as being "double jeopardy."

The majority of the Court adhered to this "judicial restraint" philosophy, until Arthur was appointed.

Arthur himself, in commenting—long after he left the Bench— on the change that took place upon his appointment, wrote:

> In summary, from these and other cases, it appeared that the Warren Court was manifesting a growing and possibly more general impatience with legalisms, with dry and sterile dogma, and with virtually unfounded assumptions which served to insulate the law and the Constitution it serves from the hard world it is intended to affect. If still not articulated, there was discernible a general groping for what might be called a "new realism" in the Court's approach, a retreat from abstraction and an increased willingness to attach broader significance to the realized human impact in the events that gave rise to legal disputes and court cases. That movement was both healthy and necessary; it responded to an increasingly apparent fact of modern life—the gap, too often a chasm, between the sometimes pietistic pronouncements of our system and its performance in fact.
>
> To me, at least, one of the most crucial challenges facing the Supreme Court today is the need to make our declared principles, our constitutional protections, into a workable and working reality for those to whom they must often seem to be the sheerest of illusion and others have spent decades molding and remolding legal doctrine, shaping it into ever more refined declarations intended to protect human liberty, expand personal freedoms, and enhance individual dignity. But it is of the utmost importance that the words match the practice.*

In a series of memorable decisions, the new majority of the Court overruled cases that had restricted the full application of the

*"Equal Justice—The Warren Era of the Supreme Court," the 1971 Julius Rosenthal Memorial Lectures, Northwestern U. Press, Evanston, p. 25.

Bill of Rights to all persons—rich or poor, black or white. Arthur tried to extend the same principle of constitutional equality to women as well as men, but the majority of the Court only went part way.

Gideon's Trumpet was heard, and in Gideon's case, a defendant who was poor was *really* accorded the right to counsel by being provided one. Evidence illegally obtained by the police, called "tainted," was suppressed, a far more effective sanction than a slap on the wrist to the police. The right to counsel where it was needed —at the police station—was assured, before the authorities could exact a confession from the accused. This prevented the trial from becoming an appeal from a conviction, rather than a genuine trial on the merits. Naturalized citizens were given the same rights as the native-born, except for the right to be President, which is denied by the Constitution. The right to travel was declared to be a precious right for all Americans.

The First Amendment protections of free speech and free press were given new life and "the breathing space" it needs if it is to survive. One man (they should have said one person, and that is still not too much to expect) one vote became the rule, and mala-portioned legislatures were prohibited.

All the above illustrate some of the changes that occurred after Arthur was appointed. There were many others in that eventful three years.

For me, the Court period offered great satisfactions. I could see with my own eyes and hear with my own ears that the Highest Court of the land construed the Constitution according to the idealism of the Founding Fathers.

It was gratifying that the Court, during the Warren period, was unanimously affirmative in civil rights cases, but I was particularly impressed by the Court's decision in the case of Mary Hamilton. She was a young black girl who refused to answer the questions of an Alabama white prosecutor who, with condescending familiarity, called her "Mary," though it was local custom to call white women either "Miss" or "Mrs." Even though the judge, too, ordered her, "Come now, Mary, speak up," she shook her head, refusing to answer until she was properly addressed.

"My name is Mary Hamilton—*Miss* Hamilton." She was held in contempt by the Alabama courts. On appeal, the Supreme

Court unanimously and summarily reversed the conviction of criminal contempt (*Hamilton* v. *Alabama,* 376 U.S. 650 [1964]). Thus, the Court showed that according to our Constitution the words mean what they say, and one may not condone any tolerance of a racial caste system, no matter how slight the apparent action may be.

On our Asian trip in 1964, Arthur quietly told that story to a large assembly of law students in Singapore, among whom were some left-wing youngsters who had been heckling him. When he finished the story of Mary Hamilton, they all broke into applause. I also used that story in some of my speeches, and once I quoted the committee report of the House of Representatives concerning the Civil Rights Act:

> Discrimination is not simply dollars and cents, hamburgers and movies; it is the humiliation, frustration, and embarrassment that a person must surely feel when he is told that he is unacceptable as a member of the public because of his race or color. It is equally the inability to explain to a child that regardless of education, civility, courtesy, and morality, he will be denied the right to enjoy equal treatment, even though he be a citizen of the United States and may well be called upon to lay down his life to assure this nation continues.*

One of the causes that I found particularly interesting was Arthur's concurring opinion in *Griswold* v. *Connecticut,* the Connecticut birth control case. It was particularly interesting to me because it illuminated the similarity between creative process in any field, in art, science, or law. First comes a search of a way out of an impasse, based partly on intuition (and intuition is thought by some to be really a vague memory of where a possible solution may be found); then there is a delving into old studies for possible new channels that may have been left unmined. Then comes an insight or a discovery.

Arthur's use in the Griswold case, of the "forgotten" Ninth Amendment to hold that the Connecticut Birth Control Act was unconstitutional as an unwarranted invasion of marital privacy was as creative a find as that in any ground-breaking work of art

---

*U.S. Code, Congressional and Administrative News, 88th Cong., 2d Sess. 1742 (1964).

or science—as exciting as the discovery of penicillin or the break-away into cubism. At least, I think so.

As applied in *Griswold,* the Ninth Amendment not only protected the fundamental right of married couples and their doctors to determine the size of their own families but had a wider potential in protecting the right of privacy of all citizens in other areas. Though our friend Justice Black criticized relying on the Ninth Amendment, it is now accepted and applauded in legal circles. It figured importantly in the Supreme Court's seven to two ruling invalidating state laws inhibiting a woman's right to obtain an abortion.

Before Arthur's time, when the Connecticut birth control case first came to the Court, the Justices who subscribed to "judicial restraint" took recourse in a legal technicality to avoid having to decide. They came out with something about doctors not having adequate "standing to sue." In *Griswold,* however, the Court disdained to use that technicality.

The Ninth Amendment says, "The enumeration in the Constitution of certain rights shall not be construed to deny or disparage others retained by the people." That supported the view that there are certain fundamental liberties not enumerated in the Bill of Rights that still must be protected under the due process clause. The Ninth Amendment makes these rights applicable to the states by virtue of the due process clause.

The right of privacy is not mentioned expressly anywhere in the Bill of Rights, but Art regarded it as one of the fundamental rights of an American citizen, protected under the Ninth Amendment, Justice Douglas, writing for the Court, also mentioned the Ninth Amendment, but Arthur's opinion placed principal reliance on the Amendment, and his concurrence brought with him the Chief Justice and Justice Brennan, thus assuring a majority of the Court for Justice Douglas—a majority that might otherwise not have occurred.

As a citizen, I believe that Art's opinion in *Griswold* had seminal magnitude for American jurisprudence. Law teachers and law students now regard this contribution on Art's part as a most imaginative one. In the Burger Court, Justices Blackmun and White, in writing the Burger Court's opinion holding state anti-abortion laws unconstitutional, relied considerably on the "forgotten" Ninth Amendment.

And when Senator Philip A. Hart spoke on behalf of the Democratic majority in Congress on March 2 of 1974, accusing the administration of spying on political opponents, I realized the deeper implications of *Griswold* and the right of privacy:

> When Government officials use Army personnel to spy on peaceful political meetings . . . your privacy is threatened.
> When Government officials send burglars to break into the offices for confidential files . . . your privacy is threatened.
> When Government officials use the confidential files of the Internal Revenue Service to harass persons on a White House enemies list . . . When Government officials eavesdrop on private conversations of political opponents . . . your privacy is threatened.

Another opinion I particularly liked and one in which all our family takes pride, although it was a minority opinion, was the case of *Rudolph* v. *Alabama.* Only Justice Douglas and Justice Brennan joined Arthur. *Rudolph* struck the first blow against the unconstitutionality of the death penalty. For the first time in the two-hundred-year history of the Court, a Justice raised the question of whether the death penalty was unconstitutional under the Eighth Amendment, a claim that is gaining acceptance.

Art, however, was convinced that by contemporary standards the death penalty itself was cruel and unusual punishment and thus unconstitutional. He got no help from lawyers in capital punishment cases, however, who, thinking it useless, never thought even to raise the question. Arthur decided that precedent supported his view that if the constitutional rights of a person are violated and the lawyer fails to raise the constitutional issue, that does not stand in the way of the Supreme Court itself applying the Constitution to protect fundamental rights.

Art went beyond raising the question in *Rudolph.* In 1963, among the certiorari applications for appeals for hearings, there were several capital cases. Art circulated an extensive memorandum to the members of the Court, elaborating upon the constitutional case against imposing the death penalty.

He received little or no support for his position, which would have struck down the death penalty across the board. Then he tried a "fall-back" position and argued in the Court conference that although he believed the death penalty was unconstitutional in *all* cases, it certainly should be held unconstitutional where the crime did not take human life.

In *Rudolph* v. *Alabama* (375 U.S. 889 [1962]) the case was one of rape, but there was some question about whether the evidence proved rape beyond a reasonable doubt and there was no taking of life in this horrible crime. Justices Brennan and Douglas supported Arthur in voting to grant a hearing to consider this limited question about the validity of the death penalty where there is no taking of life. Four votes, however, are needed to grant certiorari, and the majority voted against hearing the case.

Then Arthur wrote a dissent from their denial of a hearing. He explained to me later that his reason for filing his dissent was to alert the lawyers having capital punishment cases to begin, at least, to raise the question and to argue the constitutionality of the death penalty, and he succeeded in that. Further, he was convinced that, sooner or later, the Court would see the light. His opinion in *Rudolph* stimulated many lawyers to raise the issue. As a result, governors held up executions and more than six hundred men in death cells were given temporary reprieve pending a definitive Court decision.

His dissent in *Rudolph* relied on a 1910 case, *Weems* v. *U.S.,* and Justice McKenna's decision. In that case, an officer of the U. S. Government of the Philippine Islands was convicted of falsifying a public document and was sentenced to fifteen years of *cadena temporal*—an ancient Spanish punishment. The prisoner had to wear chains on his ankles and wrists as he did hard and painful labor. Then he was stripped of any rights he had as a parent, husband, or property owner, and all during his lifetime he had to be kept under surveillance.

Justice McKenna must have been an extraordinary judge, yet the name never meant anything to me until Art used his language. After Justice McKenna had carefully analyzed the historical experience that had led up to the need for an Eighth Amendment (and he went all the way back to the Magna Carta), he said, "Time works changes, brings into existence new conditions and purposes. Therefore, a principle to be vital must be capable of wider application than the mischief which gave it birth. This is peculiarly true of constitutions. They are not ephemeral enactments, designed to meet passing occasions. They are, to use the words of Chief Justice

Marshall, 'designed to approach immortality as nearly as human institutions can approach it.' The future is their care and provision for events of good and bad tendencies of which no prophecy can be made. In the application of a constitution, therefore, our contemplation cannot be only of what has been but of what may be. Under any other rule a constitution would indeed be as easy of application as it would be deficient in efficacy and power. Its general principles would have little value and be converted by precedent into impotent and lifeless formulas. Rights declared in words might be lost in reality [217 U.S. 349 (1910)]."

When Arthur used those words of Justice McKenna's in his *Rudolph* opinion, I felt like murmuring bravo and asked, "Who was he? Did you ask if there's a biography about him, an autobiography?"

"Yes, but there isn't any."

"Not even in the Court Library?"

"Now don't go overboard for him. You haven't done any research on him. Just because he happened to write that good opinion . . ."

"That's enough, even that one little paragraph is all a person needs to justify a lifetime."

Finally, in 1972, a culmination of Arthur's efforts against the death penalty came in a historic but divided decision of the Burger Court in *Furman* v. *Georgia* (408 U. S. 238 [1972]). There, the Supreme Court held the death penalty unconstitutional, at least where it was applied in an arbitrary and discriminatory way. Unfortunately, the Court left open the question of the constitutionality of the death penalty where the legislature of a state had required that the death penalty be imposed without any discretion allowed to the judge or the jury.

Following *Furman,* the legislatures and courts of several states have prescribed mandatory death penalty for certain serious offenses. Several such cases are before the Court as of this writing. I hope the Court will follow Arthur's lead and strike down the death penalty under all circumstances. It is unthinkable to have a ghastly mass killing of the hundreds that have been waiting in death row—the last execution was in 1967. The Furman decision brought about the reprieve from the death sentence of more than six hundred men then in death cells. Since then, some two hundred and fifty-three people have been sentenced or resentenced to death under the so-called mandatory rule. No matter what public image we proudly parade before the nations of the world, such a mass killing would prove us no better than the most brutal, ignorant savages.

In 1973, I went to Tucson, Arizona, with Arthur and heard him deliver an address on the death penalty to the law school of the University of Arizona. Mary and Tom Clark were at the same pleasant resort where we were staying. It was good to get away from the cold and ice of February in Washington but the local pro capital punishment sentiment was chilling to the spirit. Not only students came, but legislators and various politicians. I hope they listened carefully when he concluded that "the most inhumanitarian aspect of the death penalty was mandatory imposition without considerations of mercy warranted by the given circumstances and the human condition.

"The rack, thumbscrew, chains, branding, cutting off of ears and the stretching of limbs, everyone would now agree are not permissible under the Eighth Amendment. Under 'the evolving standards of decency that mark the progress of [our] maturing society,' the deliberate, institutionalized taking of human life by the state is the greatest conceivable degradation to the dignity of the human personality. Surely, this generation of Americans had experienced enough killing."

I found especially interesting Art's drive to eliminate wealth as a factor in according justice. To commemorate his going on the Court, Arthur gave me a gold bracelet on which was suspended one charm, that of the symbol of justice bearing her scales—blindfolded. I asked why justice was always depicted as blind.

The reason is that justice must not be able to see the litigant. It must make no difference whether a person is powerful or weak, wealthy or poor, brilliant or stupid. It is an ancient admonition from the Bible.

Art himself liked to quote Judge Learned Hand, as he did in an address before the National Conference on Law and Poverty in Washington, on June 25, 1965.

"Our Court recently observed that 'providing equal justice for the poor and rich, weak and powerful alike . . . is the central aim of our entire judicial system.' Judge Learned Hand expressed the same thought another way: 'If we are to keep our democracy, there must be one commandment—Thou shalt not ration justice.' "

To me, it was surprising that in the long history of the Supreme Court, however, it was only in the early Sixties and during Art's tenure that steps were taken to assure equal justice to the poor. Arthur never claimed sole credit for this. He always reminded me that he was merely one among his brethren, who felt the same. Changes for the better seem to occur slowly in law, as in science and in art, and not until the general climate of culture is ready to accept it.

It was during Art's tenure that it was decided for the first time that a poor man should be provided with a lawyer in a major criminal case—that was the case of *Gideon.* The majority opinion, written by Justice Black, said that Gideon was entitled to be given a free transcript of the record at state expense so that he could make an appeal. Arthur, however, went beyond that in his thinking. He believed that practical distinctions between the rich man and the poor man are found throughout the area of criminal law. The rich man may be summoned to the police station; the poor man is more often arrested. The rich inebriant may be escorted home by the policeman; the poor drunk is almost always tossed into jail. The rich accused is released on bail; the poor defendant cannot raise the bail and remains in prison. The rich defendant can afford the best legal advice; he can summon psychiatrists and other expert witnesses; he can afford a thorough investigation of the facts of his case and can raise every possible defense. The poor defendant, until the recent *Gideon* decision, often had to defend himself, and even today in many jurisdictions he is denied many other important tools of advocacy. After conviction, when a fine is imposed, the rich man pays it and goes free, but the poor man, who cannot afford to pay a fine, must go to jail. The rich man, who can be guaranteed a job, may qualify for probation or parole; the poor man, lacking a job, more often goes to or remains in prison.

In his Madison Lecture at New York University, Arthur said that poor defendants should be provided the same assistance of investigators, ballistics experts, laboratory assistants, psychiatric experts, and the whole range of technical services that the state or wealthy defendants can draw on. For this, he was charged by Professor Kurland of the University of Chicago and some other academicians with being "egalitarian." But Art chose to regard being called "egalitarian" as a compliment.

Once, when Arthur and I were walking up the great sweep of entrance steps to the Court (usually, the side ground entrance was used to enter his chambers), he said, "Look, how can anyone not believe as I do when you read across the top of the building, 'Equal Justice Under Law'?"

10

Death
of
President
Kennedy

On November 22, 1963, I wrote the following letter to our son, who was at the London School of Economics:

It is 7:45 P.M. of this miserable, hideous, wretched November 22, and I began this day with a letter to you and sent you a stupid recipe for pepper steak. . . . The President is dead, and the sickening reality of it is all around us. The TV is still going downstairs. Dad came home early, we sat and looked at the TV until the announcer said that the body would be brought back on the Presidential plane at six. Dad sat up and went to the phone and asked the White House operator. They all know him. Dad asked, "Who is there?" She put on an assistant doctor who said that some people had congregated near the offices, I mean in the offices, but that they were going by helicopter and it wouldn't be possible for Dad to get on the helicopter—or words to that effect. Dad hung up and asked quietly for the head of the White House police, told him we were going to the airport, but he had dismissed his own messenger and would have to drive himself and wasn't very good about directions; if anyone were going in a car from the White House we would like to be at the field too when the plane arrived and would be most appreciative of their assistance.

When we came to Pennsylvania Avenue and 18th Street, Dad told the officer we were headed for the White House and he permitted us to make a left turn. The guards at the northwest gate, which we had entered only two days ago for the judiciary reception, let us in, and one of the top guards rode with us and guided us right to the White House steps, where we parked on the circular drive in front of the last side steps leading to the rear or south grounds. He guided us to an office. It was Mr. Dave Powers' office. There were Averell Harriman, Franklin D. Roosevelt, Jr., Joe Fowler, Tony Celebrezze, Charlie Murphy, the new Postmaster General Gronowsky, and a very excitable-looking man, a Mr. McNally of transportation. A secretary took our coats. The White House mess stewards brought in coffee. It was 5:05 P.M. when we sat down there.

Dad immediately got up with Franklin D. Roosevelt, Jr., and went somewhere else. Mr. McNally said we none of us could go to the airport because Mrs. Kennedy did not want a crowd there. Then he added, "But stick around, it's been changed three times and maybe it will still be changed." Then Dad came back and said we were going by helicopter. He had called Bobby Kennedy and had said that he and I were going out as Mr. and Mrs. John Q. Public to be there when the body came home, out of respect for the President. We wanted to do this not only because of President Kennedy, though it was our sorrow, the public sorrow, that first was in mind, but because there is a certain amount of form owed to the country by its officials, and President Johnson too was returning. He had already been given the oath of office by the first woman federal judge to swear in a President, and she had been appointed by President Kennedy in 1961.

I felt so much a sense of unreality that when we walked down the lower corridor to the helicopter, leaving the White House by the door where we used to enter for so many receptions, the three guards silhouetted near Dr. Travell's office looked like wooden figures on a set.

That was the beginning of a feeling that we were walking through history backwards on a fantastic stage setting. The wind of the whirly-birds forced us to stay sheltered in the little area reception hall where Mr. McNally was doing his official duty by counting off all the high officials, saying who could go and who could not go. First the Cabinet could go then the sub-Cabinet would have to go out in cars.

All the others of the Cabinet were returning from Honolulu. They had been en route to Japan for the Second Reciprocal Trade

Delegation visit. They received word one hour out of Honolulu and turned around immediately. Mr. McNally told Dad very briskly that Mrs. Goldberg would have to go out to the airport by car. Dad shook his head. Mr. McNally again said Mrs. Goldberg had to go by car. I started to back away, but Dad (and I never saw him swing weight around that way) grabbed my arm with a clenched grasp and said quietly, while shaking his head and looking at his feet, the way he does when he stubborns up, "Mrs. Goldberg goes with me." Mr. McNally said, "Then a Cabinet officer will have to stay back," but Dad said no. I guess he knew how many seats were available, and how many Cabinet officers there were, and that there would be room for me. But I felt very much an intruder. I slipped myself on to the seat meant for three, and made a foursome; thus, I really didn't displace anyone. The helicopter went straight up and over the trees and the city was below us, but not so far away as when one rides by plane. The lights were nearer.

Over the Potomac, the land and the horizon lit by lights along piers with mourning darkness in a high space and below looked like Loren McIver's *Venice* with brave little ripples into the water from the lights above, but not clear and sharp, just blurred and mourning. We stopped, and Captain Tazewell Sheppard asked Franklin D. Jr., to keep us all in until he found out where we were to go. We waited and waited until Dad started getting restless again, and said to FDR, Jr., "This will be the same story, just like the other." He heard the helicopter officer or pilot talking into a phone and again it seemed as if Mrs. Kennedy preferred that no one be there. That was understandable, Dad said, and no one would have thought to approach her, but something is owed the dead President by his country and its Cabinet, and those close to the President in his beginnings were symbolic of the country.

FDR, Jr., said it was only 5:45, and we still had fifteen minutes, but then they decided to get up and we left the helicopter. The sight of Andrews looked like a setting for an ancient tragedy. The light of the huge press cameras for TV and the illumination of lights on the airport silhouetted people so that they looked like poles on a wharf, straight, immobile frozen sticks with masks above them, too far away to look like an Ensor, but for all the world like a Greek tragedy on a supersurrealist set.

The huge staircases on wheels, standing by, waiting, looked like Jacob's ladders that would never reach into heaven, going someplace but ending nowhere. As we drew near, I could see it was the press people, the reporters that were the masks on sticks that I had seen from afar. Dad held my hand firmly, and we walked into a crowd. I saw McGeorge Bundy, Arthur Schlesinger, George Ball, Ken Galbraith. Ted Sorensen walked like a wraith in utter disregard of even despair, as if nothingness had fallen into the moment we were all sharing and soon we would know it, as he was knowing it, but now it really was a nightmare that was unbelievable. "The commandment is a lamp, and the law is light," but not in Dallas. Sorrow swamps and inundates irony or bitterness. Mary McGrory came up to Dad, and Dorothy McCardle, newspaper friends, and he kissed them.

No one had words. There were tears too. I stayed in the shade of some huge TV structure on wheels and felt merely that we were bearing witness. Angie Duke was running forward. The plane was coming in like a huge whale-bird from the sky. Then it swiveled and a contraption with an elevator approached the door, and the doors opened, and the bronze coffin was there. It was too much. He was so young, so full of health and cheerfulness, and what on earth had he had to say to Daddy the day before yesterday, in the morning, we will never know. He said, "See you on Monday," because Daddy couldn't be late for Court, though Dad had said, "I could come up for a few minutes." "No," the President had said, "it will keep, I'll see you Monday." Oh, the very terrible pity of this day. On TV they had been showing last year's Cuba crisis, and the jowls emerge and the anxiety and the weight of the responsibility is evidenced as we listen and know that the face and the voice will soon disappear from the screen too.

We turned toward the helicopter when the coffin was slipped into the ambulance with its gray shades down. Mrs. Kennedy, Mother said (Mother had been glued to the TV), seemed composed. How horrible for her to have to face the screen. We did not see her. Mother said his sister "ran like a wild thing to a car," but I wonder if Gram really saw that. We were heading for the helicopter again when we were hailed to return to the field, because President Johnson was to make a statement. We approached and saw Lady Bird in light coat and hat walking with the new President, but we could not hear him and we did not approach him though he began to shake people's hands. Hubert Humphrey was near us. We had heard him on TV in our car as we were driving to the White House. He was on a newscast and said the usual things and that it was very sad when he left such young children. The pity is more than that. It's the brevity of the opportunity, but that is always the pity, there is so little time for living and knowing that we are living, and for the contemplative concern to become a consummated action. Still, he was responsible for the thaw in the cold war, and for many good beginnings.

Senator Mike Mansfield, Maureen, and Ann came out. Ann looked the pale shock of it. The young are unaccustomed to death anyway, and none of us, old or young, is accustomed to such suddenness, such horror.

Senator Dirksen was in our helicopter returning from the field. Again I slipped on to the seat meant for three with Ambassador Harriman and Secretary Celebrezze on either side of Dad and me. What a day this has been. It began with sun coming up over Mrs. Logan's woods across the street after seven o'clock—like any other day. It isn't cold, but it has chill, and when we landed on the White House lawn and walked through the halls and the huge lobby where the red-coated marine band had been playing just the day before yesterday in the midst of all the gayety at the judiciary reception, I ached. The place was dimly lit and no one was there but the aide who led us to our car, which was where we had left it. We were ushered into Pennsylvania Avenue in the height of the homeward traffic by the guard and turned right, then north somewhere far down, then home. And that is how a day began and ended with a sense of loss and indebtedness, for a day of life is a gift. There is an indebtedness.

The horror of that death was that it was like a death in the family. The nation's grief expressed outwardly in traditional symbols, the riderless horse, the ceremonial parade, the Requiem Mass. The bereavement pain becomes keener when the ceremony is past and the day is just an ordinary day that never can be ordinary again, or so it seems. What was "ordinary" suddenly becomes exceptional. The President's familiar face on the TV screen, in news commentators' programs, in the press conferences, in the weekly journals of opinion, in the daily papers and the photographic Sunday supplements was suddenly removed. We saved the remembrance.

Thus, Friday night, after returning from Andrews Field and bearing witness to that homecoming, I reached for the early morning edition of that day's news to save it. When I had read it at breakfast, the day had seemed like an ordinary day, but by night, the world had changed. The words of the sages are remembered by younger and older people. It is true then; it is not just a truism, a banality, that no one knows in the morning what the night will bring (or one must wait for the evening to know how good or bad the day has been). I believe that many others like myself must have saved every newspaper during the next several weeks until, finally, an ordinary day could become an ordinary day again.

There was the despair and unfulfilled promise. People naturally yearn for reassurance that hope itself is not an absurdity. The critics of the Kennedy period intimate that the New Frontier sought to make politics serve the role of religion in the lives of the people, and built up too great expectations. What was permitted to be instilled in the minds of the people was hope—not hope for an absolute success of individual and national purpose, but hope that the individual was more than a digit on a computer. Finally, his voice could be heard. Finally, the individual citizen would be able to share with his leaders the work of putting together a new ordering out of the chaos of the national environment we had inherited.

No work is too tedious if there is hope. No work is too tedious if one can believe it to have meaning in a greater good for one's children and grandchildren. When such hope goes, then everything becomes essentially the here and now.

The only thing that made the loss endurable was the same spirit of public service and a drive to work at the problems evident in President Johnson's staff, which was largely the same, except for the few who have always worked close to him. He phoned and spoke to me, after talking to Arthur, the day that he was sworn in, about ten thirty I think it was. All plans for any public socializing had been canceled. Small private groups met in homes, but the two times we were out, in the three weeks after the assassination, the talk was only of the President, his family, the loss, and the shame of it. Mrs. Kennedy's composure, which I witnessed myself (standing very near her in the Rotunda and so very near in the cathedral at the services that I could hear her whisper to John-John as he was growing restless: "Say good-bye to Daddy," then a man seated behind her took the child out), was extraordinary.

The nation's children who may have been only eight years old on that tragic Friday in November are now able to vote. What can they remember of the name Kennedy, or the people of the New Frontier?

I folded the newspapers and magazines into neat bundles for the children's children to remember. We know where we were at the time, what we did, and we remember how we clustered into small groups after the sound of taps in Arlington Cemetery to hold private wakes. We tried to talk away the meaningness of that act in Dallas. Nothing helped. Pat Moynihan, on television, stamped a bitter: "We Irish always have known the world would break our hearts."

Nothing helped, not the talking, not the sermons—though some of the verses tried. "Comfort ye, comfort ye my people . . . For ye have paid double for all your sins . . . Bring now good tidings to the humble and bind up the broken-hearted . . ."

Nothing helped, except perhaps the words that other generations had heard too. But grief was stung with the humiliation that despite all our science, all our technology, all our history, our philosophy, all our superiority, our great nation was no more immune from crimes of hatred and violence than the least among the most primitive of tribes grouping themselves into newly developed nationhood.

In future years, when I will remember this period, I will again wonder about the words to which the brokenhearted turn for comfort. We sat very near the flag-draped coffin in St. Matthews Cathedral. The Court wives had arrived in a group. We seated ourselves in alternate spaces to allow room for the men who were marching behind the caisson in the entourage that had left the White House. We sat and waited in the front pews of the church and stared ahead at the marble and the stone, listening to the drum beats grow louder. DIES IRAE. I could not remember the words of the *War Requiem.*

We had been invited by the Erich Leinsdorfs just a few months before to the Tanglewood Music Festival to hear the first performance of the *War Requiem.* When we returned from the cemetery on the burial day, I went to the libretto still on top of the spinet piano. It was buried though, under an accumulation of program notes and assorted trivia. And there were the words the young Wilfred Owen had written that had been given added illumination by Benjamin Britten's music. A few friends came to our house that evening, and we listened to the *War Requiem* again.

Poetry helped carry its share of the burden at the time. The weight of the loss was the loss of young promise, and of the unused expectant years, the crash of hope. We know how one child may see the wonder of a bird flying upward to the heights, and another may take a sling and deliberately stone the bird.

American Heritage in its supplement, December 1963, included a black-bordered poem of Emily Dickinson's, with the name John Fitzgerald Kennedy, each name on a line by itself, and another line for 1917–1963:*

> The bustle in a house
> the morning after death
> Is solemnest of industries
> Enacted upon earth,—
> The sweeping up the heart,
> And putting love away
> We shall not want to use again
> Until eternity.

A stanza of another Emily Dickinson poem came to mind, as the expression of grief took form in the weeks that followed:

> This is the Hour of Lead
> Remembered, if outlived,
> As Freezing persons, recollect the Snow—
> First—Chill—then Stupor—then the letting go.†

But the surprise was in the clearinghouse column of the women's pages in the newspaper. I always read that column, which tells how to remove white rings from the furniture, or how to travel across country with five children in a station wagon.

During the mourning days, however, in that column a hunt was on for a poem one reader required. After some days, the reply came telling her to read "Poems for the Fallen" by British Poet Lawrence Binyon (1869–1943). "You can find it in a volume of his works, namely, *Selected Poems,* published in 1924. The stanza from which you quoted is as follows:

---

* *Selected Poems and Letters of Emily Dickinson,* published by Doubleday & Co., Inc., Garden City, N.J., 1959, page 174.
† "Final Harvest," *Emily Dickinson's Poems,* selected by Thomas H. Johnson, Little, Brown & Co. Boston, 1961, copyright 1929, © 1957 by Mary L. Hampson. Poem #341, p. 73.

They shall not grow old, as we that are left grow old,
Age shall not weary them, nor the years condemn,
At the going down of the sun and in the morning,
We shall remember them."

We remembered the deep, high-piled snow of the Inaugural balls of January 1961, the high-hearted celebrating that looked ahead to 1968, and how we danced into the morning. Now there was only this hour of lead, remembered, if outlived, as the country remembered the death of Lincoln. We begin to understand what is meant by history being a cast shadow. Even now, the skilled historians dutifully sifting through mountains of paper in a library, work with shadows, reflections through words. The historian may be a good craftsman, like one who makes silhouettes. Something may be evoked by chalking an outline against a wall or on paper, but the object itself, the action itself, the person himself, in all the fullness and roundness existing in our space, is gone.

At the holidays that year the cards piled up as heavily as usual. One had a photograph of a young daughter smiling on the outside, and within the fold a few words from Gandhi:

In the midst of death,
   Life persists;
In the midst of darkness,
   Light persists;
In the mist of untruth,
   Truth persists.

11

---··❦··---

The UN Period
of
Our Lives

On Tuesday, July 14, 1965, Adlai Stevenson died in London.

On Friday we attended the funeral service at the Cathedral Church of Saint Peter and Saint Paul. The great pressing crowds assembled for Adlai Ewing Stevenson for the final time. The service was according to the Book of Common Worship of the United Presbyterian Church, and the anthem, from Ecclesiasticus 44:1–9, 14, was in the black-bordered leaflet I took away with me.

> Let us now praise famous men, and our fathers that begat us. Such as did bear rule in their Kingdoms, men renowned for their power, leaders of the people by their counsels, and by their knowledge. Such as found out musical tunes and recited verses in writing: All these were honoured in their generations, and were the glory of their times. And some there be, which have no memorial; who are perished, as though they had never been. Their bodies are buried in peace; but their name liveth for evermore.

The memorial ceremony at the United Nations General Assembly Hall on July 19, 1965, was marked by tributes from Secretary General U Thant and others in high office. I was impressed by Archibald MacLeish's comments about Stevenson's reluctance to accept power:

Power fascinates us, and the exercise of power, and we judge our public figures by the power they dispose of, by the offices they hold which give them access to the thrust of power. . . .

He had no taste for power, no desire for it . . . there are some things in the life of a democracy more important than to come to power—more important ultimately than the possession of power . . .

His great achievement was the enrichment of his time by the nature of his relationships with his time. . . . It was himself he gave in word and thought and action, not to his friends alone but to his country, to his world. . . .

Although it has been many years, the question is still asked, and it is time that the answer is finally given.

On *July 16, 1965,* Arthur was working in his chambers at the Court when his secretary said that President Johnson was calling him. The President said to Arthur that it was necessary, because of a crisis in the UN involving the Article 19 dispute that threatened to destroy the UN, to fill Adlai Stevenson's post with an outstanding American, and that he hoped Art would consider leaving the Court and accepting this post. The dispute was caused by the unwillingness of the Soviet Union, its satellites, and France to pay their dues. The President said that he desperately needed a man of Art's judgment and experience, who was as acceptable to Congress as to the public, to resolve the UN crisis *and* to guide him to an early settlement of the Vietnam War, in which we had become increasingly involved, to Arthur's increasing dismay.

Many years later, after President Johnson's book came out, I overheard Arthur saying to the President on the telephone that the comment in his book that Art had solicited the appointment was completely unfounded and that the President knew that he thought he *was* serving the country on the Court, but that he would give his offer consideration after talking to me and considering it thoughtfully.

Art felt that he owed a great deal to the country, that had honored him publicly and had afforded him great opportunities, and he was convinced—as was really the case—that the country was in great trouble over the Vietnam War as well as over the UN crisis. So Arthur left his chambers in the late afternoon to join me at my mother's bedside in the hospital. While there, he received another call from the President, who pursued the matter and strongly urged that he accept.

The next morning Arthur called on President Johnson at the White House. In the anteroom of the President's office, Jack Valenti, merely making conversation, Art thought, inquired whether he might not also be interested in the post of Secretary of the Department of Health, Education and Welfare.

Arthur told Jack Valenti that that post held no interest for him whatsoever and that he had no interest in discussing this with the President.

"I'm not an applicant for any post—including the UN one," he said, And he repeated that the Court was the highest post to which he ever aspired and that the only reason he was responding at all to the President's call was the President's strong plea.

When Valenti went in to announce his presence to the President, he must have advised the President of Art's reaction, because he never brought up the subject of HEW. The President again pursued the matter, and Arthur again deferred his decision. At that meeting, or perhaps shortly thereafter, we were invited to accompany the President to Bloomington, Illinois, for Adlai Stevenson's funeral. On the plane, returning from the funeral, the President and Arthur had a long private conversation. Arthur told him it would be a very grave step for him to leave the Court and that he would need assurance before giving a final word of acceptance not only that the UN ambassadorship would be elevated in general foreign policy-making but that he would be a principal advisor and participant in all decision-making leading to a negotiated peace in Vietnam.

Arthur asked the President point-blank if he were committed to such a peace. The President said that he was and that one of his basic reasons for asking Art to assume the UN role was to get the benefit of what he termed "America's greatest negotiator" in reaching a peaceful solution, and soon.

Arthur called Chief Justice Warren before finally accepting, and the Chief's reaction was, of course, one of great dismay. But Warren said: "You and I have both been soldiers when our country needed us, and while I personally and officially do not want to lose you as a friend and colleague, nevertheless our country is at war and I can understand that you cannot refuse to put on the uniform again."

Then Arthur called Justice Black, and he said as much. Justice Douglas, however, wrote a letter strongly pleading with him not to leave, but later in conversation with Art said that he too had come to the same view as Warren and Black.

The very weekend before he submitted his letter of resignation we were both guests of the President and Mrs. Johnson at Camp David. On Sunday afternoon of that weekend, Bob McNamara presented a proposal for calling up the reserves for service in Vietnam. Arthur told the President that if that were done, he would withdraw his acceptance and not submit his resignation letter because, to him, calling up the reserves meant the equivalent of a formal declaration of war. President Johnson did not give the order.

The three years on the Court were like three days. There still was so much Arthur could have given to the law. When I thought of all those years of his work that neither of us had ever dreamed would be rewarded by so exalted an appointment, providing opportunity to truly serve; when I thought of all those preliminary years of "bicker and bargain and bustle"; when I thought of all the corporation lawyers' astonishment that anyone could arrive at the most revered position in the law doing everything the wrong way, the hardest way, then I had no heart for the usual public-face smiles of the devoted wife at the thought of his moving off the Bench.

Now he was being asked to exchange the Olympian heights for daily sparring in the jungle again. Once more there would be the round of punctures and wounds, once more the blasts of arguments, once more crowds of strangers. Once more all that noise.

Perhaps a wife should say "No—a thousand times no" when she feels as strongly as I did. Arthur's life, every part of it, was law-oriented, and the High Court was a surprising culmination, vindicating his work. I would not assume that I revered it more than he.

Then I recalled an incident that had happened shortly after Arthur's oath-taking. We were invited to a dinner at Decatur House. Most of the guests were strangers to us, as we were to them, though there was a smattering of diplomats and White House officials and a Cabinet officer or two. Subsequently, I learned that many of the guests were "cliff dwellers," that is, natives of Washington because their families may have been in business there or in the government.

I found myself standing near a dowager with a sharp interest in everybody, and an equally sharp tongue. She measured every guest and asked me for whatever information I might have about them—not once, but several times. When a Cabinet member passed, she asked, "Who's that?" I told her.

"Hm, a politician. Politicians—they come and go. And who's that?" she asked, pointing with a crooked little finger.

"That's his excellency the distinguished ambassador from France, Hervé Alphand."

"Hmn, a diplomat. Well, diplomats—they come and they go."

Then she appraised me for a moment. "What did you say your name was?"

"Goldberg."

That gave her a moment's pause. She wiggled the tip of her tongue over her upper lip. "Miss or Mrs.?"

"Mrs." I said.

"And what does your husband do?"

I took a patient breath to sustain me: "He has just been appointed to the Supreme Court. I hope it cannot be said of the Associate Justices of the High Court that they come and they go."

Remembering that old woman, I was doubly rankled by the new appointment. When the family was photographed at Arthur's swearing-in ceremony in the Rose Garden, my expression was unmitigated Stone Age.

Bob, the two new clerks—John Griffiths and Dan Levitt—Fran Guilbert, and Bob Suttice, Arthur's messenger, drove us to the White House.

The guard said, "Is this all family?"

"Yes."

Marvin Watson, a Presidential aide, asked the others to wait outside. Bob and I waited in the doorway with Art. The President had not heard us enter. We waited on the threshold briefly, but Bob cleared his throat in a discreet cough. The President looked up, "Excuse me." He had been writing something.

He got up, kissed me, shook Art's hand warmly and said, "Sit down and listen to the statement. I cut it some. There are less words, but I want you to hear it—in case you want anything changed."

Then Dean Rusk came in, gave Art an "embracio" and kissed me and wished us luck. And also George Ball and Mac Bundy. They all seemed to think it was the greatest news.

Bob was introduced and he and I listened. The President had put in all Art's stipulations—particularly immediate access to the President and to be a part of the Cabinet and in on policy-making conferences.

The President was called to the Rose Garden to receive some new foreign ambassadors who were then brought in to meet Art and the others. While the President was out, the conversation touched upon newspaper speculation that the new ambassador was Jewish and how that would affect his handling of Israeli-Arab matters. Arthur said to Mac Bundy and George Ball and Rusk the same things he later told the President about his devout belief in Israel's messianic role and that, as a Jew, he really believed that and he would not change his words or his mind because of Arabic pressure. He would do his best to bring peace, if at all possible, because it was good for the Arabs too. But he could not pretend to be different from what he had been all his life.

It was a sacrifice to leave the Court. Those who now express reproach overlook the fact that Arthur's successor on the Court was Justice Abe Fortas, who basically shared Arthur's views and would have voted more or less as Arthur. How would Arthur have been able to foresee the unfortunate Wolfson episode that caused Justice Fortas to resign?

Louis Wolfson, a virtual stranger to us except that our children were at school together for a brief period in the third grade, had offered to extend the same kind of financial help to Arthur on his going to the UN.

Arthur was astonished that the offer should even have been made, and replied to that offer of "help" by saying it was inappropriate for Mr. Wolfson to have made such an offer, notwithstanding the modest salaries paid to Supreme Court Justices and to ambassadors. By going to the UN Arthur was taking a $10,000 salary cut, as well as giving up lifetime security and status for himself and the pension for me that wives of Justices are entitled to receive.

Surprisingly enough, Mr. Wolfson himself released Arthur's reply, which was, in effect: "I thank you, but I have always provided for our needs. I deem it inappropriate for a public official to accept any financial assistance. I shall try to take care of my own security as best as I can." And that was the last he ever heard on the subject.

For my own part, I hasten to say here, and I know that Arthur shares my feelings, that I feel that what Justice Fortas did was certainly a regrettable indiscretion, but it was *not* venal, and I am sure that whatever Justice Fortas' understanding may have been with Mr. Wolfson that it never affected his decision-making in the slightest.

Although I finally concurred with Arthur's ultimate decision, my own opposition was shared by everyone in the family, particularly the children, who were incensed about Art's even being forced to make such a choice. In an interview to the *Chicago Sun Times,* Barbara said in response to the query "What do you think about your father stepping down from the Court?": "My father did not step down; he took a step aside to do another important work."

Although Arthur had asked for advice from all of us, I had not wanted to take responsibility for a decision of such gravity, fearing that my opposition might have been motivated by my own personal interests—my mother's illness, my unpreparedness for the upheaval of moving at that time, my disinclination to move to New York, and my natural tendency to conservatism when confronted by the unusual and the unexpected.

The world might survive, as it already had for several years, without Dorothy Goldberg's original paintings, but Arthur was an artist, too, of another kind. I knew better than anyone his talents for negotiation of conflicts in crises, and it was a question whether the United Nations could survive the crisis then facing it. The Soviet Union and France were threatening the very existence of the UN by their dues-paying defections, and those who had regarded the United Nations as the hope for a better world would see it go the way of the moribund League of Nations.

It was ridiculous to think that world peace was dependent on such a little thing as my views about moving to New York. Arthur would have heeded me because he enjoyed his work, and life tenure was not to be lightly dismissed. Still, whether it was an overinflated sense of self-importance or not on my part, I opted for giving him a chance to achieve a great good—however frail, however slight the possibility.

Besides, whatever miracles may have happened in times past could be regarded dubiously; and whatever miracles might happen in a future time could be regarded similarly, but the miracle that happens in one's own time is undeniable. This ancient thought often expressed by others in other contexts had become a personal testament.

To me, it seemed that Arthur's appointment to the High Court was one such miracle. That was enough for one lifetime. I looked for no further miracles at the United States Mission to the UN, but there was still a sense of indebtedness, and an appeal to serve one's country further, when made by the President himself, cannot be lightly disregarded.

Later, after seeing the way the United Nations functions and the work that Arthur was called on to perform, I gradually ceased to feel a sense of numbness over his having left the Court. Indeed, before we left the UN for private life, I had completely changed my mind about the decision he had made. When people ask me which office I had liked the best, I honestly say the United Nations, for the reason that nothing a person does before arriving there, and nothing one may do afterward, is commensurate with the feeling of exhilaration in the hope that maybe, just maybe, it is possible to work for a better world. And this I think is true for most people who are sent there to represent their countries.

Isabelle Shelton, in her column in the *Evening Star* on September 12, 1965, had a little paragraph labeled, "An Unusual Day":

> The proclamation by the District Commissioners declaring this Friday as "Dorothy Goldberg Day" is highly unusual, if not unique.
>
> The proclamation which honors the wife of UN Ambassador Arthur Goldberg for her "significant humanitarian and cultural contributions" to the District is something we've never done before except occasionally for a visiting African leader, or a long-dead hero such as George Washington Carver, says Walter N. Tobriner, president of the District Board of Commissioners.

Dorothy Kurgans Goldberg Day was officially September 17, 1965. Two thousand people came to say good-bye to me at the Statler Hilton Hotel. The Statler gave their grand ballroom gratis, but the guests bought their own drinks at the bar.

In the large entrance corridor to the ballroom, tables were set up, with pages to be autographed by the guests who were coming because of a special reason (e.g., whatever new project they were working with or cared about). Then those pages were bound in a large red-leather album embossed in gold, "Dorothy Kurgans Goldberg Day" (not "Arthur Goldberg Day"—I couldn't help gloating).

People from all the projects came, and also dear friends. The Chief Justice and Nina Warren came. My family had been invited from Chicago. My sister, Anna Lehnhoff, came, but my mother was not well enough to come. Her doctor said the excitement would be too much.

At the breakfast table that day mother said wearily, "When you make your speech, tell them I wanted to come but couldn't, not only because you're getting the honor, but because a part of me is in you—all those coffees, teas, receptions right here, all those cookies I made, all that talk I had to listen to . . ." Then she smiled, "Never mind, just you remember I didn't help just for you, but because I cared about the others being helped." And I knew that really was why the two thousand came to say good-bye—not for me, but for the work that was still continuing and to which all of them had given so much.

I enjoyed all the eulogies and ceremony—all the politeness passing by—trying to keep my pleasure from being too obviously apparent, but it was a most unusual experience to be alive and able to hear people solemnly talking about me as if I already were embalmed and covered with roses.

But try as I did, I could not manage to assume any saintliness of expression. I just was very pleased with myself and everybody there and enjoyed the moment fully without any trace of irony.

12

———————·◇·———————

Apartment 42-A
and the People
of the USUN

After the first flurry of commotion about Arthur, the press turned as usual for human interest material to the new ambassador's wife.

How did I feel about moving into the Waldorf Towers? I dryly commented that I could not get overenthusiastic because after all it had no basement nor attic.

Perhaps it would have made a better story for them had I confessed to being overwhelmed by the luxury of an apartment with a rotunda and a large, mirror-lined dressing room of my own, never having had a dressing room all to myself in my whole life.

The *New York Times* article on the subject was captioned: "Mrs. Goldberg Stymied by Suite Without Attic." Another newspaper captioned their account: "What, no basement?"

Redbook magazine inquired about the possibility of my writing an article on exactly what I did have in our basement and attic that I felt I couldn't get along without. Their readers would be interested in knowing because apparently the lack of those facilities was causing me to regard the new move dubiously.

The new apartment, 42-A at the Waldorf Towers, had ten rooms if one counted the rotunda. The house on Albemarle Street had had nine rooms with a large basement for laundry, a work-room with stacks of racks for paintings, a separate studio room, and freezer storage area. The attic had room for all the records and files in transfer cases about Barbara, Robert, and Arthur that I couldn't bear to throw out.

The implication of the query was obvious. Considering the Goldbergs' modest beginnings, Mrs. Goldberg had become spoiled.

So I wrote an article for *Redbook* telling them what was in all of those cartons and files. To my dismay, they captioned it, "How to Live with Memories."

The major mistake I made in setting up the new apartment was in not noticing that the telephone was on my side of the bed.

No sooner had we begun our long-anticipated Labor Day holi-day than war broke out between India and Pakistan, and because the presidency of the Security Council is held on a rotating basis, and it was our country's turn, Arthur found himself president of the Security Council, the highest office under the UN Charter.

To ensure high-level responsibility, Arthur asked that Zulfikar Ali Bhutto, then the foreign minister, now the prime minister, of Pakistan and Foreign Minister Singh of India fly here to partici-pate in the discussions.

The UN Security Council, in emergency session late on Satur-day, September 4, unanimously backed Secretary General U Thant's appeal for a halt to the fighting by adopting an urgent cease-fire resolution.

That crisis in September 1965 was confronted differently from the same crisis in 1973 when our country "tilted" toward Pakistan. As president of the Security Council, it was possible for Arthur to introduce a new technique that is now accepted as routine practice.

Formerly, the Security Council would go into public debate automatically. The galleries would be filled, the press would be ready to rush to report, and the two main opponents, with great emotion, would inevitably emphasize their differences. Having the prestige of the Security Council presidency, Arthur used the office to patiently conduct a series of negotiations.

Despite a highly inflammatory speech by Bhutto, largely for the benefit of his domestic Pakistan press and the galleries, he admitted, Arthur succeeded in getting agreement for a cease-fire and the return of both sides to where they were before the shooting started on August 5.

As a rookie in the galleries of the Security Council, I stared and listened, trying to make an order for myself. It was the first of a long series of visits there for me that caused our friend, the Mexican ambassador, Cuevas Cancino, to marvel once: "Dorothy, we get paid to sit through all this, but you subject yourself to it for nothing." It was not for nothing. There never would be such an opportunity again to widen my own horizons about world politics and foreign affairs without having to wade through ponderous tomes. The names of Rawalpindi and Tashkent were to be heard more often than Brooklyn and the Bronx. Gradually I began to feel a bit more at ease with the new environment—though not "at home" in it.

I kept my translator-earphones tuned to the French to try to perfect my understanding of that language, but not when the Russians came on. I gave them undivided attention in English translation. I wondered if they were jumping on Arthur because they might have "kept a little list." Did they remember that it was Arthur in 1948–49 who, as the CIO counsel, had kicked out the communists and fellow travelers from the American labor movement?

During this opening period we were getting to know the new team at the mission. Charles W. Yost became chief deputy. A career diplomat who had been ambassador to Asian and Arab countries, an aide to Stevenson, he had also written a novel and books on foreign policy. After Charles Yost left, to write, he was succeeded by Ambassador William B. Buffum as deputy permanent representative. Again, Arthur was very fortunate in having so excellent a foreign service officer as his right hand; he was selfless in his willingness to serve Arthur's needs at the mission and, like Arthur himself, kept team morale consistently high. Dr. James Madison Nabrit, Jr., the president of Howard University, took a year's leave to replace Charles Yost as United States representative to the Security Council. He had been a lawyer active in civil rights cases and Arthur had confidence in him.

When Kitty Teltsch reported on "The Goldberg Team

Takes Over at the United Nations" in the *New York Times* of August 29, she said: "As never before, the United Nations delegation, now led by Arthur J. Goldberg, will have to do its campaigning on two political fronts. . . ." One, the General Assembly; two, "The fresh team he personally has selected will be concentrating on Washington because he apparently is well aware that in some congressional circles opinion about the United Nations has dipped to a low level. . . .

"Aware of these currents . . . his selection of the delegation . . . includes members with a background of experience in domestic politics who will have status with Washington officials. California Congressman James Roosevelt is one. Another is Eugenie Anderson, the former ambassador to Denmark and Bulgaria and Democratic National Committeewoman."

The other representatives were William C. Foster, director of the Arms Control and Disarmament Agency; Congressman Barratt O'Hara; and Congressman Peter H. B. Frelinghuysen, whom we liked very much. I found Bea Frelinghuysen to be a great help too—a retiring and most unassuming person, but nonetheless of a calm and efficient approach to her duties as a congressional wife, and a most conscientious mother. I knew Bea from Washington, and had always felt a bit guilty about having been on the Blair House Restoration Committee in 1964 when the exquisite paneled antique fruitwood dining room walls they had contributed were cavalierly painted white, although I had not had anything to do with that decision. I also liked Bea because she had a sense of humor, and people with whom one can laugh easily become friends more easily.

Dr. Nabrit's wife, Norma, I recognized as a kindred spirit. The wife of a college president surely must relate to faculty and students and the community outside in the same way as an ambassador's wife.

James Roosevelt's wife, Irene, also was a help to me in various events arranged for and by mission wives.

Richard N. Gardner, formerly a deputy assistant secretary for the State Department and then a law professor at Columbia University, was a senior advisor that year. He and his beautiful wife, Danielle, became our good friends. Danielle, Italian by birth, could speak several languages, as could Irina Yost.

We found the permanent staff to be "salt of the earth" people —particularly Richard F. Pedersen, minister and counselor of the mission, whose wife, Nelda, was a willing aide to me in our various projects. John A. Baker, Jr., was on Political and Security Affairs and his wife, Katharine, we also regarded warmly. Katharine certainly baked her share of cookies for the various events given for United Nations wives. The Clarence I. Blaus we had known from Washington also and I was so glad to see them. Our children had gone to the same schools.

Of the rest of the representatives, I knew the wives better than the men because we had coffee sessions every month. Admiral Jack McCain, however, I liked very much and not only because he made his little navy plane available to us so that we could leave for Washington on our own schedule. (Several times I had to hurriedly dress in my evening finery in the women's room of the National Airport and once I saw Marietta Tree in the same predicament. After that Arthur arranged for a little *pied à terre* for us at 4000 Massachusetts Avenue.) Vice-Admiral John Sidney McCain, Jr., had come to the UN just two months before Art's appointment and was installed as vice-chairman of the U. S. delegation and U. S. Naval Representative to the United Nations Military Staff Committee. Although before Admiral McCain that post was not regarded as more than a good preliminary-to-retirement spot, he went from there to ultimately become the overall commander of the armed forces in the Pacific (Compac). Roberta McCain had an identical twin sister who stayed with them frequently and who looked so much like her that everyone asked the admiral how he could possibly tell them apart. He said, "That's their problem, not mine."

When the military staff entertained on the top floor of the mission building, I had to admit their buffets were far more ample than our budget could afford. Roberta McCain was one Navy wife who never stayed home. She made a deliberately planned schedule of every art museum in the New England area that could be reached and visited within a day's travel time or, if necessary, longer. I envied that, but it was impossible for me to accompany her.

Michelle Cooper's husband, Charles I. Cooper of International Organization Affairs, was also an adviser. I would see her often listening attentively behind the press section in the Security Council and she, like Dorothy Carpenter, was responsibly committed to the UN Delegations Women's Club. Mrs. Carpenter's husband was the press officer.

Perky Cates' husband was Jack Cates of Latin American Affairs. His sense of humor and help in the selection and arrangement of some of our after-dinner events made them outstanding. Benedicta Monsen's husband was the press officer who succeeded Carpenter. She too was helpful. The Peter Thachers and Don Toussaints, as well as the Cateses and the Seymour Fingers and others on the staff, were invited frequently also to our receptions. Peter Thacher was a "special assignment" to the permanent representative—that meant Arthur; and Don Toussaint was assigned to Political and Security Affairs—both were career officers on the permanent mission. Their wives too helped me bear the responsibilities of host country entertaining.

During the three years of Arthur's mission, a series of people served on the delegation, and Art persuaded the President to give them the personal rank of ambassador during their service, which was generally for one assembly.

Outstanding among them were Harding Bancroft, executive vice-president of the *New York Times;* Patricia Harris, former ambassador to Luxembourg; I. W. Abel, president of the Steelworkers Union. For us, one of the fringe benefits was that they not only gave Arthur and our government the highest type of conscientious service but they also became good friends.

Robert and Jean Benjamin, an unusual couple, made individual and joint contributions of great value to the mission. Robert S. Benjamin, chairman of United Artists, was the principal and most devoted supporter of the United Nations Association and a member of the delegation for one of the General Assemblies; he also served conscientiously on the Legal Committee. Jean Benjamin served as an advisor to Morris Abram, the American delegate to the Human Rights Commission. Arthur Krim, co-chairman of United Artists, and his wife, Matilda, made a valuable contribution as private citizens to our government and to the UN through the open and warm hospitality they so frequently accorded the African delegations.

At the USUN Mission, too, Arthur received devoted service

and wholehearted support from Norma Garavente and Jane Merrill, his two secretaries, and from Imogene Dutton and Lillian Liccardi.

Kathleen Gaumond, wife of the chief administrative officer of the USUN, often came forward to help. Few of the mission wives other than those at the very top level had met one another previously and they liked the idea of a once-a-month coffee session in 42-A, as the "embassy" was always called.

A consistent attempt to meet with the wives of delegates at all levels from other nations developed after a sad happening at the United Nations Delegation Club. Early in the autumn, I met a charming young African woman from Malawi, Mrs. G. T. K. Mwalilino, who was with the newly arrived ambassador's wife from the same country, Mrs. Bridges W. Katenga. Olive Mwalilino, the wife of the second secretary of the permanent mission of Malawi, was shy and delicate in her movements and speech, with a fresh eager smile. I was surprised to learn she was at least twenty, and had two little children. She looked younger.

A few days later, I was stunned with horror to see her photo spread over the papers, with pictures of the skyscraper apartment from which she had flung herself and her two children to instant death. I at once paid a call on Mrs. Katenga, who lived in a distant suburb. She too was shocked, and when I asked if she had had any inkling, she explained that she was very recently arrived herself and scarcely had met Mrs. Mwalilino before I saw them together, being preoccupied with unpacking, adjusting to the new home, children of her own and with only a fourteen-year-old niece to help. When I asked if there were others from her mission in the area, she said she would go with me to the home of another young woman whose husband was on the Malawi official staff. There I met a young African mother of three, with no help. Her first-grader arrived soon after we did, bubbling with eagerness to tell of his experiences. The other child was in a carriage and she wheeled the carriage as she spoke to pacify him. Her home, her person, her children, her gentle manner toward them—all bespoke more intelligent organization and dignity than that of women much older.

"She was my dearest friend," and her sadness was making

speech difficult for her, "but they lived so far away in New York and I could not help her."

I began to ask other wives of ambassadors if they had any responsibility to those in their mission. Mrs. Morozov told me that at the Soviet Mission she met with them at breakfast almost every day.

There was a hospitality committee at the United Nations, but it existed largely to invite women to various events, and I thought it was geared more to top-level wives than to those of officials at lower levels. At our own mission I asked what had been done about host-country obligations.

I was told that there was a brochure detailing for the wives the various places they might need to know, but it was only with some difficulty that I finally was able to locate a copy. It was four years old, out-dated, incomplete, inadequate. I thought there should be a new one. In fact I thought that all the strange nongovernment agencies listed there ought to provide more up-dated information. There was no money for such a project.

Finally, through the United Nations Association, I was put in touch with Ronnie Codel of the New York Chapter of the United Nations Association, who had formerly been in advertising. She had no use for volunteer work now, having done more than enough other years, and preferring freedom to travel with her husband—but the project appealed to her.

Ronnie and I were distressed to learn how little some of the nongovernmental agencies were contributing to extend a warm friendliness to the strangers in our midst. A number of them were paper organizations. Only those providing a valid service were included. The "Information for Delegations" that the United Nations Headquarters distributed would be of no help to a young woman thousands of miles from her home and family, plunged into a cold environment, and the Hospitality Committee in the United Nations was challenged too.

Ronnie planned the investigation, developed the questionnaire, performed as general director while doing the interviewing herself. Barbara Carroll of Fort Lee New Jersey was recruited by Ronnie and came faithfully and shared willingly. First Ronnie asked pollster Lou Harris for counseling, and at the end brought him the little mimeographed brochure of "New York Night and Day—A

Guide to Community Services." Ronnie said he offered her a job but she declined smilingly, preferring to keep her "amateur status."

The lack of money, the crying need for volunteers, the volunteers' ineffectuality because of their status-conscious leadership were subjects for provocative thought. After hearing Mrs. Malecala's solution for the embassy of Tanzania, I was overcome with awe and admiration for a tribal system that worked better than all our theoretical social-worker abstractions.

Mrs. Malecala, a poised and intelligent wife and mother of great energies, lived in an attractive suburban home. When a wife of a member of their official team was expecting a child and there was no one to take care of her and her older children, Mrs. Malecala had devised an ingenious solution: While the wife was in the hospital, the husband and the children moved into Mrs. Malecala's home in Mt. Vernon. During the day, the children went to school with hers as their guests after she had prepared ahead of time with the teachers. In the afternoon, they played with her children. In the evening, the children and their father shared their dinner, but after dinner it was the father's responsibility to supervise their baths, their clothing for the next day, and to spend some time with them. On the mother's release from the hospital, she too was enveloped in Mrs. Malecala's household commune. For two weeks, her entire family moved in. And Mrs. Malecala told me, "It's nothing at all. They took care of themselves. All I did was put more food on the table."

Nothing at all!

In the United States Mission to the United Nations, Mrs. Margaret L. Gerstle became liaison employee with the Host Country Advisory Committee. She was sympathetically aware of the needs, the previous impasses, and all the possibilities.

The tragedy of Olive Mwalilino revealed a great untapped reservoir of goodwill for the United Nations, but the mission had no funds to set up a small office with one or two professional supervisors of volunteers, and I myself could not do that.

Whenever I walked up the few steps to the entrance of the USUN, I would draw a contented breath. If there was no time for gallery openings or museum visits, at least the mission itself glowed like an intimate little museum. The works of art on all twelve floors could be glimpsed whenever the elevator stopped, and passengers might reflect that if the only reason to save this miserable world is to save the works of the human spirit, among those works, art is numbered.

With the help of René d'Harnoncourt, director of the Museum of Modern Art, we arranged for an Advisory Council on the Arts to the USUN Mission, comprised of the curators of painting from the Museum of Modern Art, the Whitney Gallery, and the Metropolitan Museum of Art; the twelve floors of USUN were filled mainly with art loaned for Arthur's tenure. The galleries of Betty Parsons and André Emmerich loaned exciting works. On the right wall of the lobby was an Okada mural in ochres, whites, grays, beiges. On either side of the sliding glass doors leading to the outside courtyard were two handsome sculptures—for the traditionalist a Remington, *Bronco Buster,* and an abstract of a chambered obelisk by Ruth Vollmer. To the left, near the elevators where Imogene Dutton, the receptionist, cheerfully welcomed all visitors, were works by Joseph Albers, Alexander Liberman, and Franz Kline. Imogene had a mimeographed catalogue of all work on loan available at her desk to answer inquiries about identification.

There were works throughout by Thomas George, Neil Williams, Miriam Schapiro, Ellsworth Kelly, Morris Louis, and Alexander Calder. The Alexander Calder stabile called *The Object in Five Planes,* unlike the others, was a permanent gift to the mission.

At the "embassy"—the apartment in 42-A—the paintings were by Anuskiewicz, Bearden, Rauschenberg, Motherwell, Noland, Prendergast, Childe Hassam, Rattner, Frankenthaler, and Joan Mitchell, and the Pratt Contemporary Graphics loaned a miniature exhibit of international prints that were mounted on a door. Corning Glass provided Steuben art crystal. My own paintings were hung in the bedroom and in the small study we used when we were home—once in a while.

Poetry, too, is among the works of the human spirit that world peace would preserve; so with the help of my friend Myra Seitz and Galen Williams of the Poetry Center of the 92nd Street YM–YWHA (Young Men's–Young Women's Hebrew Association), a popular community center, we arranged several unique programs, with readings by Marianne Moore, John Hall Wheelock, and Robert Penn Warren, with discussion participation of other literary greats such as Richard Eberhardt, Stanley Kunitz, Arthur Miller—others.

My time was also occupied with arranging for tours to the UN, beginning with those for congressional wives. I saw no reason why only congressmen should receive briefing; Arthur agreed that wives should be invited so that they might be able to interpret the UN to their husbands' constituencies.

A few congressional wives took me aside to say they would prefer being briefed apart from their husbands because the husbands thought they knew more than they actually did and that made them reluctant to ask questions in their presence. My friend Lindy Boggs, then wife of the House Democratic Whip from Louisiana and now a congresswoman in her own right, coordinated the Democratic wives, and Bea Frelinghuysen coordinated the Republican wives, with some help from Mrs. Hugh Scott. The pattern that was set was followed by leaders of groups from many women's organizations, as well as volunteer organizations in Washington and New York. After the briefings I invited UN wives to meet the American women.

Washington volunteer leaders arrived by chartered bus, leaving Washington about 5:00 A.M. Mrs. Robert H. Jackson, wife of the former Supreme Court Justice and chief prosecutor in the Nuremburg trials, who was not as young as the others, nonetheless energetically participated in one of these with the Lawyer's Wives of Washington. Visitors arrived in time for a 10:00 briefing at the USUN, visited the General Assembly and Security Council, and sometimes one of the committees, and toured our apartment and the mission to see the art works.

There were no funds for functions sponsored by an ambassador's wife. My cousin, Abe Kurgans of Chicago, learned of this, and kept me supplied with an excellent coffee that I used for this purpose. No small matter when one considers that between August 1965 and June 1968, according to Rosemary Spencer of the Department of Protocol, who kept the official entertainment record, Mrs. Goldberg gave 48 coffees/teas at which 1,738 guests were present, 18 luncheons for 315, and one reception for 60—a total of 2,113 guests. The total number of guests entertained by the two of us was 16,094. (During the same period, the protocol report showed that in addition to events we hosted I attended 85 others.) The staff wives volunteered to provide the cookies when we set up a series of film showings and hospitality gatherings at the mission for wives of all officials of the various UN missions, not just the ambassadors' wives.

When we had an exhibition of the work of American craftsmen for two weeks on the top floor of the mission, Mrs. Vanderbilt Webb, chairman of the board of the Museum for Contemporary Crafts, and Mr. Paul Smith of the museum's staff gave it all the personal attention and interest they would have accorded a formal showing. The imaginative resourcefulness of the presentation stimulated questions and provided an opportunity for examining the economic potential of crafts in the various countries.

It was at that affair that Katherine Baker baked eleven loaves of banana bread, and other mission wives enthusiastically contributed their own home-baked creations. Someone had told me that when the wives of any of the other delegations entertained at the Church Center, they provided their own national delicacies, and some of them thought the American women had no such talents, that they were either so affluent that they had cooks to bake for them or that, always being in a hurry, they used mixes. Well, the USUN women really showed American talent in this respect. And the event was one of such friendliness and warmth that whatever the men may have achieved that day across the street, the women more than duplicated it in goodwill, and that year and the next there was a little more friendliness among us.

Art thought I should write Congressman Rooney, chairman of the House committee that set funds for our expenses, about an item that appeared in Drew Pearson's column about our mission not having enough money to buy cookies for my teas—the women did not *have* to do that; they *wanted* to help with home-made delicacies. I did not write about it, for unquestionably the morale of the women was more like that found in a village church bazaar than in a great impersonal organization.

The professional women on the staff contributed toward staples —sugar, lemons, etc.—but everyone with a kitchen baked something. There were so many goodies that when the guests had left and the mission men wandered in to sample the pastries, their wives made packages for them to share with their colleagues. (By that time it was after hours.)

Roberta McCain and the wives of the military staff arranged table settings, flowers, in addition to bringing sandwiches and baked goods. Roberta sent the silver tea service from the Admiral's Quarters and I sent the new one purchased for the embassy residence. Everything sparkled, and the visitors said it was a smashing success—so much so that other embassies asked to have an opportunity to do as much on their own premises. It was hard work, but worth it to hear the surprise expressed by the guests that American women at the U.S. Mission could bake.

13

———————— ·◦⟨∞⟩◦· ————————

Official Duties
and
Our Private World

On September 25, 1965, the *Chicago Daily News* in a full-page
article by Georgie Anne Geyer for the "For and About Women"
section displayed a picture of Arthur and me with a banner headline: *Who'll Be Guest? Oh, Lyndon and the Pope.* I winced, not
having said that—although they had not put the headline in
quotes.

"Now the Chicago girl who 34 years ago married the poor
striving lawyer in Chicago (the son of immigrant Russian Jewish
parents who lived on 13th St.) is the American woman who is to
face the world in our names. . . ." However, the article, displaying
a certain local-girl-makes-good hometown pride, and despite the
flippancy attributed to me by the headline, read: "It is this apartment and this couple who will be America's neighbors to the
world, and the quality of their neighborliness is something that
will influence every American. According to Dorothy Goldberg
it will be a new kind of neighborliness.

"The emphasis . . . will not be on decor and cuisine."

Not only the Washington press corps of newswomen were interested in visiting the apartment and interviewing me, but the large
corps of the international press as well. I took a deep breath and
applied myself to the job of preparing for the arrival of the Presi-

dential party in connection with the Pope's visit. Arthur was bringing me all sort of directives from the Department of Protocol.

There was considerable conjecture about where our government would extend hospitality to the Pope. Finally it was decided that it would be most appropriate to hold the reception for the Pope in the Waldorf's Presidential Suite. I could not understand the reasoning behind the change from our residence to a suite of hotel rooms (a Presidential suite is wherever a sign is placed to that effect), but Arthur explained that our residence was official United States Government territory, and that the Pope was really coming to visit the United Nations and not the United States Government.

Our residence was, however, to be the setting for a dinner that Arthur and I were giving for President and Mrs. Johnson. At least that was how it began; then it was to be in honor of the U.S. Delegation to the United Nations. The President kept adding to our guest list, which included United Nations officials, Governor and Mrs. Rockefeller, Mayor and Mrs. Wagner, and U.S. Mission ambassadorial associates. First President Johnson wondered if he could bring the Catholic members of his staff—Valenti, Califano and others—and their wives. Then another call inquired about the Catholic members of Congress. And at the last minute, Congressman Rooney, who oversaw UN appropriations, and the Vice-President.

Our dining room table seated fourteen, sixteen if we squeezed little gold chairs around. For any number beyond that up to twenty-eight, we exchanged the family-size table for a banquet-size understructure. For thirty guests, we brought in three round tables of ten; but the very most that could be seated comfortably, without being endangered by waiters carrying soup, was forty people around four tables of ten. (Most of the time when we were serving crowds we had cold soup—Senegalese or jellied consommé—to avoid that very possibility.) The final listing came to seventy-six.

I tried to keep acid out of my voice when I asked Art, "Why not the Grand Ballroom? Don't you think that would be more comfortable and make it much easier to plan?"

"No, I do not, and neither do you, so let them handle it and it will be all right."

"Let who handle it?"

"Whoever did before." But nobody had ever before given a formal dinner for seventy-six guests in that apartment.

"Oh, stop making a federal case out of it." But it *was* a federal case. The President, the Secretary of State, the Majority Whips of both Houses of Congress, their opposite numbers in the Minority, the members of the U.S. Delegation to the United Nations, the Secretary General, the president of the Assembly, Cardinal Spellman, the Apostolic Delegate, and everyone else from the United Nations and the New York area whom the President wanted to meet would be present.

The Protocol Department of the mission, headed by Miss Rosemary Spencer, performed valiantly. They addressed the invitations and verified them and carefully lettered the place cards. Protocol arranged the seating according to ranking, no small job. The way we finally arranged it, the President and Mrs. Johnson would be in the living room at a table for forty-four. The dining room would have four tables of ten.

I asked that the menu be printed on little eagle gold-crested cards similar to those used for dinners at the State Department and the White House. One might have thought I was asking the mission to climb Annapurna. Everyone was extremely budget-minded and shivered at Congressman Rooney's denunciations of extravagancies. But the menu cards would make the dinner a bit more of an embassy dinner, and not just another Waldorf Hotel event, so I merely smiled and listened in silence to demurrals, until menu cards were found to be possible after all. At the top of the card was the notation:

Dinner in Honor of the President and Mrs. Johnson
given by
The Representative of the United States of America
to the United Nations
and Mrs. Goldberg

The head of catering at the Waldorf Towers was an enthusiastic young man of about thirty-two. A Swiss, Carl Zimmerman was a graduate of Cornell's School for Hotel Administration. He was bubbling with energy and goodwill. I trusted him more than I did some of his more experienced associates, who were rigid in their attitudes. I suggested that we meet with the chef who would have responsibility for the actual preparation. I had gone through my file of menus saved from all the embassy dinners we had attended during the Kennedy administration and during our Supreme Court period, as well as State dinners, White House Dinners, and menus from various embassies overseas. I had saved them all. I consulted the thick gourmet cookbook that Bob had given me for my birthday four years before and was ready with one or two changes of sauces.

The chef, in his tall white hat, arrived and looked dubiously at my cookbook. He looked as if he were hoping to find a way of not hurting my feelings. Then he said, "Hmm-n," and cleared his throat. "I've got one of those too." Pause. "You don't need it."

Mr. Zimmerman, his eyes dancing with the pleasure at the challenge, was extolling a side of beef—the best, the choicest, the greatest—from a prize-winning steer; after all, that's what Americans like best, and they were mostly Americans, weren't they? No. Anyway, they knew that that was what the President liked best. *They* had phoned the White House to inquire. I asked if that was their practice. Were they perhaps expecting regular lists of our guests so that they could ascertain what preferences in food they might have?

I gently reminded Mr. Zimmerman that the embassy residence was not the Peacock Alley.

In the end we settled on:

Quenelles of English Sole, Lobster Sauce
Roast Sirloin of Beef
Château Potatoes
String Beans Forestière
Bibb Lettuce, Sauce Vinaigrette
Wisconsin Brie Cheese, Crackers
Crown Waldorf
Maréchal Strawberries
Petit Fours
Demi-tasse

I insisted on putting the Waldorf staff through a rehearsal despite their executive superciliousness about it. The first rehearsal was a week before the dinner, using only half the drawing room and half the length of table. The rugs were removed, the furniture moved aside, and the table and the chairs brought in so that we could measure and count, because the living room had never before been used as a dining room.

Security arrangements were made by the White House. Every inch, every closet, every item was checked thoroughly and inspected, as were the walls and the wiring. A tangle of telephones was installed. Strangers were around wherever one looked. They were all very polite, but I had no way of knowing if someone was there legitimately, or if they had just wandered in out of curiosity.

There was a minimum of confusion because our neighbors, Senator and Mrs. William Benton, had made their apartment next door available to us. Thus, we could accommodate a cocktail reception for the President beforehand for a small group in our little red study, and a larger group at the Benton apartment. The entertainment afterward—we had decided to ask Anna Moffo, the Metropolitan Opera star, whose singing the President enjoyed— was also to be held in the Benton apartment.

The chief of the Waldorf staff and I checked the Benton apartment together with Miss Kay Hart, Senator Benson's administrative assistant. I was concerned about the Bentons' beautiful collection of objets d'art, and they were put into a small room that was closed to guests. But it was the paintings themselves in one of the bedrooms that Miss Hart thought should concern me more. There were a number of nudes that gave *me* no misgivings, so I said, "Well, let's think about it"; none of them would have swept the administration out of office. (Some one, however, had them summarily removed for the party.)

Then we gauged the number of little gold chairs that could be comfortably placed in the Benton apartment for the musicale, and several of the staff and I considered logistics. I went through all the motions as if I were a guest coming out of the elevator door.

There would be coat racks in front of a screen near the Benton apartment and, in the Benton apartment, coat racks for the women's furs and wraps in what the Waldorf still calls "the boudoir." There would be a little table outside the Benton apartment where guests could pick up little crested Embassy of the United States cards with a diagram pointing to where they would be sitting at the long drawing room table or telling them, "purple ribbon table, dining room." (The four tables were designated "red ribbon table," blue ribbon table," "green ribbon table," and "rose ribbon table" and identified by small velvet ribbons in those hues placed around the base of the flower centerpiece on each side. I had gone to the florist downstairs for the ribbons as an after-thought—rather than labeling the tables 1, 2, and so forth.)

The second rehearsal on the Sunday of the dinner gave us enough time to make actual changes where needed. Then the room was cleared for Operation Presidential Dinner.

The incoming and outgoing traffic had to be considered. If the dining room emptied as usual, the apartment entrance would become a bottleneck and people would bump into one another. Further, the apartment facilities would be needed for those women guests wanting to change their make-up and freshen up. I asked the wives of mission officers to be on the alert for guests in the dining room and to help share the hostess role there. I also asked them to suggest that people exit through the guest-area foyer of our apartment so that they would not crowd the apart-ment on their way to the Benton apartment and to help as host-esses for the dining room after dinner, in case guests wished to use the facilities.

These little details are routine for a White House or State De-partment event, and presumably for the great embassies in Paris, London, and Rome, but the embassy residence had not really been regarded as more than just another apartment before, although some beautifully planned parties had been held there.

The Protocol Office anticipated other needs, planning for our meeting the Presidential plane, for instance, and arranging for the interpreters that would be needed.

At about six o'clock I went into the living room for one last check of the table, which stretched from wall to wall and filled the entire room short of about four feet, but the white brocade sofas with the raspberry velvet pillows, placed on both sides of the center doors, gave the room an air of normality.

We had to use Waldorf china, glassware, flatware and silver-plate candelabra, but with the tall tapers lighted and the tiny flicker lights in the crystal chandeliers, the atmosphere and the setting could have done justice to an official residence of any United States Embassy anywhere. (Later, the State Department would provide us with a measure of what they allowed our other embassies overseas.) Elegance was not an objective, but dignity was, a warm hospitality and dignity.

Then as I turned to get dressed for dinner, I noticed the table itself. I had taken that for granted, and now I saw that at forty-four place settings there were forty-four bread and butter plates and forty-four little butter knives.

Mr. Zimmerman was standing near. I just looked at him. "What's the matter?" he asked. "Is something wrong?"

"No, not much, but please remove the bread and butter plates right away."

"Oh, Mrs. Goldberg, I think you want them. Where will they put the rolls then?"

I said, "Please tell the waiters to take them away."

Two of his assistants glared at me, I think they were tired. Inwardly I was annoyed with myself for being preoccupied with the removal of bread and butter plates, which are quite acceptable and even necessary at lunch but for no good reason are considered improper at formally set dinner tables by long-established custom. What difference would it have made to any but the fluttering spouses of certain moneyed officials who happened to have a mistaken sense of values? The Foreign Service career wives were not usually snobs. I had been in public life, however, long enough to recognize the degree of supporting application to their husbands' duties given by other embassy wives. Many of those in major embassies gave full-time consideration to their consort status roles. I was determined that the wife of the host country ambassador would give no less.

At approximately 8:30 P.M., the Presidential party—those who had been having cocktails in our apartment—went to the Bentons to form a receiving line consisting of the President and Mrs. Johnson, Arthur and myself. They went from this receiving line either across the hall to the dining room or around the corner into our apartment. In either case, they could find their places easily because they had to pass the little table with the direction cards on their way.

Even as we were being served, the people behind the scenes were also being served. The Secret Service? Poor men, I never did know how they managed those late engagements, but they always said, "No, thank you."

Everything was delicious, and I suppose that is all that mattered. The waiters restrained any impulse to march into the room with the lights turned off and the Crown Waldorf aglow on trays held high above their heads. The service was quiet and efficient, and I was very glad that we were in a hotel and not in a private house.

The dinner turned out to be a great success from the President's standpoint. I supposed I should also regard it as a success, if only for the fact that Congressman Rooney and his wife became good friends of ours. The congressman was not the ogre I had been led to believe he was. I never thereafter had to worry about his not understanding the reasons for any request I might consider necessary. And for that matter, neither did Arthur.

One of the reasons for this development in our relationship with the chairman of the Appropriations Committee was that on his and Mrs. Rooney's arrival late Sunday for the Presidential dinner at the last-minute invitation of the President, Congressman Rooney had phoned me in dismay. They were delighted to come but had not been told that a papal audience early the next day, Monday, was possible, and the only dress that Mrs. Rooney had brought along was flaming red—inappropriate for the all-black required at a papal audience. Though Mrs. Rooney was taller and a few sizes larger, I found a new black chic dress for her to wear —after some hurried alteration in my own closet. A soap-opera solution to that critical situation, but both Rooneys became my friends, and Art often said that he wished he could send me to the Appropriations Committee to testify on budgetary needs of the mission.

The fact is that Arthur, as ambassador, had none of the contest that poor Adlai Stevenson had to contend with from head of the Appropriations Committee. Arthur was always given a respectful hearing and granted every request.

At the dinner, the President himself was not too communicative. Much of the time he merely sat in a brooding silence or was absorbed in the talk across the table where Art was sitting with Lady Bird at his right. Or he may merely appeared to have been thus absorbed to avoid having to engage in conversation, and no wonder, because the next day he entered Bethesda Naval Hospital for that much publicized abdominal operation.

He kept looking, however, at the large paintings on loan from the Museum of Modern Art hanging in the living room.

"These yours?"

I told him mine hung in our private quarters.

"How come I never got one?"

I said I never gave them away—it would be presumptuous—but if he really wanted one, I would send him one. When Arthur phoned Mrs. Johnson at the hospital afterwards and the President was well enough to take the phone, Art thrust it in my hands after saying, "And Dorothy's right here and wants to talk to you."

Before I could make an appropriate remark, the President asked: "Where's my picture? You said you were sending me one."

I did not know what to send him, not having painted new canvases for five years. Bob and Barbara had appropriated a good number for their houses, and whatever they had not taken was either on the farm or in Arthur's office.

"Oh, find something," Art said, "After all, it's the President."

I admired the President's courage for coming to dinner and also for facing the tedious ordeal of the next day. So I went to Art's office and removed from the wall near the door a painting in mixed media called *We the People,* that treated the Constitution as a long-lost ancient scroll.

(The administrative officer, Ed Gaumond, arranged to have it crated and shipped to the ranch where it hung until the President, in his retirement, wrote his book.

In Johnson's book he wrote that the reason he asked Arthur to leave the Court and become UN ambassador was because of his undeniable ability but also because he had heard that Goldberg was bored with the work on the Court. This statement about "boredom," which was so contrary to the truth, outraged Arthur particularly because he had heard from a newspaper man a considerable time before Johnson's book came out that the President had made a similar off-the-record statement to that reporter. At that time, Art had made a point to speak to the President at the White House to ask him whether he really had made such a statement. The President denied making the statement and said that he knew of Arthur's great contentment with his work on the Court and that he was keenly aware of the sacrifice Art made in leaving his judicial post. And then the President asked one of his aides to bring in the public statement that Johnson made at the time of Arthur's resignation from the Court and appointment to the UN post. He reread it to Arthur, pointing out particularly that he had used the word "sacrifice" as well as Art's statement that time about his regret at leaving the Court. Thus when Arthur read Johnson's distorted version of why he left the Court, he was so outraged that he phoned the President, insisting that I get on the extension. He told him that I was there and said, "I want her to hear me tell you what I think." Then he said, "And one other thing. I want that painting of hers she sent to you. It's mine and you don't deserve it.")

I actually found myself enjoying the Presidential dinner project and tackled the frustrations and obstacles and contrasting absurdities with zest. I suppose that it might be regarded by some younger women as the sad deterioration of a creative mind. But I would like to point out, if lamely, that some of the great masters of Renaissance painting were also engaged by princes and dukes to plan and execute court fêtes. If I think about that dinner in the light of the new Conceptual Art, then my planning, if mounted on a light Bristol Board with appropriate diagrams and graphs using markers and acrylics, could be regarded as an example of Conceptual Art too. Certainly my detailed approach and the execution of the plans was no less valid than a series of cliffs in some Australian remoteness.

Before the younger women begin to challenge me with making too great a case for the hostess-wife (after all, it took a great change in the cultural climate to finally remove the corporation wife's personality from her husband's dossier—and who wants that?) let me point out that to make innovative change requires more than a creative innovator. It also depends on the warmth of the climate and the degree of public acceptance of what the innovator has to offer. If one is not permitted to testify adequately or at all on the importance of his or her work, no matter what one knows or hopes to achieve amounts to anything without funds for carrying out a program. And occasionally a wife, by lessening the pressures, may help just a little, if only by chance, in changing the climate. For my part, it was satisfying to even be there by chance to help a little.

May I pause here to clarify this somewhat, because I would not want any granddaughter of mine to think that being the wife of an ambassador is preferable to being an ambassador herself. She certainly cannot make any commensurable contribution, but should she choose wifehood, that also allows for great satisfactions that are not necessarily always vicarious. And I do not doubt that this is true even if one's husband is not an ambassador but just a labor lawyer or, for that matter, not even a plain lawyer but just a laborer working in some plain vineyards. There is much to be said for working as a team for similar goals if there is communication and mutual respect and if there is a mutually accorded opportunity for each to grow whether that growth is achieved concomitantly or in relay stages.

And, of course, there is always that certain something called simply love. That helps very much.

In October my mother wrote to me that she had been watching the television presentation of the preparations being made for the "Pop's" arrival. "The poor Pop. What do they think he is? He is not a giant, and neither are you. Get some rest." Pop? I wondered if mother really was herself. Maybe it was her way of telling me to keep a sense of humor, to keep a sense of balance. I think in Russian the Pope is called "Popa." For mother, who read Tolstoi, Turgenev, Dostoievsky in the original Russian, the Pope became a "Pop."

But it was not only the visit of the Pope that was on my mind in October. I had accepted an invitation from Presidential aide Douglass Cater to be a participant in the newly organized Task Force for International Education, which resulted from a speech the President had made proposing a "new and noble adventure" in international education. The task force was "to recommend a broad and long-range plan of worldwide educational endeavor."

A glittering list of celebrities were on that task force. Dean Rusk was chairman. John W. Gardner, Secretary of Health, Education and Welfare, was at the first meeting. Others were Francis Keppel, U. S. Commissioner of Education; David E. Bell, administrator for the Agency for International Development; Charles Frankel, Assistant Secretary of State for Educational and Cultural Affairs; Leland J. Haworth, director of the National Science Foundation; and several university presidents including John Fischer, of

Teachers College, Columbia University; and Charles Odegaard, of the University of Washington. Besides myself, there were two other women, Margaret Clapp, president of Wellesley College, and Pauline Tompkins, general director of the American Association of University Women. On the formal listing, my name stood out nakedly plain: Mrs. Arthur J. Goldberg—no title, no job, no constituency.

Once or twice I wished I had declined. I sat between the Secretary of State and Douglass Cater. Dean Rusk smiled benignly at me, and Douglass Cater opened the session with: "If anyone's wondering what Mrs. Goldberg's doing here, it's because the President said she had to be invited. He wants her here; that's all."

That was touching and I felt warm toward the President, thinking that DKG Day publicity occurring on the same day as his speech might have impressed him. But if the President wanted me there, it was not just to sit and beam; thus, I again wondered what would be my role. And why should it be so surprising to be invited as one ordinary citizen representing no official group?

Still, no one there represented an art interest; although Leonard Marks could speak for the United States Information Agency, which had had experience with art exchange, but he would necessarily have other areas in mind too. My role could be also that of "generalist"—the one who puts simple basic questions to the specialists, like the first one I asked. "Why do we need this task force? Doesn't it duplicate the objectives of UNESCO?"

If it was an opportunity, it was also a responsibility, particularly if no one there was including art in his or her thinking about international education needs. I became aware of a certain slight sensitiveness on the part of a few professionals on the USUN staff toward a nonprofessional like myself, although it might have been the boss's-wife syndrome. While Ambassador Jimmy Roosevelt could have not have been more pleasant at the few meetings to which I was invited where the permanent staff specialists, as in all government agencies, discussed implementation of the President's task force proposals, I was conscious of a certain patient indulgence of my presence there. They sent their own recommendations to the Secretary of State, but did remember very kindly to send me a letter.

I asked the advice of Lois Bingham of the United States Information Agency, Catherine Bloom of the U. S. Office of Education, and, for the private sector, Ralph Colin, the executive director of the Art Dealers Association, and, of course, private artists I knew such as Pietro Lazzari, the sculptor, and Jack Perlmutter, the printmaker and painter.

It was work; still, I very much enjoyed the task force. While I made no pretense of being an authority, I was glad that I was there to put other simple questions to them, like what did they mean by "education" and by "international education"? Simple—yes, but provocative and I liked the discussion that ensued.

I really tried again to put a word in about creative minds and the difference between such a mind and a merely well educated one, and about how dependent a country is on its creative minds. I suggested, in my written recommendations, a conference on the nature of creative thinking. Well, nothing ventured, nothing lost. It was a good idea nonetheless.

In the final version, the recommendations for the International Education Act focused on the legislative side of the program, on an act to strengthen the international aspects of American education at home and less emphasis on the major international intercultural meaning of the full program.

On October 29, 1966, the President, on a visit to Chulalongkorn University in Thailand during his seventeen-day Asian tour, signed into law the International Education Act of 1966.

Although Public Law 92-318 extended the programs of the International Education Act in 1972 for three years, it is still not funded as of this writing. There are some worthwhile blueprints contained therein for some other era, some other President, some other Congress, some other students, who will "provide for the strengthening of American educational resources for international studies and research."

Early in November, I was greatly alarmed when Arthur came home before noon from the Security Council having suffered a dizzy spell. Until we were reassured that stroke was ruled out and that it was simply an inner-ear infection, I feared for him and was glad the doctor insisted that he rest in bed. Relieved of the greater anxiety, I tried to maintain the entertainment schedule as much as possible so that we would not fall too much behind before the close of the Assembly in December; Adlai Stevenson understandably had had to allow many obligations to go unmet even months before his last illness.

I did what I could, therefore, to avoid sending continuing regrets while Art was out of circulation for twelve days. Virginia Rusk, instead of Arthur, went with me to the Royal Danish Ballet, but the Danish ambassador's face, much as I liked him, was a study in suspicious politeness. He evidently thought Arthur's "indisposition" was more diplomatic than actual. At other functions, the host's jaw dropped visibly if I arrived without my spouse, so I decided the thing to do for those delegations to whom we owed hospitality was to entertain the wives at luncheon. It might not have been much to write home about, but it was better than nothing in an ambassadorial report to a foreign minister about his contacts with the ambassador of the United States Mission to the UN.

I invited only as many women as I could seat comfortably around the dining room table, so that I could use one of my own tablecloths and try to make the luncheon as intimate and home-like as possible. And the hotel staff was really trying hard to please. Jane Lahey was the apartment-based secretary that year. She had been in Robert Kennedy's office when he had been Attorney General, and neither she nor I knew that we should have cleared with Protocol first. We sent one list of invited guests to Rosemary Spencer, who called at once to inform me breathlessly, "Mrs. Goldberg, we don't do that—we don't invite Turkey, Greece, and Cyprus at the same time."

"No? Well, I cannot rescind the invitations. On the Supreme Court, no matter what their differences, they sit civilly together at lunch and dinner."

Rosemary said, "I'm sorry, but the State Department is not the Supreme Court."

So, I gave that little problem my best thoughtful analysis and decided to place Mrs. Eralp of Turkey at the south end of the table, Mrs. Liatris of Greece at the north end, and Mrs. Rossides of Cyprus across from me in the center of the table, with the other guests strategically placed to prevent the three combatants from tearing out one another's eyes or stabbing one another with their forks.

What happened was that the three, who knew each other fairly well, were given their first opportunity in many months to exchange pleasantries and friendly inquiries. No one had been inviting them to the same parties. After luncheon, they deliberately chose to sit near one another and appeared to be having a good time.

Sylvia Caradon of Great Britain was guest of honor and first to leave, and I saw her to the door. She whispered with such emphasis it was almost a hiss: "You got away with it this time, Dorothy, but take my advice—*don't go trying this with the Arabs and Israelis.*"

We both laughed, but it really was no laughing matter.

"I mean it," she repeated, "very seriously."

Why, I wondered, could not the diplomats be as civilized as the Justices? Perhaps if the differences were disregarded and more such invitations extended, they might be able to engage in dialogue as humans, not combatants all the time. Or perhaps the solution for peace in the world is that more women should be diplomats.

When I spoke to Zena Harman, wife of the ambassador from Israel to Washington, about the parting comment Lady Caradon had made, she smiled quizzically: "I would be glad to come, but it's not comfortable to try to talk to someone who promptly turns her back on you. I don't feel like giving them more opportunities to do that." It seems Arabs would walk out of a room at once if Israelis were present. The Arabs on the UNICEF Committee had participated in an unanimous vote to have Zena, who was an alternate representative on the Israeli delegation, head a most important committee, acknowledging her fairness and objective professionalism. But that implied no personal acceptance of her in any other situation.

Evidently, even a fairly amicable relationship could not be expected. Frequently at luncheons, dinners, and various events, I met Mrs. El Kony, wife of the Egyptian ambassador, and liked her. She looked exactly like the painting of an ancient Egyptian woman—excellent carriage, sloe-eyed, a Biblical figure—and was cultured and knowledgeable about UN affairs. In a small group she allowed her own smiling personality to surface, but in a large UN gathering where Israelis might be she congealed into a removed silence. Both Arthur and I found Ambassador El Kony unfailingly courteous. In the heat of debate, he was always mind-

ful of the amenities, unlike the bitterly vituperative style of
Jordanian ambassador, Dr. Muhammad H. El-Farra. Yet when
El-Farra was host, his parties were the liveliest and the cuisine
superb. At one of them the ambassador from Afghanistan, Abdul
Rahman Pazhwak, did a graceful scarf dance with Mrs. El Kony.
El-Fara is Deputy Permanent Representative of Jordan. Saudi
Arabia's ambassador, Jamil M. Baroody, and I were seated near
each other and I was surprised at the erudition and culture of a
person who was so obnoxious on the floor of the Security Council,
strutting like a barnyard rooster and crowing and screaming with
bigotry. Then I remembered that learning and culture had no
automatic humanizing effect. The Nazis read Rilke and Goethe.

Still, I had to concede that his shrill hysteria against Israel was
his public image. In private he said, "I hope, Mrs. Goldberg, you
do not become offended by what I as my country's representative
must say." Although I had been shocked by his vitriolic outbursts,
I replied, "Whatever my feelings are, Mr. Baroody, I cannot have
as real a malice in my heart toward you as I should because you
look like my Uncle Ruben."

He gulped, paused, then said, "I hope he is a young Uncle
Ruben."

At the buffet luncheons for the ambassadors' wives, I went out
of my way to try to sit next to the ones I was not supposed to be
friendly with—Cuba, Mongolia, and Albania. It takes courage
and poise to be silent and alone among a chatting crowd.

Once I invited Bertha Jackson, wife of Admiral A. McB. Jackson, who had replaced Admiral Jack McCain, and we sat at a table
with Mongolia and Albania. Language was very much a problem,
but one of them had a fair command of English and somehow
could translate for the other. So we began with the usual opening
gambit, namely our children. They both had young adult children
of whom they were proud. I am not certain about their careers,
but I think one child was in medicine, another was an engineer—
both prestigious vocations in any case. We were getting along
famously, despite the language barrier, until they asked Bertha
Jackson about her daughter. Mrs. Jackson is gentle, slow speaking, and gracious, devoid of any tendency to self-assertiveness, but
when she was asked, "And what does your daughter do?" she
hesitated for a moment and then said almost apologetically, "My

daughter is a nuclear physicist." They stared. I doubt if they believed it and thought perhaps it was American one-upmanship, but it was the truth. Still, it made for little icy silence the rest of the time, so as I sipped my coffee I resolved never again to open with, "And do you have children?"

At the Waldorf Towers, except for our own long-time housekeeper, we had no personal staff but depended on the hotel employees to service the apartment and to serve the many diplomats whom we were obligated to entertain. We discovered that in all the time the American Embassy had been at the Waldorf, the staff had never been invited. We thought it only right to give a party for them. On December 7, 1965, we entertained the maids, elevator operators, bellmen, telephone operators, doormen, waiters, and the many skilled and very competent working people who helped us represent our government at a reception with all the appropriate hospitality.

Another "first-time" USUN event occurred later when we invited the Vice-President and Muriel Humphrey. That was for the 1,528 United States citizens who worked at the United Nations. Most of them had never been invited to the United States Mission to the United Nations, even though it was just across the street. In June, Arthur invited them to celebrate "American Day" at the mission and to meet Vice-President Humphrey.

One woman told me, "I have worked here for twenty-years and had come to believe that I was a nonperson, that I didn't exist so far as my own country was concerned, but now I feel better. I know that I too am somebody." A man came to me to say, "I cannot hope to reach the ambassador in all this crowd; would you please tell him for me that what he has done here today means so much to us, talking to us about what our mission is doing, and letting us meet and hear from the Vice-President."

Arthur had not participated in labor controversies since he left the Department of Labor, but somehow his radar picked up grievances in the air. Now there was a United Nations one. Since 1960, the Secretariat employees who were United States citizens had been subject by law to U.S. Social Security tax. Since the UN cannot be taxed as an employer, employees were taxed at the high "self-employed" rate which pinched many of them.

So Arthur was involved in another labor settlement. The Secretary General had ordered a study to be made, the result of which was a formal request from the Secretary General to the U.S. Government, through Arthur, for agreement that appropriate relief be given these U.S. citizens by the UN.

To have this victory announced on American Day at the U.S. Mission made it doubly welcome, and added much to the warmth and camaraderie of the day. It was horribly hot, but no one seemed to mind being pressed together in the too small courtyard when Arthur said:

> Now, I am also your collective-bargaining agent. I have received through the Secretary General a collective-bargaining demand. But I have had some very good help, as the collective-bargaining agent, in presenting your request to our government. I have had the help of our distinguished guest here today—the Vice-President. I am very glad to announce that the Secretary General's proposal to the American government that you no longer be taxed as self-employed people, which you are not, has been accepted. Now isn't it a remarkable coincidence that we should make this announcement on American Day at the UN?

Everybody just cheered and cheered. It reminded me of January 21, 1961, when Arthur and I were in the motorcade that left the Capitol after the swearing-in ceremony of President Kennedy.

In the midst of the crowded schedule of official entertainment, there were occasional opportunities for private dinners where guests could talk and listen to one another, but these were rare. The official receptions allowed for no more than a cursory handshake and the usual amenities. Even at a pre-dinner cocktail hour, ostensibly a period for relaxing, if a pair of diplomats went off by themselves, a hostess was well advised not to interrupt them blithely with, "And what are you two talking about?" "Wouldn't you care to move nearer the window and meet . . . ?" They wouldn't. They might be discussing a counterargument to the Soviet bloc on the Security Council for tomorrow morning's meeting.

Official dinners, night after night, tend to become somewhat repetitive and often a little dull, particularly when the men take too long for after-dinner liqueurs and coffee. I do not want to think that Arthur may have been as responsible as any other gentleman for those extended discussions; *all* of them would return with an I-wasn't-the-one-causing-this-belated-reentry-to-civilized-society expression. At least Art would tell me about their discussion (unless, of course, it was classified). Often the men exchanged viewpoints and suggestions helpful to one another in their work. The women frequently missed extremely interesting exchanges, as, for example, the account of the coup against Nkrumah in Ghana while he was in China. I felt especially annoyed for Ambassador Eugenie Anderson, who properly should not have been exiled with the women after dinner.

I did remind Arthur once how bitterly Senator Maurine Neuberger had inveighed against this obsolete custom. In 1961 Senator Neuberger had been invited to a private dinner in honor of Arnold Toynbee, whom she was most anxious to meet. There was a galaxy of other ranking officials, some of whom had higher priority.

She found herself placed so far below the salt that however she strained she could not hear any of Toynbee's comments. She consoled herself with the hope of a more favorable after-dinner possibility; but after dinner, the hostess marched the women to an upstairs bedroom for coffee, where they were held captive until all had availed themselves also of the "little girls room." By the time they had marched down again, the guest of honor was in the foyer putting on his overcoat and taking leave.

Maurine said later, and not laughingly, "I really think, after such an experience, it might be a good idea to ask a hostess, before accepting, how much of the evening she intends to keep the women segregated."

Although a dinner party appears to be social, it really is to provide the diplomats with an opportunity to appraise each other, speculate about one another's position on a given resolution, and to duly include that information in their reports. Occasionally, during our United Nations years, I wondered if the hostess might have been under instructions from her ambassador-husband to extend the after-dinner coffee period. When that happened, one of the longer-posted, more experienced diplomatic wives usually arose, stretched a bit discreetly and remained standing until the hostess also rose to suggest brightly, "Well, shall we join the men?"

Among themselves, the women might talk about how the children were affected by their parents almost nightly absence; of the presumptuousness of the high official visitors; the women talked of being left in the lurch by the cook and staff hours before an important dinner party and how they managed by calling on the staff of another ambassador's wife. It was helpful to learn their techniques for coping with the unexpected, and I enjoyed the friendliness and the warmth when only ambassadors' wives were present. With strangers, the talk could be even more excruciatingly trivial.

While I was under no delusions about the purely business nature of even the friendliest social occasions, there were a few women with whom laughter came easily. Oddly enough, I related better to the foreign wives than to our own. When I met them at official parties or receptions, the Americans seemed a bit more strained, more serious even in their trivialities. However, Ruth Bunche of the Secretariat and I became as good friends as Ralph and Arthur.

SCHEDULE
DKG

Monday, November 1

2:00—Meet with Ambassador Roosevelt at the Mission
6:30 to 8:30—Vietnam Reception   UN Dining Room
5:30 to 7:30—UNICEF Reception at the mission   12th floor
7:30—Dinner in honor of Ambassador and Mrs. Anderson [U.S. Ambassador to Portugal] given by Admiral McCain and Mrs. McCain Quarters "A" New York Naval Shipyard   BLACK TIE

Tuesday, November 2

1:00—UN Wives Luncheon
8:00—Dinner M/M John Chambers Hughes   BLACK TIE

Wednesday, November 3

1:00—Lunch with M/M Sol Linowitz (you and the Justice are to go to this)
4:00—Tea and film showing, Madame Lekic [wife of

Yugoslav Ambassador] (You have handwritten in the appointment book—"Eve—Fanfani's Michelangelo ship. Check with Art if we must)

Thursday, November 4

    10:30—Sabatini Bros. Warehouse re: Museum of Modern Art

6:00 to 7:30—Andrew Heiskell and Editors of TIME Reception TIME-LIFE Building

    8:00—*Madame Butterfly*—New York State Theater in Lincoln Center

Friday, November 5

    10:00—Selections from Museum of Modern Art arrive

    1:00—Luncheon with Irina Yost

6:30 to 8:30—Tanzania Reception   UN Dining Room

Saturday, November 6

Sunday, November 7

    1:00—Luncheon with Amb/M Plimpton, Huntington, Long Island

    7:30—Premiere of *Eleanor Roosevelt Story* Cinema Rendezvous followed by reception at Persian Room of the Plaza   BLACK TIE

There were other schedules of more substance than this, but if my mother had been at the apartment as we had planned, I am sure she would have said again: "Parties, they have, all the time parties and so many people starving in the world." But the business of getting to know one's associates both at the mission and the United Nations is an imperative, so the parties were not exactly social, and in the beginning one hardly knows which are the "musts."

A stranger telephoned and told the first secretary assigned to the apartment that she did not know me but wanted to introduce me to the right people.

The right people? What people? At the UN?

No, New Yorkers that we should invite when entertaining ambassadors. Again—"She thinks she can help you meet the right people."

I was tired, the correspondence was piling up, and I felt no inclination at that moment to be diplomatic. "Tell her, no thank you, I know too many already."

My mother died in Chicago on the last day of the year, while I was with Arthur on the peace mission. During the long travel in the jet Air Force transport plane, with Arthur as the only other passenger, I had plenty of time to consider her life.

She died thirty-five years to the day after my father had died. I think she may have willed the hour of her going in a last defiance of that death she had never been afraid to joke about with us. My sister, however, told me that she thought, toward the very end, she detected an anger creep into her eyes as they suddenly opened. I felt a pang at that helplessness, at her being so humiliated by an entrapment of tubes, catheters and gauges. Then, for the first time, I felt a stab of guilt. ("When Arthur asks you to go with him, go.")

Perhaps, as the oldest in the family, had I been with her instead of with Arthur, I might have been able to persuade the others that we free mother from our devoted concern, from the best of medical science, when she might have preferred to take her leave earlier. Yet years before she was stricken, she had told Art and me very firmly that should it be cancer when her time came, she did not want to know. She preferred to hope to the last minute, and she wanted to receive all the benefits of current research and new techniques while hoping till the end.

Still, the night before the operation when I visited, her eyes held mine just a little longer, as if to tell me she really knew, and she delayed her slow smile even more when I said, "Good night, darling . . . see you in the morning."

In the very early morning, the day of the operation, Art arrived in time for us to get to her room before the first spinal anesthesia was given to her. I said to her: "Remember, you must live to be a hundred. That's the best gift you can give us." (We were being so matter-of-fact.) And she said, "You mean a hundred and twenty. What's the matter with a hundred and twenty?" She really brightened when Art kissed her, and she clung to his hand.

Then, never letting go of her hand, he and my brother, who held her other hand, walked alongside the rolling table escorting her through a long corridor to where a sign on the door of the operating room area said, "No Entrance." She knew we planned to leave for the Bahamas to get a long-delayed rest, but that we would wait until after the operation to hear the surgeon's prognosis. If everything was going as anticipated, we would return in a week to see her again.

We waited until she had returned from the recovery room. She was under sedation, but the doctor said that while no miracles should be expected she might well be spared for several weeks, perhaps months.

Then we left for the island of Eleuthera in the Bahamas, accepting the kind invitation of Mr. and Mrs. Frank Gledhill to use their cottage. For one day we walked the beach enjoying the solitude. I gathered small white shells slightly tipped with yellow marked with black zigzags to stare at while I thought of what I wanted to save in writing about my mother. Then while Art read a mystery, I began writing about her on a yellow legal pad, but at every paragraph I would pause to look at the gulls and the clouds; and in my ears I could hear her admonishing me: "Now, why must you do that? The first free time you have, you waste it with all that writing. Go wading, take a walk, or lie down and get some sun on your face. A person should do what she's supposed to do when it's the time to do it. Stop writing. Rest."

But the writing about her helped me feel nearer to her.

In Eleuthera the bedroom cottage was a few yards away from the little dining-living-room cottage. It was open on three sides but shielded from bugs by screening. In the middle of the second night, a stranger, a sailor from the naval base, awakened us to take Arthur to the naval base where he said a telephone call had come for him.

When Art returned about an hour and a half later, he said it was the President. He wanted us to go to Europe, to see the Pope at the Vatican, to NATO, to de Gaulle—maybe other places.

As soon as we could get to the naval base phone again in the morning, we called Chicago. Mother was doing as well as could be expected. We were again told not to expect miracles, but there was no telling—she might be spared whatever time her strength and her will allowed, perhaps a few weeks, possibly even months.

We left Eleuthera and flew to New York where we hastily packed winter clothing. In between, Art kept trying to locate his political officer, John Baker, to accompany him, but he had gone to the theater and there was no way to find him. So at about nine o'clock we left from Bennett Field in the Air Force transport jet, and I was his only aide. I didn't do much aide business. Once his zipper got stuck in a strategic place right before he had to leave to meet de Gaulle (it was unthinkable to keep de Gaulle waiting) and his other suit was at the valet's. I had to dive into action with a nail file, attacking with a bobby pin, yanking desperately to get it back on track. What else? Not much, really, except that whenever he left that attaché case with classified material for a minute I had my eye on it. If he put it down for a second, I moved up and stood near it so it could never be confused with any other attaché case belonging to someone else.

I think all I was good for was just to keep him company and to share that particular trip with him. He really needed no aide, in fact, but he did need a vacation, and when he was not reading and studying we could talk. We could talk about where we were going, where we had been, and where we now found ourselves. And if *Le Figaro* had an article about M. Goldberg, representant des États Unis à l'O.N.U. Reçu aujourd'hui à l'Élysée, my French was adequate.

A traveling wife is a fair enough substitute for an aide, unless experts are needed to assist in specialized negotiations. And if the envoy happens to be one of those strong-minded individuals who listens politely to aides but follows his own judgment, he might as well be accompanied by his wife. With a wife along, they are invited frequently to dinner, amenities are exchanged, and cherished friendships sometimes develop. Without their wives, happily married men have fewer interesting options in the evening; dinner is usually spent with the same aides, who take shop talk to the meal.

In any case, Arthur wanted me to go with him, and I was not sorry I went. In Rome, Gabriella Mellon, wife of Sidney Mellon of the United States Embassy there, very kindly devoted her time to showing me sights not generally seen by tourists. She was a member of a weekly archaeological study group and our trips were diverting. I spent time looking for a bed jacket for my mother.

We were in our rooms at the Hotel Raffael when our Bob called to break the news about "Grammie." He who had loved her so joyfully now spoke subdued in a voice unused to sadness. But at least, my sister and brother and others in the family had been privileged to stand vigil. Whenever her eyes opened, she saw their love. That was a solace.

Arthur said he would cancel the appointment with correspondent C. L. Sulzberger of the *New York Times,* which he had already canceled twice before. I said, "Let Sulzberger come. Just don't say anything about mother."

Mr. Sulzberger said NATO was very disappointed that Art had not told them more. But there was no more. Art told him that he wondered at the simplicity of their thinking. "First of all, I was under no obligation to report to NATO. What did Belgium, Turkey, or Denmark ever do for us in Vietnam?"

"Besides," he told me later, "anything I would say would have made all the papers, and as a guest of France, after all, I couldn't speak for de Gaulle. The French diplomat at NATO would have carried back a story that I had insulted him."

"How?"

"Because I would have had to say de Gaulle was de Gaulle."

I was feeling disenchanted—so little was accomplished—and tried not to express it. Art had said some people thought that Ho Chi Minh would turn into another Tito and then would sit down to negotiate, but that it just wasn't that way.

The hard truth was that impasse now confronted us. That was what the NATO diplomats, the press, and the public found so exasperating, so frustrating. There was a fervent longing for a change to bring an end to the war, but nothing was happening.

New Year's Eve in Paris was grim—rainy, altogether dispiriting when I looked out the window. About five o'clock in the morning, I heard a few horns tooting that broke the quiet of the Avenue Kléber. I felt no grief yet, just a pang that mother no longer could choose life at the New Year. We phoned Chicago again, then Arthur arranged for our departure. There would still be time for him to call on Prime Minister Harold Wilson and the United States Embassy in London.

While he was at his meeting, I visited our friends from Washington, the Philip Kaisers; he was deputy chief of mission with the rank of minister. Hannah Kaiser, an efficient and sensitively understanding Foreign Service wife, was receiving London political friends, some of whom, Lady Gaitskell among them, we had met previously. It all seemed normal. The deep pain of mourning had not yet struck.

Our huge plane returned to Chicago. The children were there to take us to Arthur's sister Jean's home, in Evanston, where we always felt cherished. A motorcycle policeman guided us through traffic. I felt no grief, not even when our beloved Jacob Weinstein, friend and rabbi, led our family at the graveside in the recitation of the Kaddish—the Magnificat—in which we express gratitude for intelligence, faith, and memory and ask for our heart's peace —even as mother was knowing the final peace. I felt no grief until we had arrived at 42-A in the Waldorf Towers and saw the room that was still waiting for her. Then the loss struck me very hard.

I answered more than two hundred letters by hand, weeping every time. The President had sent a basket of flowers to the chapel and a telegram:

> Lady Bird and I just heard the news. We're sorry to hear of your mother's death, but we hope you are comforted by the knowledge of your husband's returning to the States to be by your side.* He has served his country well—and we know he will serve as a great source of solace for you at this difficult time.
> Lyndon B. Johnson.

Nothing was a comfort. But there was understanding in a little note from my poet friend, May Miller Sullivan, who had been so great a help in the Washington School Arts Enrichment Program, and it succinctly states the void between the public and the private life:

> Grief is such a private matter that friends can only stand outside the closed door and think of you. . . .

That closed door on my mother's vibrant life, with the "No entrance" sign above it shutting out so irrevocably all in our family who so loved her, made it hard to go about my affairs as usual. Now I was glad for all the pressures that compelled my attention to the far more grievous losses of others in the family of nations, and was grateful to be able to serve.

---

*Apparently the President thought that I had preceded Arthur in returning home or that I had not accompanied him.

BOB AND BARBARA'S WEDDING

In the midst of sadness, of international crises and public pressures, a joy entered. Bob and Barbara's wedding day was February 13, 1966. The date had been moved ahead in the hope that my mother would be well enough to attend. The preparations lessened the hurt of our mourning temporarily.

We were happy that during her last years she had had an opportunity to know and love Barbara Sproston, and we recalled Mother's pleasure in helping her prepare for a White House costume party given by Linda Bird Johnson. Mother had fussed over Barbara's straw sailor hat and her blouse, her tiny-waisted skirt with a wide belt, and told us what she used to wear in 1907, when the style was popular. It was she, not I, who stayed up late to hear details of the party.

For my part I was filled with a sense of relief that Bob, who was so devoted to his grandmother, had so sweet a love of his own to blunt the edges of loss that all of us felt.

The guest list was made up solely of relatives and a few very close friends. To my relief and gratitude, too, our rabbi's wife and my own good friend, Janet Weinstein, attended to details that made the ceremony an intimate, a lovely event.

I had been so preoccupied with the changes in our lives in New York that I had not had time or thought for realizing those of our close-knit family. Only Arthur and I were at home without the children; without mother. I was not troubled that home was a strange apartment in New York. Home was wherever we were together. I felt only relief that each child had a life with love, so it was not mourning for their being launched into lives of their own apart from ours, but mourning it was nonetheless. It was unthinkable not to be able to share all details with "Grammie," as the children called my mother, and I missed her greatly. A private grief that surfaces in a public place is a diminution of a precious intimacy, as well as a vexing embarrassment. I was so glad not to have spilled tears into the wedding joyousness, and I sang and danced and particularly enjoyed the music by brother-in-law, Sheppard, played at the ceremony itself.

Still, returning to Apartment 42-A at the Waldorf Towers, I was in mother's unused room responding by hand to 273 letters of condolence, acknowledging contributions to various charities in her name, and kind Masses arranged for her by a number of Catholic friends.

14

Mission: Peace

We arrived in Rome in an Air Force jet transport plane about 4:00 P.M., bringing to the Pope a personal message from President Johnson to thank him for his pre-Christmas appeal to the world, which was helpful in bringing about the bombing truce. At least, that was how it was described in the press. December 30 was the sixth day of the bombing halt.

The events leading up to the peace mission really began on November 11, when two Italian visitors conferred in Hanoi with President Ho Chi Minh: "I am prepared to go anywhere to meet anyone," is what it is reported he told them. On November 20, Italian Foreign Minister Fanfani sent a summary of their remarks to President Johnson, and on December 4, Secretary of State Rusk replied to Mr. Fanfani saying, "The United States does not agree with elements of Hanoi's four points for peace settlement but we are prepared to include these . . . for consideration in any peace talks." And he asked Mr. Fanfani to get a clarification. On December 13 Fanfani told Dean Rusk that a summary of his reply had reached Hanoi and he would inform him as soon as he received any reaction.

On December 17, the State Department revealed the exchange

and said it awaited Hanoi's clarification. There was some concern that the disclosure of the peace feelers might imperil the plan.

On December 29, we landed in Rome. Ted Morello, of the *World Telegram* staff, New York, wrote on January 15, 1966:

> Goldberg travels light. When his plane landed the Ambassador for his peace parley with Pope Paul VI, Roman newsmen were astonished to see only the two Goldbergs step down from the ramp. Where, the Italians demanded, was the Ambassador's entourage of aides? Gesturing toward his wife, Goldberg grinned, "Here she is."

In Rome, Art had a fifty-minute private interview with the Pope in the Papal Library, urging him to continue to use his influence to effect peace. From there we went to Paris, where Arthur called upon de Gaulle. President de Gaulle told the newsmen at his New Year's reception following Arthur's visit (it lasted 55 minutes, beyond de Gaulle's customary lunch with his wife; Art then learned it was one of the longest de Gaulle had ever accorded a visitor) that Art was one of the few Americans who made any sense.

On his arrival in Paris, Arthur received a cable from Dean Rusk; it was, however, obviously from President Johnson. "You are to report to de Gaulle our peace moves, but you are *not* (repeat NOT) to ask his advice as to how to settle the war in Vietnam." Johnson did not trust de Gaulle.

Arthur decided to go alone, without any accompanying chargé d'affaires; the ambassador was away. De Gaulle liked that. It appealed to him because he himself was alone; he had not invited Couve de Murville, his prime minister. He greeted Arthur on the steps of the Élysée Palace. In his grand manner he said, "Monsieur l'Ambassadeur, you are the personal emissary of the President of the United States, and I am at your disposal."

"Monsieur le President," Arthur replied, about exhausting his French, "I shall open our discussion by reading to you my instructions from my President," whereupon he read the telegram. De Gaulle broke into loud laughter. Art continued solemnly, "As you see, Monsieur le President, officially I cannot ask for your advice on how to get out of the Vietnam mess, but the telegram does not restrain me from asking you personally for your advice. Therefore, in my personal capacity, and not as a representative of the President, I would welcome it."

De Gaulle replied, "I got out of Algiers. You get out of Vietnam. It will not hurt the United States; it has not hurt France. I am aware that in the long run, Vietnam may go communist. None of us wants this, but Asian communism is no menace to the Western world, as China demonstrates. It will be more a menace to the Russians than to us."

Art agreed, but asked, "Are they ready to make peace now?"

"Probably not. But you must pursue it as I did in Algiers." After that de Gaulle said, "Let us talk on pleasanter subjects. I have a thanks to express to you."

"For what, Monsieur le President?"

"I know that as an officer of the American Army in London, and since, you have been a friend of mine and of France, and that, Mr. Ambassador, is saying the same thing. De Gaulle is France, and France is de Gaulle."

Arthur was a bit taken aback and said, "Well, it's true I was a de Gaullist in the difficult days of London and North Africa when FDR was not your friend. But in the spirit of frankness which characterizes our discussion I must say that you are not an easy man. You have taken positions toward the United States that I think are unjustified."

Again de Gaulle leaned back and laughed. Art went on: "But I have something to thank you about today."

"What's that?"

"You gave me a good hotel, the place I stay in Paris, the Raffael." Art had read in one of the news magazines that de Gaulle had used the hotel briefly before taking office.

De Gaulle wanted to know, were they treating Arthur right, was the service good? And Arthur responded very seriously that yes, the concierge was very friendly, but that it all cost too much. Perhaps de Gaulle enjoyed the respite from the grave problems hovering in the background. And perhaps, too, he may have relished the fact that Arthur was not overawed or unduly adulatory. He was forthright in saying, "You are a troublesome fellow. You cause even your friends trouble by the statements you make about them, and, just as you are devoted to France, so am I devoted to the United States."

Ultimately, Secretary of State Kissinger used the French as intermediaries to arrive at a settlement, but at that time it was difficult for Arthur to get Johnson to agree that Paris would be a good place even to conduct negotiations.

The UN years were kaleidoscopic and exciting and though at the end Art told newsmen he felt only a dismal sense of failure over Vietnam, there were some achievements that should be mentioned.

In the Vietnam War, as the United States records show, Arthur pushed President Johnson and our government, despite their considerable resistance, steadily toward a negotiated peace settlement. He did this both publicly and in private counsel, as David Halberstam's book reports, but reports only in part. Arthur saw the utter futility of the Vietnam War and its calamitous consequences for our country. His March 1968 memorandum to Johnson after Tet, it is universally conceded, was a decisive factor in suspending the bombing and accelerating the President's decision not to run again.

In December of 1965, when I asked Art why did he not resign, he said it would make a one-day news story and the President would still have no one in there speaking forthrightly. He intended to keep on speaking his mind in the hope of ultimately having some effect, keenly disappointed as he was.

From almost the first day that he accepted the mission to the United Nations, Arthur, both in private conversation with the President and in written memoranda, urged that the bombing of North Vietnam be stopped and that negotiations be pursued. To this the President was not receptive; Presidents are generally allergic to outspoken criticism of their conduct.

On December 4, 1965, Arthur sent a strongly worded memorandum to President Johnson, saying that military actions ordered by the President contradicted the President's Johns Hopkins' speech, in which he advocated negotiations. That memorandum said in effect to the President: Stop the bombing and come to the UN yourself and say you're prepared to negotiate as you said at Johns Hopkins.

When the memorandum was received by the President, Art received a call from Bob Kintner, then an aide to the President, saying that the President wanted the memorandum withdrawn.

Art replied heatedly that he did not understand the request. If any attempt were made to expunge his recommendation, he would resign at once. Art said: "The President can always throw a memorandum in the wastebasket, but I have a copy of my memorandum and I don't withdraw a word."

Soon after that, he received a call from Bill Moyers, Johnson's personal assistant and press secretary, saying that Art had misunderstood the President's request. Art said it had not been misunderstood: "He goddamn did mean it and you shouldn't be a party to it." What he had told Kintner stood. And then he said, "Part of the trouble with the whole Vietnam business is that responsible administration officials give the President the advice he wants to hear rather than what he needs to hear."

Arthur then said he would not be a party to such procedures. In his memorandum he had expressed himself frankly to the President and he was telling Moyers what he had told Kintner— that he would not be a party to doctoring up the historical record. And he hung up.

The President reconsidered, suspended the bombing for thirty-eight days, and then sent the so-called peace missions scurrying around the world—including ourselves.

Shortly after that, at a meeting of the National Security Council, Arthur asked for the floor and, in the presence of the President and all the other members, repeated the substance of his memorandum.

We met Bob Kintner again on January 19, 1973, at a party at Luvie Pearson's. He said he was contemplating writing about his own experiences and that he intended to say that Art was the only person close to the President that had "guts enough" to face his displeasure and to speak up for his beliefs openly at the National Security Council.

Here is what happened the other times he tried to resign in 1967:

When the news was bruited around that Art was giving Johnson trouble and intending to resign, Hubert Humphrey came to see Arthur in New York. He didn't say that he came from Johnson. He was sympathetic: "I see you have strong views . . ." etc.

In fact, Art had said he wanted to leave before the Middle East situation broke in 1967. He was not satisfied with the way Vietnam was going. Hubert, obviously bearing a message from the President, suggested that if Art was thinking of resigning, would he consider a U. S. Court of Appeals assignment? Hubert had no authority to offer anything. Art replied, "Hubert, don't you be a messenger for Johnson. The answer is no."

Bob McNamara also called on Arthur about the same time and Art said he was surprised that he would act as a messenger boy for the President. What held Art there in 1967 was the Middle East, and then, after he tendered his resignation formally and irrevocably in 1968, it was Dean Rusk and Bill Foster who came to see him on separate occasions. Their appeal was identical. Both said, We cannot get the Non-Proliferation Treaty through the UN without your taking charge because you have acceptability and also can do the negotiating.

They appealed to him in behalf of that great move toward disarmament, to stay until the Non-Proliferation Treaty would be approved by the General Assembly. Dean Rusk brought a consensus report from our National Security Council expressing the views of both the nonmilitary and military members urging Art to stay and negotiate the approval by the General Assembly of the Non-Proliferation agreement in the interests of our country and world peace and survival. So Art stayed to do that job.

Then George Ball came to see Arthur and he said, "I don't have the acceptability and the experience at the UN. I'm regarded as a non-UN person. [He had made speeches and written a book and articles to the effect that the UN was ineffectual.] You would be doing a great thing for me personally if you would stay on and see this through."

Bob McNamara called on Art strongly urging him to stay because for the treaty to have acceptability it had to be approved at the UN where all the nations except the two nuclear powers were not enthusiastic about it.

George Ball said, "Foster and Rusk are right that your staying on assures the ratification of the Non-Proliferation Treaty." So Art agreed to stay.

As soon as the treaty was ratified by the General Assembly, the resignation he had submitted the day after the President had announced he was not going to run in March of 1968 was accepted by the President at Arthur's insistence, and the U. S. Mission to the United Nations was turned over to George Ball.

At the UN, Art had to struggle to get Vietnam placed on the agenda. Finally he got the votes and I was hoping this would be another successful fight like his vote-getting on behalf of the Anti-Recession Bill when the Senate Finance Committee reversed itself —an unheard of thing. His object in bringing Vietnam to the UN was to get UN moral support for having it referred to the Geneva Conference, the forum which had previously dealt with it.

An excerpt from my journal notes of February 1, 1966, is from my behind-the-scenes point of view:

Art is on the phone talking to Hugh Caradon [Lord Caradon, Britain's ambassador], telling him to go quietly to the Russians and say to them is there anything serious about Geneva. "If there's any real possibility we could put this off in the Security Council. That's where it ought to be—Geneva."

I asked him: "Why did you bring it to the Security Council then?"

"Well, we tried to get it to Geneva just a month ago. Harold Wilson went at our request and the Russians said no. Now if they'll go to Geneva—good."

I still thought maybe there might be some hope because this time Fedorenko [Soviet ambassador] when confronted with a fact that made him squirm merely said Art was distorting the facts whereas a few years ago the Russians would have shouted, "Lies, lies, lies," trying to intimidate polite Americans.

Khrushchev's shoe-banging episode was childishly ridiculous. Maybe the UN now is causing them to behave more diplomatically mature or maybe Art's way of making such outbursts backfire is the reason. Still, he dropped the "distinguished" when referring to Art. That should have been a tip-off because it's a commonly used courtesy. Fedorenko was trying to appear calm, dispassionate, but to a calm dispassionate listener the truth was finally being uncovered. *They* do not want Vietnam brought before the Security Council and neither does France.

At lunch Mrs. Adebo (wife of Chief Adebo, Nigeria) pointed directly to the reason that the vote went so heavily against us. We were at the monthly first Tuesday Ambassadors' Wives luncheon. She wanted to know what had I thought of Mali's speech (Ambassador M. Sori Coulibaly). I said, "Well, I wished he had voted with us." Mrs. El Kony (Egypt) was standing near, listening, but noncommital. Mrs. Adebo said, "But it's not logical—your position.

You don't have Hanoi, Peking, Vietnam here. They should be at the UN if a vote is taken; otherwise it's just talk."

She was right and it was my turn to squirm, but Arthur's object was to get the moral support of the UN to refer it at least to the Geneva Conference.

He hoped the Africans would realize that they cannot expect to have apartheid in South Africa condemned as immoral by the moral force of the UN and then deny that same world moral force of the UN to the people of Vietnam who should have the right to choose for themselves what type of government they want. The stalemate, the impasse is staggering. Jordan is the swing man (Waleed M. Sadi). He suggested postponing the vote until tomorrow afternoon. Jacob Weinstein was in town and sat with me in the gallery. Mary McGrory was there too. When she wondered why the postponement, Jacob said, "Probably to get directions from his king." Everyone is probably calling the king tonight—the Russians, our people, their own people.

You really begin to understand what it means not to have France as our ally. This morning Roger [Ambassador Seydoux] brought Art a telegram from de Gaulle saying complimentary things, but still they voted against us.

Throughout, Arthur was the only one who openly spoke up at the meetings of the National Security Council and expressed vigorous opposition to the war.

His memorandum of March 15, 1968, to Johnson bluntly said that the President had lost the consent of the governed; that it was necessary to seek a political rather than a military solution of the conflict; and that the first step required an end to the bombing.

After that memorandum, Johnson summoned his Senior Advisory Group on Vietnam, a blue-chip Establishment group. These were the great names of the Cold War: McCloy, Acheson, Arthur Dean, Mac Bundy, Douglas Dillon, Robert Murphy. And over a period of two days they quietly let him know that the Establishment —yes, Wall Street—had turned on the war; it was hurting us more than it was helping us, it had all gotten out of hand, and it was time to bring it back to proportion. It was hurting the economy, dividing the country, turning the youth against the country's best traditions. . . . At one of the briefings of the Wise Men it was Arthur Goldberg, much mocked by some of the others, who almost single-handedly destroyed the military demand for 205,000 more troops. The briefing began with the military officer saying that the otherside had suffered 45,000 deaths during the Tet offensive.

Goldberg then asked what our own killed-to-wounded ratios were.

Seven to one, the officer answered, because we save a lot of men with helicopters.

What, asked Goldberg, was the enemy strength as of February 1, when Tet started?

Between 160,000 and 175,000, the briefer answered.

What is their killed-to-wounded ratio? Goldberg asked.

We use a figure of three and a half to one, the officer said.

Well, if that's true, then they have no effective forces left in the field, Goldberg said. What followed was a long and very devastating silence.*

That Senior Advisory Council was a much more sympathetic group than the National Security Council. Many of them, like Acheson, who had long supported the President had by this time changed their minds. After he left office, the President acknowledged, on television and in his book, that Arthur's memorandum had had an important impact on his decision to stop the bombing and start serious negotiations.

In the face of considerable resistance, Arthur pushed toward recognizing mainland China. Although completely unsympathetic to its totalitarian ideology, he thought that recognition was "not a good conduct medal." It made no sense that Russia and other military dictatorships should be recognized while China, the most populous nation in the world, was denied. Thus, he advocated as a first step a committee to study the question, an idea only timidly accepted by Johnson and Rusk but which was understood by both China and Taiwan to be a precursor of a new China policy by the United States.

In the *Pueblo* crisis, despite a recommendation by the Joint Chiefs of Staff that we liberate *Pueblo* and its crew by military intervention, Arthur, with Rusk's support, persuaded President Johnson to use the United Nations as an escape valve to allow justified emotions to flow against North Korea's illegal capture.

And it paid off. While the debate was going on at the UN, the

---

*David Halberstam, *The Best and the Brightest* (New York, 1973), pp. 653–54.

Hungarian ambassador, Karoly Csatorday (the unofficial representative of North Korea at the UN) received word from North Korea to communicate to Arthur that they were prepared to negotiate the release of the crew.

Arthur took particular pleasure, too, in personally negotiating the Space Treaty. In recognition of Arthur's work by our government, his signature was affixed to the treaty along with Dean Rusk's.

By this treaty, nuclear weapons were banned from outer space and astronauts were protected from being treated as spies if they landed by accident on unfriendly territory.

Rudolph and *Griswold* were the two Supreme Court opinions of Art's that I found most noteworthy; the NNPT was the one for the UN period in which our family takes the most pride. It was for this that President Johnson asked him to postpone his resignation: to guide the Nuclear Non-Proliferation Treaty to a successful UN ratification. In Geneva, despite the acknowledged skills of William C. Foster, Director of United States Arms Control and Disarmament Agency, the unaligned nations had begun muttering protests at the two great powers. It would be Arthur's job to persuade them that ratification was in their own interests. Vasily Kuznetzov, the veteran first deputy foreign minister of the Soviets, acknowledged Arthur's leadership here. In a move unusual for the Russians, he asked Arthur to take the lead in negotiating the ratification in New York. He said frankly that he trusted Arthur's negotiating ability and knew that Arthur's acceptability and credibility among the delegates were greater and better than his own.

Newspaper reports have emphasized Arthur's role in getting American support for the Rhodesian embargo. This embargo was, to the great discredit to our country, weakened during the Nixon administration, although our country is bound by treaty to enforce UN Security Council resolutions.

One further contribution is a symbol of Arthur's mission to the UN. It was made over the protests of Charles Bohlen and other State Department Kremlinologists. As chief of the United States Mission to the UN, Arthur personally took over the Human Rights Commission representation to give greater emphasis to the American position in protest of the Soviet persecution of the writers Yuli Daniel and Andrei Sinyavsky.

In a statement on March 6, 1968, he pointed out, "It is the plain duty of the Human Rights Commission to be concerned about transgressions against freedom of opinion and expression whenever and wherever they occur. No country, including my own, can claim a perfect record, although we are fortunate in having an independent judiciary which has given increased protection to our own Constitutional safeguards of freedom of expression, of the press and of conscience. If therefore I today call attention to current and serious transgressions in the Soviet Union it is in discharge of the plain obligations of this commission and not to make cold war propaganda."

Chip Bohlen's objection was that such a high-level protest would interfere with détente. Arthur's position, however, was that, under the Universal Declaration of Human Rights, human rights was everyone's business. Genuine détente, he said, would not be prejudiced.

His emphatic protest caused a bitter argument. But after that episode, Kuznetzov and Arthur cooperated together on the Nuclear Non-Proliferation Treaty and on Resolution 242.

The good relations with the Russians had personal ramifications as well. Arthur and I went to Moscow during the summer of 1969 when, after his return to private life, he led a UN association delegation. We traveled with Robert Benjamin and his wife, Jean, and with Porter and Susan McKeever. Kuznetzov entertained us all royally, although Arthur assured him that he was no longer in office or associated with the government.

When Kuznetzov left our country, Arthur and I drove to the airport where there was a small farewell reception to say good-bye to him and his party. Harry Reasoner, the television newscaster, was there and interviewed Arthur: "Mr. Ambassador, wouldn't you say this is unusual? I can't recall any other American ambassador extending himself in this way for a Soviet foreign minister."

Art said, "Well, I don't know about the others, but this foreign minister is a statesman and a friend. We have worked cooperatively, and my wife and I feel warmly toward him."

Kuznetzov went out of his way to afford us other courtesies, which included facilities for us to visit the birthplace of Arthur's father and mother in Zhinkov, an area otherwise prohibited to foreign visitors. In fact, Kuznetzov overrode the initial demurrals made by lesser officials to this request. They claimed that a new road was being built and that recent rains had made the old ones impassable.

There is one other quite charming story about Kuznetzov and Arthur. Our distinguished ambassador to the Soviet Union, Llewellyn E. Thompson, complained bitterly to the State Department that when he returned from the United States on a visit, the Soviets insisted on examining the contents of his personal crates despite his explanation that the crates contained purely household items. Normally, as an ambassadorial courtesy, the Russians permitted an embassy truck to meet the plane and transfer these effects, a courtesy that was reciprocated for Ambassadors Dobrynin in Washington and Fedorenko in New York.

The Russians offered to release Thompson's personal luggage, but he would not accept and insisted on remaining at the airport until, after a long humiliating delay, the Russians released the entire contents of the plane.

Ambassador Thompson correctly pointed out to the State Department that this obviously harassing tactic must not be overlooked and that to avoid a repetition, any high-ranking Russian diplomats arriving in Washington ought to be subjected to the same treatment.

The State Department demurred, believing that this would impair discussion of important matters such as space and the Nuclear Non-Proliferation Treaty. So Thompson cabled Art directly, asking his cooperation. Art immediately agreed; he also believed the Soviets must answer for such shabby treatment and he was sure that it would not affect the larger negotiations in the least.

The next highest-ranking diplomat to arrive in New York was Vasily Kuznetzov. Much as he respected him, Art carefully instructed his officers, who in turn advised the Customs and Immigration officials, that Kuznetzov was to be treated precisely as Ambassador Thompson had been treated.

At the Waldorf, it was almost midnight. We were about to go to bed when Art received an anguished call from Dean Rusk saying that Kuznetzov had been placed under arrest at Kennedy Airport. Art told Rusk to relax. "I'll look into it. Leave it to me."

Then he called his aide, Joseph Glennan, a career foreign service officer. Joe Glennan immediately went to the airport and reported to Art that it was a fact that Kuznetzov was being *detained* in a private arrival room while his crates were being leisurely inspected. Several hours had by then elapsed, which counterbalanced Thompson's harassment, and Art ordered everything released. He asked why his original instructions to merely hold the crates and release the foreign minister and his personal luggage had not been followed. He discovered that an overly zealous and overly anti-Communist Customs official had taken it upon himself to detain Kuznetzov.

The next morning Kuznetzov filed a formal complaint. Art regretted it, saying that Kuznetzov misunderstood; that actually he had not been detained, only his crates. Kuznetzov made this complaint personally and in the presence of his ambassador. The atmosphere was frigid, but after his official rejection of the complaint, on the spurious ground that Kuznetzov had not actually been "detained," Art spoke privately to Kuznetzov.

"Mr. Minister, I owe you frankness. You were detained. This was contrary to my instructions to the Customs people, to treat you only as you fellows treated Tommie Thompson, but the reason I've rejected your complaint is that your government brought this on yourselves. You had no business treating Thompson the way you did. Now having officially rejected your complaint for this reason, I want personally to apologize to you for what happened. And now, Mr. Minister, the two of us have important business to enact. We simply have to work together to get these two important treaties through the Assembly."

Before getting into his limousine, Kuznetzov looked very thoughtful for a moment and then said after a pause to Art: "I like your frankness. You are businesslike." (Ironically, the highest compliment any Russian will accord any one.) And he said, "Okay." (He was trained at Carnegie Institute of Technology in Pittsburgh at the Ford plant and knew our vernacular.) "We'll forget it. Tomorrow morning let's have breakfast and we'll discuss our strategy for the Assembly."

Art said, "Okay," and they shook hands. So Art was right and the Kremlinologists at the State Department turned out to be wrong about how to get along with Russians. And that's why we went to the airport to see Foreign Minister Kuznetzov and his party off.

The foregoing controversies, sketchy as they necessarily are, unfortunately cannot include the many nuances of bargaining that occurred. The Mideast crisis in 1967 certainly requires more detailed accounting than can be given here so far as Arthur's role is concerned. I think it is enough to say that those who are familiar with that agony of negotiation recognize that although the Resolution 242 was offered by the British, it was a result of an agreement between Arthur and Kuznetzov that neither of the two superpowers would sponsor the final resolution.

The resolution itself—the concept and the language—was Arthur's work. And it is this Resolution 242 that even now, at this writing, everyone still agrees, should be the basis for a final Mideast settlement.

Much of what happened while Arthur was at the UN was of major historic significance, and while it is impossible to tell about events here substantively, it is possible to highlight several.

Again it was disconcerting for me to realize, as every involvement made the front pages, how cursorily I had read about them previously. Oh, the headlines were scanned, yes—but not the complex details about everybody living everywhere in the world. Suddenly the whole world did become the breakfast-lunch-and-dinner business and talk in our household.

Arthur, of course, had always been interested in foreign affairs.

Through the years I had attended meetings with Arthur in Stockholm, visited steel mills in Kiruna, listened to British steel officials and workers at their Metal Workers Conferences, but my notebooks were quick sketches of landscape made in passing, trying to note and isolate the uniqueness of a place.

Now the very stuff of everyday living for us began in some faraway place with problems—international problems. They began with the storm of conflict between the two great powers—the Soviet government and its satellites, and our country, though France, too, was becoming a serious factor in its willingness to see the UN collapse because of controversy over Article 19 of the UN Charter.

I think it was the Article 19 dispute which brought Arthur to the UN. Had any of the other crises been imminent, important as they were, I doubt that he would have thought seriously of leaving the Court. That dispute, however, threatened to destroy the United Nations, and our own country, locked into a diplomatic vise, was contributing to the possibility as much as the Soviet Union, its satellites, and France. Those three had balked at paying their assessments because of the Congo.

While Art was against the Russian position of refusing to meet her obligations, his own judicial sense compelled him to believe that if the situation were reversed and the United States were assessed for a UN peacekeeping operation to, say, insure Castro's continuity in Cuba, the Congress would similarly balk.

After all, the UN operation in the Congo, whether by design or accident, would keep Soviet Communism from dominating the Congo and, presumably, the rest of Africa.

Thus, Art's first act as the new American ambassador to the UN was to promote a strategic withdrawal from the inflexible United States position. The rigidity was the result of Secretary Rusk's, Adlai Stevenson's, and the administration's having assured Congress that if the Soviets and their sympathizers refused to pay their dues, the United States was prepared to enforce the issue to its obvious end. That was a polite way of saying we were willing to have the second-largest power and its cohorts expelled from the United Nations.

That much we had discussed at the table at home even before his appointment, when we had no inkling of our ever becoming more involved in a situation so remote from our lives. It was not exactly prudent on the part of the United States, Art said, to have allowed itself to become so boxed in by a rigid diplomatic stand.

We were at a luncheon in my honor given in the Capitol by Lola Aiken and Florence Lowe from Metromedia for sixty women including the women's press, when he made his first move as an ambassador by phoning former President Eisenhower. President Eisenhower had released a press statement in support of the Republican position, shared as well by a good many Democrats, in favor of a showdown with the Russians on the Article 19 dispute.

Arthur had always maintained pleasant relations with former President Eisenhower, whatever their political differences. He believed that Eisenhower, though a great soldier, was also a man of peace. He knew, moreover, that Eisenhower was also a firm supporter of the United Nations. So he asked if the former President would receive him at Gettysburg that same evening. Then he flew down in a White House helicopter. It was only forty-five minutes away.

President Eisenhower received him cordially. In the helicopter, Art decided that he would not ask him directly to reverse his publicly taken stand. At the meeting he stressed instead the immediate danger to the United Nations if we insisted on our justified legal position. The former President listened carefully, making no comments other than to say quietly that under no circumstances should the risk be taken of allowing the United Nations to fall apart.

While Art was returning to Washington, Eisenhower issued a statement supporting Arthur's view: that instead of expelling the Russians, the United States should take the simple position that the Russians, their satellites, and the French were wrong in their position and that the United States would reserve its right to withhold payment of special assessments should we ever regard a special assessment unfavorable to our own interests.

After Eisenhower's statement the anti-UN Republicans and Democrats had to drop further efforts to pull our country out of it.

The vestige of an old domestic labor controversy arose during the UN period. Although Art had, after leaving the Department of Labor, set a rule for himself to remain apart from labor bills and controversies, a situation arose that drew him into a problem.

It was about a bill to make the railroads arbitrate the size of crews operating the diesel engines. There is nothing for a fireman to do on a diesel engine; there is no fire for him to stoke, no work, but the labor unions insisted that he remain, and that sparked an old controversy. The negotiations had fallen apart and the unions were intending to strike. The administration had offered a bill to require them to arbitrate this controversy.

Arthur had not been involved, and told President Johnson, as he had told President Kennedy, "You've got a Secretary of Labor; it's his problem. It's not appropriate for me to advise you." But after a Cabinet meeting in the White House, the President invited him to stay for a private chat in the Oval Office. Thinking it was a matter concerning international relations, Arthur accepted. But as he sat down, the President remarked that he hoped Art would

not mind George Meany's coming in to see him for a few moments
—and, "He'll be glad to see you too."

Art asked that he be excused if Mr. Meany already had an
appointment. The President said no, it wouldn't be too long and
for Art to please stay. George Meany then stormed in belligerently
and at once exploded to the President. "Mr. President, we're
gonna have to oppose this arbitration bill. Labor's against imposed
arbitration and won't take this."

President Johnson seemed to fumble a reply and came up with,
"Well, George, I had hoped you'd be with me on this," and then
there was a silence. Art thought the whole scene was silly and that
neither had been thoughtful about the problem, but the silence and
the sulk were obvious. It was not illegal to help the President
under the circumstances, though the President knew of the rule
Art had imposed upon himself, so he said: "Okay, since I'm here,
and I shouldn't be, I'll make an observation." And turning to the
President, he said: "Mr. President, you cannot expect George
Meany not to act like a labor leader. He has a constituency. His
situation would be like asking Proxmire to come out for importing
cheese at the expense of Wisconsin cheese, or Hubert Humphrey
to come out for oleomargarine instead of Minnesota dairy butter
—so George can't be with you on this bill.

"But, George, I have something to say to you. The President
can't permit a nationwide railroad strike now. There'd be too
much damage to the economy. There's no other way the President
can go than for an arbitration bill. The unions and the companies
are at loggerheads—nothing's moving."

Then he proposed: "George, you go ahead and testify against
the bill. That'll satisfy the railroad unions—but don't turn out the
troops."

By that he meant that Meany should not turn the problem into
a burning controversy warranting a full-fledged lobbying effort,
listing with COPE (AFL-CIO's Committee on Political Education) all the votes pro and con on the bill. Then Arthur turned to
the President: "And you, Mr. President, stick by your bill as you
have to and get it through as you have to, but don't get into a
shouting match with George Meany and name calling. George
simply has to express opposition. Okay, is it a deal? So shake
hands." And they shook hands.

(We were reminded of this recently when the Israeli secretary of labor under the new Rabin administration in Israel asked George Meany and Arthur how a labor minister is to get along with a government. Previously, the Histadrut, the labor organization, was essentially the government. Art said it's simply a matter of government having to act like government, and labor having to act like labor, but labor must never forget it's *their* government and has to modify demands and actions accordingly.)

To this day, almost wherever we go, people constantly say, whether they are conservatives or liberals: "We're sorry you're not still on the Court," and ask why Arthur left. It was not easy to parry such questions.

Arthur was asked the question often by the news media, once on the "Meet the Press" program. Usually on these programs, with their limited time, a question that produces an answer of more than twenty seconds is considered "long-winded," and Arthur has, on occasion, been charged with long-windedness by some news commentators. When he was asked on "Meet the Press": "Do you now regret leaving the Court?" he answered, as he had been answering the newspaper people, in one word—"Yes." The TV reporter was nonplussed, recognizing that he had something newsworthy. Being a good reporter, he pursued it further: "Will you elaborate on that?" to which Arthur merely said, "No." That was a technique he used in dealing with President Kennedy on occasion.

(President Kennedy, who often was impatient with long answers to complicated questions, sometimes expected what Arthur thought were impossibly brief replies. When Arthur submitted his recommendations to the President with regard to the Commission on the Status of Women, for example, the President looked up and said, "What's this all about?" Arthur summed up the entire case for the new Commission in one sentence: "What it says, Mr. President, is 'Are you for or agin women?' Sign here." The President laughed and said, "Okay, you made your point. Now tell me what it's all about.")

For my part, I gradually ceased to feel a sense of numbness over his having left the Court. Indeed, after seeing the way the United Nations functions and his own contributions there, I completely changed my mind about his decision. I remember too that he was *not* asked during the UN period, "Why did you leave the Court?" In theater lobbies, at benefits, in hotel lobbies, in planes, at various private and public gatherings where strangers come forward, no one said then, "We're sorry you're not still on the Court"—not when he was instrumental in helping stop the India-Pakistan war of 1965 from spreading. Nor do I recall anyone saying that when he "defused" the Cyprus crisis of 1967; or when he changed our government's Rhodesian and South African policy into one that was sympathetic to African rights; or when he made strong government protests against the Soviet Union's repression of the rights of Jews and other political dissenters; or when he was "defusing" the *Pueblo* crisis in Korea; or when he was personally negotiating the Space Treaty which prevented nuclear weapons from being stationed in space; or when he was guiding the Nuclear Non-Proliferation Treaty to a successful conclusion; or when he was the main architect of the Middle East Resolution 242 after the Six Day War, which even today everyone agrees should be the basis for settlement; and no one said that when—from the very beginning—he was determinedly overcoming (as President Johnson's own memoirs show) the President's stubborn resistance to unwind the Vietnam War.

That war Arthur regarded from the very beginning to be an unmitigated disaster. I do not remember anyone saying they were sorry he left the Court when he was working so hard to provide the basis for a change in our China policy or when he was healing the breach caused by the defection of the Soviet Union and France because of the dues-paying controversy in connection with Article 19, which saved the UN then. Had that particular controversy not been solved by a person of Arthur's stature and his general acceptance to former President Eisenhower and Congress, it easily might have resulted in the dismemberment of the United Nations.

Admittedly, it has not been easy for me, at least, to parry such questions, but they brought home to me how much more had been sacrificed; namely, a certain distance that envelops the Justices and separates them from the noise of the crowd.

When I try to make order for myself out of the hectic period we spent at the UN, one thing is clear—it was not a fool's paradise. We had no illusions, but at least the day we left was not as black as the day in February 1965 when Secretary McNamara predicted before the House Armed Services Committee that 122 million Americans would be killed in an assault on our military targets, 149 million if the attack included urban centers. Life itself became meaningless when gauged by the statistics.

No wonder the young people revolted. What choice was there, with the clock hands moving toward midnight? The rage of the young people was understandable, and so was their laughter mocking all principles and values as sham for power-seekers. But understanding why the young hate did not make it possible to reach out to them.

The helplessness of the individual in the face of monolithic government and its unresponsiveness to protest, estranged the generations during the Sixties. Although we were spared that, because of our children being older, we grieved for those parents whose children were alienated and lost to them. No matter what we felt or thought or said or did, we were part of the government and had to endure the onus.

But at the UN I recognized that all choice was not blocked. The individual is still given the privilege of working for peace in the world at various levels of responsiveness. The very fact that the UN exists makes the world less of an absurdity. The UN Charter lists the alternatives to war: negotiation, inquiry, mediation, arbitration, judicial settlement, resort to regional agencies or other peaceful means of a nation's own choice.

I have not lost faith in the United Nations, but I must say that the recent actions of the General Assembly on the Mideast are no credit either to the Assembly or the UN itself. The spectacle of a pistol-packing nongovernmental person addressing the Assembly and being accorded an ovation cannot be justified nor the betrayal by Unesco of its own charter when it excluded Israel.

True, the alternatives to war as listed in the UN Charter read better than they work, but still it is more than just a list. The UN is reproached for being just a debating society, but potential combatants can stand up and try to reason together there, instead of murdering each other. Each day spent talking is one more day of life to a soldier on the front, one more day that may allow the rage and hate to cool a little so that he may not need to be killed.

In 1967, I was asked to be one of the judges of college students' films about world peace. One student had filmed four cavemen wearing skins and carrying cudgels, squatting, tearing the meat of some animal apart with their hands, grabbing one another's women, fighting. Then, noticing a strange object sticking out of a hill of sand—obviously a rusty hinged door of an abandoned truck—they stare blankly, shrug and start fighting again. All without words. I thought that should get the prize for the world of tomorrow without a UN.

The absurdity of some recent UN actions is lessened, for me, at least, when I think about something I read in Raymond Aaron's *Peace and War.* He found it fascinating to contemplate that humanity today behaves like a ten-year-old child—that is, if we accept J. Fourastié's estimate about how much time there is still left in the future for humanity to live. The latter estimates that humanity still has nine-tenths of time left to be lived in the future. "Humanity today would be to mature humanity as the child of ten is to the old man."

While that thought may lessen the meaninglessness of existence —to know that humanity is only infantile and not doomed by instinct to be forever aggressive—it does not lessen a certain despair. After all, a child of ten playing with matches can burn the house down. Still, it allows for a slim hope that maybe with patience, with better education for world peace, the stupidity of war can be outgrown—if only there is enough time for outgrowing infantilism.

If there is another war, all the treasures of the civilized mind in all the libraries of the world will be lost, and all the cherished art in all the museums of the world will mean nothing. And all the personal strivings for individual identity will mean nothing. So when finally I try to make order out of the years at the UN, I look for similarities with the little I know of human culture. Culture is not just painting, poetry, the other arts. It is the quality of life lived in a certain place in a certain time.

I thought that the United Nations had become the medium that the human spirit in our own time has created for affirming its own life. I still hope so despite recent disappointments. It is inadequate. It has great failings, but it is a beginning.

In January of 1968 I signed a two-year contract with the W. Colston-Leigh Lecture Bureau for speaking engagements at universities, community forums, and women's organizations. One of my three subjects was "The UN: Is There an Alternative?".

The UN is not just a hope of starry-eyed dreamers; it makes plain common sense. As we know from the tragedy of Vietnam and our own bitter experience, the war cost us more than 50,000 American lives and more than a hundred billion dollars. Surely, the UN peace-keeping forces that cost us only paltry sums of money and no American lives demonstrate the practical worth to us of the UN as well as its promise and potential.

And right now it is the UN peacekeeping force which is helping maintain the fragile peace that exists in the Middle East. It is the UN that stands between the equally dangerous division in Cyprus. Desperately we rely on the UN for the peacekeeping in those two beleagured areas, and fervently we hope the UN will grow in its capacity for peacemaking, too.

15

Penultima

People who leave public life and the perquisites of power often feel that nothing worthwhile remains available to them. And an increasing number of young people now look at public service dubiously after the Watergate scandals. Recently, when a young friend of ours was worried about accepting a promotion in the Nixon administration, in an independent agency, Arthur told him, "It is never a dishonor to serve our government and the people of our country honorably."

But for the ones who honorably have held high office and power in public life and may regard their return to private life as being less worthwhile, we remind them of the glory of time to spend with one's children and grandchildren. Happy portents of the private years to come in the midst of the pressures of the public years were the births of our first two grandchildren. On October 3, 1967, our first grandson, Daniel Maurice Cramer, son of our daughter, Barbara, and of David Cramer, was born. At the age of four months, they brought him to Apartment 42-A where Arthur and I delighted in welcoming him, and Arthur proudly bore him in his arms to present him to Secretary-General U Thant.

Then on April 10, 1968, Esther Fiona Goldberg was born,

daughter of our son, Robert, and Barbara Goldberg. Esther, named for my mother, of blessed memory, is our only grand-daughter. Four other grandchildren arrived to illuminate our return to private life—Matthew Alan Cramer and Jesse Samuel Cramer; and Angus Ephraim Goldberg and Duncan Abraham Goldberg.

We remind those who may feel a sense of loss at the advent of private life of the pleasure in having unhurried time to spend with old (not purely official) patiently understanding friends; of neighbors, urban and rural, not particularly impressed by title and high office; the joys of anonymous privacy in the city and the pleasure of time in the country where the sun still rises and sets and so does the moon. That is hardly "nothing." The leaves still change color in the autumn, and when they fall we do not weep.

If Art does not have political influence, he still has access to the pen, not an insubstantial resource for public good, as the press showed with Watergate. Now there is time to include more non-work pleasures, in the evenings and on Sundays, without worrying about settling strikes or the Sunday Security Council meetings or the pile of certiorari.

Public life had its share of triumphs, as well as troubles, but there was much enjoyment for both of us. Maybe it does not allow for that "stillness of spirit" to be found in art, the country, or the contemplative life, but it has a certain poetry of its own. There are satisfactions that come with applying oneself to a work one enjoys, and to serve the public trust is a worthwhile work. I am glad we had the opportunity to serve.

Although today it is easy to scoff because of the recent Watergate scandals at words such as Honor, Integrity, Fidelity as used by or applied to government officials, I don't know any other words for those qualities, but I have written about the deeds of one public servant from my point of view.

We met other high government officials during our years of public life who were true to the hope and ideals they had held when they were young. Now as the Bicentennial nears and the nation reexamines the young hopes and ideals of two hundred years ago, let the young take care what they ask in their twenties (to paraphrase Goethe), for in the sixties of their lives they will have it. I understand the satisfactions of of a homestead or organic garden of one's own to which the new youth movement turns. They hope to escape the callous indifference to human values of a power-driven industrialized economy. But that alone can't make an American Garden of Eden. We must earn the right even to have freedom to make such a choice. I think we earn the right to live in freedom through participation in politics beginning at the grassroots.

May it be in the honesty of free men and women uncorruptible by power or wealth, without fear of holocaust or nuclear terror; patient in their understanding of the newness of our democratic concept of government that makes for such exasperatingly slow progress when confronted by forces that prefer the quicker ways of kings to the public interest. We are, after all, only two hundred miraculous years young compared to thousands of years of authoritarianism. May it be in a much-loved land whose natural resources are protected and preserved in a much-loved nation at peace with itself and the others that struggle so desperately for a better world.

Index